THE
SNIPER
MIND

THE SNIPER MIND

Eliminate Fear,

Deal with Uncertainty,

and Make Better Decisions

DAVID AMERLAND

ST. MARTIN'S PRESS   NEW YORK

www.stmartins.com

Designed by Steven Seighman

The Library of Congress Cataloging-in-Publication Data is available upon request.

ISBN 978-1-250-11367-2 (hardcover)
ISBN 978-1-250-11368-9 (ebook)

Our books may be purchased in bulk for promotional, eductaional, or business use. Please contact your local bookseller or the Macmillan Corporate and Premium Sales Department at 1-800-221-7945, extension 5442, or by email at MacmillanSpecialMarkets@macmillan.com.

First Edition: November 2017

10 9 8 7 6 5 4 3 2 1

For Ben Moskalensky. In dealing with circumstances beyond his control he displays the fortitude of a trained sniper and the resilience of a true warrior. And for vets everywhere, we never acknowledge your worth enough.

PERMISSIONS

TABLE OF CONTENTS

INTRODUCTION

From 600 yards away, a man running at 8.6 miles per hour between two points of cover is a low-resolution dot a few inches high; in military jargon he is called a "limited opportunity target." Even when viewed through a high-powered sniper rifle scope as a human-sized, stationary target on a calm day at the range, hitting him presents a physics problem that appears almost humanly impossible to solve.

In 2004 during Operation Vigilant Resolve in the Iraqi city of Fallujah, marine sniper Sergeant John Ethan Place would have to solve it under the most difficult conditions imaginable. The variables that make the shot so difficult are daunting in their number alone. These include distance, elevation, air temperature, and wind speed. Gun barrel temperature. Type of ammunition being used. The target's own behavior. The sniper's heart rate and mental equilibrium. Physical factors such as fatigue, mental exhaustion, and even the tiredness that an eye experiences as it looks through a sniper scope for a time longer than thirty minutes.

Operation Vigilant Resolve was a fast push into the city of

Fallujah by a combination of US units. Political rather than military imperatives at the time had pushed up the timetable of the operation, which had affected some of the preparation. The day the operation started Place found himself in overwatch position, the only sniper protecting Echo Company. During the battle that raged for thirty days, Place would pretty much clear the area known as Jolan Heights, save countless Marine lives, and act as a fearsome force multiplier robbing the enemy of the tactical advantage of using an urban area they knew well to fight regular US Army forces. Morale among the Iraqi insurgents would plummet.

Over thirty days Place would be credited with thirty-two confirmed kills. His longest shot took down a running insurgent six football fields away. His trained sniper's mind successfully calculated the insurgent's speed based upon his understanding of average human speed, factored in all the variables affecting bullet trajectory between him and his target, extrapolated the man's behavior as he ducked and ran, and decided to fire a shot aimed 8 feet ahead of him, placing a bullet where the man would be, in order to take him down. He did all that in a window of opportunity just 2.8 seconds long and while in the middle of a raging battle, with all the other distractions that entailed taking place around him.

This book is an examination of such seemingly impossible feats and seeks to understand what makes them possible and how we can learn from them. The trained sniper is a complex fusion of hard skills such as weapons knowledge, situational awareness, tactical experience, and knowledge of ballistics and physics, and soft skills such as emotional stability, empathy, inner calmness, and a stoic acceptance of the hardships associated with a particular set of circumstances.

The premise is simple: If we can all learn to create that same synthesis of hard and soft skills in our own lives, we'll be better at our jobs, in our relationships, and in our executive decision-making. Our life choices will be better weighed. The outcomes we want to achieve placed within our reach.

Each chapter of this book presents a particular skill set that snipers possess. It explains the science behind it and then how it can be acquired and applied in a business environment. Each chapter starts with a sniper story and also features the ideas, opinions, and thoughts of trained snipers who consented to being interviewed and quoted.

Early business models were based on a hierarchical army structure that reflected not just the "command-and-control" approach of the military but also its focus on structure and modularity. Business operations, mirroring their military origins, were also modeled on strategic, operational, and tactical procedures. Over time, businesses forgot both the skills and the debt they owed to the army. They increasingly borrowed its language but forgot its culture of discipline and its practice of focus and intent to achieve the desired outcomes.

This book redresses that imbalance. The military of today, like the businesses of today, faces unprecedented operational challenges. Its work is carried out in the open with social media providing transparency in a way that would be unthinkable in the past. Its wars are fought among shifting local populations whose needs have to be taken into account. Businesses also face an incredibly fluid, challenging marketplace which demands a high degree of capability, initiative, focus, and ingenuity from their staffs.

We know that military men are capable of outstanding performance because of their training. A 2006 Korn/Ferry International study reported that ex-military officers are three times more likely to become CEOs than other American men. Ross Perot, Bill Coleman, Fred Smith, and Bob McDonald, who led Procter & Gamble, have all done time in the military.

Each chapter of this book breaks down a specific skill into its constituent parts. It presents its effectiveness. It shows you how to then achieve the transfer necessary and apply it in what you do. In twelve steps, which is what each chapter represents, you learn how to become more focused, more self-aware, more self-assured, more confident in your ability, and more positive in your frame of mind.

If you are in business, if you are running a company, if you are a solopreneur, if you are looking for a way to employ the wealth of knowledge the military has built up over centuries to simply improve your own skill set and your own abilities so that you can become a better version of you, then this is the book for you. The army learned long ago that there is no "magic bullet" to anything. Average individuals can be taught to do incredible things by training them properly, supporting them adequately, and acknowledging their worth.

It's a simple enough formula that can be applied to any business model. "You have to believe in yourself," wrote Sun Tzu in *The Art of War*. This book shows you how. Use the knowledge. Do incredible things.

David

THE
SNIPER
MIND

You make a sniper by taking a human being and reengineering him. You go down to the essence of who he really is and then you build him back up from there . . .

—CRAIG HARRISON, *THE LONGEST KILL: THE STORY OF MAVERICK 41, ONE OF THE WORLD'S GREATEST SNIPERS*

1

Seeking a Competitive Advantage: Develop a Sniper Mentality That Makes You Controlled, Analytical, and Effective

THE VALLEY OF MUSA QALA is at the central western part of the district by the same name in Helmand Province in Afghanistan. At an elevation of 3,422 feet (1,043 meters) above sea level it is an inhospitable, mostly dry place, whose rough terrain is boiling hot in the summer months and freezing cold in the winter. During the Taliban resurgence it was also the place that saw some of the most intense fighting between Afghan troops, the British forces supporting them, and the Taliban.

Musa Qala means "Fortress of Moses." A Google search of it brings up images of ragged mountain men dressed in robes and turbans brandishing AK-47s and rocket-propelled grenades. British troops come up, too, framed against different backgrounds. Their state-of-the-art vehicles, body armor, and modern equipment is in stark contrast to the ancient, often dilapidated places captured in the images behind them. There is a sense of desolation associated with Musa Qala. There is a faded, washed-out look and feel to the place that is the clearest indicator of how far removed it is from anything we are familiar with in our Western, urban lifestyles. The very name makes it destined for a starring role in either a first-person shooter video game or the kind of mythology military regimental history is made of.

For British Corporal of Horse Craig Harrison, both analogies apply, equally. It was a November morning in 2009, two years after British forces had driven the Taliban from the area and the newly formed Afghan army was being taught how to take control. The usual patrol would be a few dozen Afghan soldiers on foot, backed by a handful of British troops in armed patrol vehicles. Sometimes they would be overwatched by a sniper, his invisible presence adding an extra multiplier to the power of the punch a modern military force can deliver.

In modern warfare, overwatching is a force protection tactic: one small unit or military vehicle supports another unit as that unit executes fire and movement tactics. The overwatching, or supporting unit takes up a position where it can observe the terrain ahead, especially likely enemy positions, and provide either covering fire or warning shots.

As Harrison recounted later, it was a perfect day for shooting. It was clear with great visibility and not much crosswind. Positioned in a crumbling old wall on a hill, he was a good mile and a half away from where the British troops and the Afghan forces, which they were supporting, were deployed, dug in with his spotter right beside him.

He'd watched the troops for some time as they made their slow, painstaking way across the treacherous ground. Although there was little obviously amiss that day, Harrison knew that Afghanistan was never predictable. Days have a way of turning into nightmares very quickly in that region.

Any ambush worth its name has to happen with as little warning as possible. If Musa Qala is hard to navigate on foot, it is even harder to navigate through the crosshairs of a sniper scope that is situated more than a mile away. Under the clear light of an unblinking sun, the nondescript background of the region leeches contrasts out of the scoped image and creates a homogenous backdrop that appears to blur with the passage of time. Shadows thrown by the changing light of the sun's movement tire the eyes and make the terrain feel uncertain. Deep gullies weathered by time offer impenetrable darkness. Static objects acquire moving shadows. Like much of Afghanistan the landscape reveals itself and hides in plain sight at the same time. It offers up everything to look at and still gives you nothing of substance to see.

When the ambush came Harrison almost did not notice it at first. The Taliban had chosen the spot with care. The Afghan army soldiers and their British escort were overlooked by hills. They were at the farthest point of their sweep from base and nearly one and a half miles away from their sniper overwatch.

As muzzle flashes started to register and bullets started to rain on the metal hulls of the British vehicles, Afghan and British soldiers alike melted frantically into the landscape. They tried to make themselves seem inconspicuous. Invisible. Harrison, from his sniping position, had a clear eye view of the ambush site and things did not look good. He was galvanized into action.

A layperson conditioned by a lifetime of exposure to Hollywood films has an imperfect and flawed understanding of a sniper and what he does. Films, out of necessity, focus on the equipment.

There are the weapons, the crosshairs hovering over a target, the bullets being slowly loaded into the gun, the rifle sights being set. The scope that magically brings a target that's far, far away into sharp relief, almost as if he is standing in front of the camera (which in Hollywood films, he is). They build up a picture that projects almost omnipotent power. They lead us to believe that the moment the crosshairs align on a target a sniper can't miss. It's not quite like that, as we shall see.

THE IMPOSSIBLE SHOT

The history of sniping, in contrast to Hollywood lore, has consistently delivered a pattern of exceptionalism in many of its feats. Snipers have always managed to do more with less. In sniper history, across the ages, a scenario repeats itself. Working under pressure, against the odds snipers manage to transcend the realms of the ordinarily human and enter into a different plane altogether.

The pattern that often repeats itself across history, cultures, and countries, has distinct moving parts. There is no underestimating the enormity of the task facing a sniper. Becoming familiar with just five of the variables that make up each shot, however, helps us understand it a little better. In many cases they appear all at once. In others only a couple pop up, but they are at their most extreme:

Impossible conditions—The weather's too hot or too cold for your average battle conditions, placing the human body under instant, physical stress. There are crosswinds or updrafts. There is glare or the visibility is poor. Nature is simply refusing to play ball. The terrain is too flat or too mountainous. Its colors are monochromatic, making it difficult to spot movement from a distance.

High stakes—Lives are about to be lost. Friends are in danger. Comrades are under attack, besieged from all sides and, sometimes, wounded and running out of ammo. The sniper himself may be coming under fire or he may be behind enemy lines, operating on the fly, without a spotter. The myriad calculations of each shot now resting only with him.

A ticking clock—Time is never on the sniper's side. The situation is always tense. Anxiety levels are always high. It is only a matter of time before a position is overrun and colleagues are killed or captured. A high explosive device is being placed in the path of an unsuspecting patrol or a machine gun that's pinned down friendlies needs to be silenced. There is never enough time for the careful deliberation and planning we see in the movies.

Changing variables—As if having to calculate all the variables that can affect a shot isn't enough, the variables themselves keep on changing. Targets move. The wind changes. The situation on the ground becomes worse. The sniper who lingers too long over his calculations risks never getting off a shot that will do any good to anyone.

Distant targets—The universe has a sense of humor. It doesn't matter how powerful a sniper's rifle may be. How high energy the ammunition being used is. When the crisis hits the sniper will always have to take a shot that's beyond his weapon's effective range and somehow still make it work.

If this were a Hollywood set piece, all of this would add up to the scene titled "The Impossible Shot."

Being a sniper in these circumstances is not only not glamorous or punctuated by the kind of tense deliberation that Hollywood films make out but, as any gamer who's into first-person shooters will attest to, adrenaline and excitement alongside the tension of the game create overreactions that force obvious mistakes. A sniper attempting a shot that's against the odds has to battle a combination of all the difficult conditions the situation throws up to his face, plus his own human nature.

There is a Rudyard Kipling poem called "If—". It was written in 1895 and its opening stanza goes:

> *If you can keep your head when all about you*
> *Are losing theirs . . .*

In his autobiography Kipling left clues that it had been inspired by Leander Starr Jameson who was to become the tenth prime minister of the Cape Colony in what today is South Africa and the man who led the failed Jameson Raid that sparked the Boer War. Kipling might as well have been thinking of snipers. "If—" is an inspirational poem about enjoying a natural competitive advantage through discipline of thought.

On the morning of November 2009, as his comrades came under attack, Craig Harrison may not have been thinking of Rudyard Kipling. His brain, engaged in its calculations, had little capacity to think of itself and the situation he was in, in terms of poetry or Hollywood films. He was, however, about to exhibit exactly the extraordinary type of mental discipline and concentration that Kipling's poem celebrates.

As he watched the ambush unfold through the lens of his sniper scope, he did indeed, keep his head. His training coolly took over and he started doing what he had been conditioned to do. Over the course of three hours Harrison used his long-distance and elevated position to harass and suppress as much of the enemy as he could in an attempt to create opportunities that would help his fellow soldiers escape. It was at the end of that three-hour stint, when human concentration levels begin to flag and mental and psychological fatigue kick in, however, that Craig Harrison made shooting history.

The Taliban had managed to set up a two-man machine gun in an elevated, well-covered position on a hillside. From there it started bringing down a hail of fire on the exposed British soldiers in the plain below, pinning them down in the open. The British unit that Harrison had been protecting up to that point was suddenly threatened with being overrun.

Through the scope of his rifle Craig Harrison could see the men behind the machine gun, lying prone on the ground. He knew that he did not have a lot of time to do something to help the troops pinned by the machine gun's withering fire. The problem he was facing, however, was one of distance. The L115A3 long-range rifle Harrison was using is designed to achieve a first-round hit at 2,000 feet (600 meters) and harassing fire out to 3,600 feet (1,100 meters). British snipers have recorded kill shots with it at 5,000 feet (1,500 meters). The machine gun Harrison was looking to silence that day, however, was positioned more than 3,000 feet (900 meters) beyond that range.

As he recalled in *The Longest Kill*, the book he wrote about his time in Afghanistan: "All the evidence said that it couldn't be done; that this shot was impossible. It was far outside the recognized range of the rifle."

I was out of adjustment in my scope and my position was appalling. Every time the rifle recoiled a little chunk of wall broke away and I had to hold the bipod with my left hand just to stop it falling off. Accurate shooting is all about the minimal transference of interference to the weapon. I was struggling with that one today.

None of all this factored consciously into Harrison's thinking. All too aware of the catastrophic scene that was about to unfold he was busy changing the settings on his scope. To make things interesting, along with the five factors that make up our staged Hollywood "impossible shot" scene we shall now add a slightly more technical sixth. It's called the Coriolis effect. Put most simply, the Earth rotates. It spins around its axis at a speed which at the equator reaches 1,040 miles per hour. When we turn and talk to a person standing next to us they appear stationary because we are both connected to the planet. We are both standing on it. So the relative speed of our friend and ourselves is exactly the same. Like two speeding trains running side by side at the exact same speed, objects with the same relative speed do not appear to move at all. But this courtesy does not extend to flying bullets.

The moment a bullet leaves the barrel of a gun it is on its own. It is not connected to the planet. Whatever momentum it carries with it from its time in the gun barrel is constantly bled off with distance while the sniper who fired it and the target he fired it toward, continue to speed, along with the planet at speeds of up to a thousand plus miles per hour.

For Harrison the problem was compounded further. The advertised muzzle velocity of his gun is 3,070 feet per second (936 meters per second). It sounds like a lot but it's not constant. With no other motive force beyond the initial velocity of its firing a bullet's reach is a factor of its weight, height, angle of elevation, air temperature, muzzle velocity, and the temperature of the bullet itself. At that speed and with no other factors to take into account, a target's drift due to the Coriolis effect is just a few inches to the left or right (depending on the Earth's hemisphere the sniper is in) and up or down (depending on his elevation). The Coriolis effect is at its maximum at the Poles and totally negligible at the Earth's equator.

Afghanistan is approximately halfway between the North Pole and the equator and the Coriolis effect can produce noticeable drift there. At the distance Craig Harrison was shooting from that day, when combined with all the other factors he had to take into account and the bullet's six seconds of flight time to reach its target, it made all the difference between scoring a hit and a complete miss.

As I am writing all this I am introducing each element sequentially, building up the picture of that day one careful sentence at a time. This is not how it happened however. The day Harrison made sniper history everything was happening at once. He was mentally and physically fatigued, anxious, pressured by time and constrained by distance and the limitations of his equipment. Because of the extreme range he was shooting at, his scope was of little use to him. The target was beyond its settings so he had to fire test shots, see how they flew there and where they hit, gauge what adjustments he should make manually using guesswork and his own knowledge and experience, and fire again, hoping his guesswork had made an improvement possible.

Yet, within less time than it's taken you to read and digest all this, he'd fired off nine shots to gauge firing conditions and find the range.

One of those shots found its mark. The bullet flew across the 8,120 feet (2,475 meters) separating Harrison from the enemy machine gun position, its flight path changed by the day's heat, the updrafts it was encountering, the temperature of the gun barrel and the Coriolis effect, and curved all the way to the man lying in the prone position behind the machine gun. It had been unerringly guided by a mind that in that moment of extreme stress calculated everything and fired off a shot into the future so that the bullet would intersect with where the target was going to be.

And then, as if this seemingly superhuman feat was not enough, Harrison repeated it a few seconds later, neutralizing the second of the two-man team who'd taken up the machine gun and cementing his name in military history with an identical shot.

How?

When it comes to snipers there is a virtually universal air of quiet confidence that goes hand in hand with the seemingly superhuman way with which they deal with problems, stress, and human limitations. Understand this: the problems we face challenge who we are. Sometimes they are technical and we are worried that we don't have the skill set, qualities, and tenacity to see them through, and at other times they are circumstantial and we are afraid they will make us fail by first showing to ourselves and then to anyone who happens to be watching just how weak and powerless we are.

This is the internal monologue of self-destruction. Problems are not problems faced outside ourselves. They are problems that cast deep shadows inside us first. If we cannot find a way to deal with those shadows, the problems appear overwhelming. They raise up fears we all secretly have that can tear us apart.

IMPOSSIBLE IS AN OPINION

One man who faced perhaps more than his share of self-doubting fears and had to struggle to master them was the late Muhammad

Ali. Distilling the kind of attitude that allowed him to overcome severe practical limitations in his life and become the heavyweight boxing champion of the world three times, he had this to say on the subject of impossibility: "Impossible is not a fact. It's an opinion. Impossible is not a declaration. It's a dare. Impossible is potential. Impossible is temporary. Impossible is nothing."

If impossible is an opinion it can be overcome through self-conviction. Snipers seem to be masters at this, capable of changing the negative narrative which comes with the fear of failure and delivering positive outcomes against the odds. To do so they focus on what they can do and work out the details of how to do it, rather than worry about why it cannot be done.

That is an awesome superpower to have, right there. But there's more to it than just that. If success against overwhelming odds was just a mind-set, things would be simple and this book would be short. But there is a lot more going on when snipers can, with such great regularity, raise the performance bar to what are superhuman heights compared to the rest of us.

To find out how they do it, I had to go directly to the source. In the writing of this book I interviewed over one hundred snipers. Some had retired and were more than willing to talk. Some still served and they were reluctant to open up. It would take several attempts and dozens of e-mails to get through to them. And others had used their sniper skills in different ways. They are successful in modern life. They run companies and lead people. They straddle the divide separating military life, deadly training, and hostile battlefields from civilian life and regular careers. These were the most interesting folks to talk to of all.

"When you expect things to be different your body betrays you," was the cryptic remark made by Ghost Dog, a serving marine who insisted on using the moniker to hide his identity. He was answering my question about how to do the physically impossible. How can you keep calm under tremendous mental and physical pressure? How can you take fatigue and thirst and pain and edit them out so that all that matters is the task at hand?

What is the secret recipe that allows a person to actually become so incredibly efficient?

"It's like coming in from the outside," Ghost Dog explained in an e-mail exchange over a period of weeks. "You feel that inside is warmer or cooler. Depends where you are. More comfortable. But you don't know the temperature. You don't know what it was outside or what it is inside. You don't monitor your body's own temperature levels. So what you are really registering is the difference. You respond to the difference in temperature because you expect it to be there. But what if it wasn't? What if the outside and the inside were the exact same temperature? You wouldn't feel any difference at all."

It took me a while to digest what he was getting at: No difference.

It was the difference that created the feeling, not the conditions themselves. Discomfort, like feeling hot or cold, is a sensation, but it is a sensation that can become debilitating only if we focus on it. We focus on it because we know there is an alternative. Something better. That is the game our minds play on us. The contrast of what's better makes the current sensation difficult to tolerate. Amoeba-like we want to move away from the discomfort and inch toward comfort. Our brains, complex as they are, engage in all the possible scenarios that would make that happen. Even subconsciously, mental and emotional resources are devoted to this task. It distracts us.

A sniper's skill, I understood, is all in his head. If I really wanted to learn the sniper's secret to excellence under pressure I had no choice but to get inside the heads of trained snipers and find out how they changed their opinion of what was possible and what was not.

THE COMFORT RESPONSE

The Google Maps image of the Musa Qala region in figure 1.1 shows the kind of distance we are talking about when it comes to appraising the range of Craig Harrison's two history-making shots that day. The one and a half miles translate to over 7,000 feet. Even the powerful sniper rifle scope Harrison was using that day could not bring the targets close enough to see them clearly. A lesser person would have faltered right there. Someone less well trained and conditioned would have given in to any number of legitimate excuses that clearly stated that what he was attempting to do was simply not possible. And as Harrison himself recounted, the conditions were less than ideal for the shot he was attempting. The variables of his gun position kept changing with every shot, meaning he had to automatically reset the calculations to compensate for the change in firing position. On paper, it all appeared to be a futile task mired in a hopeless situation.

There is a familiar dialogue of negativity that goes on inside our heads all the time. There are always legitimate reasons why something cannot be done. Because few situations we face are ever perfect, technical limitations that make what we want to do appear impossible are easy to list in almost every context. When it comes to itemizing and then cataloging the obstacles that prevent us from successfully performing a challenging task, our brains exhibit a remorseless logic that builds everything up bit by bit. There is a good reason why this happens. Biologically, we share a basic trait with the amoeba. We are also hardwired to avoid pain and to seek pleasure, or at least comfort.

Everything that happens to us and everything we do is first modeled inside our heads. Our internal world is a construct made of data, information that's collected by our senses. Writing in the *Journal of Consumer Research*, researchers from the University of Chicago and the University of Arizona explained, "We tend to infer that something is good based on the bodily sensation of approaching it or bad based on the sensation of avoiding it." It's an amoeba-like response even if amoebas don't figure much in studies of consumer behavior.

The way information is processed inside our heads is revealing. Everything about our design is ergonomic, driven by the need to optimize the use of resources. Our brain accounts for roughly 2 percent of our body weight and yet consumes a full 20 percent of the body's available energy resources. With that

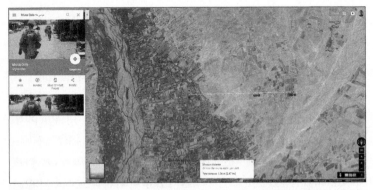

Fig 1.1 A Google Maps image of Musa Qala captures the inhospitable landscape and shows the incredible distance of Craig Harrison's two shots by stretching a 1.5 mile marker over two points in the region.

kind of load there is not a lot of room for redundancy. The same centers of the brain that process physical pain, process mental discomfort. The fear of failure lights up the same mental centers as the fear of predators does.

This has the potential to paralyze us.

Suddenly the shot we may miss in that all-important game, the words we may garble in a public speech, the critical exam we can flunk, or the career-defining presentation we can screw up are situations filled with anxiety and stress. Inside our heads they are magnified by anxiety and boosted by uncertainty.

A brain faced with such a fluid situation experiences a massive cognitive overload. Neural centers spark all over the place in what can only be characterized as a mini electrical storm. As processes become disrupted even fundamentals such as breathing and moving become a struggle. The brain seeks to defend itself by shutting down, and because that's not a real option, it frequently just goes to pieces. Grown men mentally revert to an almost infantile state and the brain invokes the comfort response.

Unlike most organs in our body that can experience pain the brain is in a position to do something about it to escape. As the cognitive overload increases the brain finds it harder and harder to make critical decisions. It can get so bad it feels like an immense effort to make your body move. With analytical thought severely disrupted the brain seeks comfort by burrowing into the relative warmth generated by itself. It opens up its internal doors and pulls us into flights of fancy made up of fantasy and nostalgia. When everything is a mental construct the risk that the brain can play such tricks on itself (and us) is a very real one. And it can happen to anyone.

The Special Air Service, otherwise known as the SAS, is

Britain's elite special forces unit. The men who serve in it have been drawn from active duty from other units of the British Army and have passed a grueling process known as "selection" that along with the probation period can be as long as eighteen months. With a rate of attrition that on average reaches 90 percent selection is a legend in itself, often attracting elite military units from the armed forces of other countries who want to try their hand at it, to test their mettle. You expect the men who are in the SAS to fear nothing, balk at nothing, and be able to face the toughest situations without flinching.

Even their brains, however, are not immune to stress and fear and the invocation of the comfort response. In 2015 Britain's Channel 4 ran a documentary in which SAS veterans put hand-picked members of the public through a miniature and, by almost every military man's account, highly sanitized version of selection. In a newspaper interview that publicized the TV program, an SAS veteran affectionately identified as Foxy talked about his war experiences: "There's a night I'll always remember," he said. "We got into a long firefight. There were a lot of bullets flying around, from both sides. I got into a ditch and I remember feeling so tired that I just wanted to be back at home, as a kid again, with my mum."

Foxy is a rugged, angular man with a face chiseled by hard physical training and a stare that is a little unnerving. He talks quietly in a clipped, precise way that makes sure each word has an exact meaning. It's a little surreal to hear him say that in the middle of a firefight he was momentarily transported to an infantile state. A hardened, deadly warrior pining to be taken care of by his mom. The tendency of the brain to shut down on us, to seek to numb itself, to transport us somewhere else when things get tough, is a response that those who develop mental toughness have learned to recognize. When it happens they can blink it off, embracing it rather than fighting it, drawing strength from it rather than feeling helpless and weak, emerging from it in control instead of feeling helpless.

Did Harrison feel something like that before he took his record-breaking shots? Most probably, though he didn't say. What he did do though was seize back control of his mind, using all its resources to focus on what needed to be done. It is a paradox that while humans are unique our skills and abilities aren't. What one of us can do others can learn to do also. When one brain manages to understand something it opens up the pathway for many other brains to also understand the same thing.

In scientific circles they call this simultaneous discovery. It's the hypothesis that most scientific discoveries and inventions are made independently and more or less simultaneously by multiple scientists and inventors. It's not limited just to thoughts and ideas however. It relates to actions too. Before Roger Bannister broke the four-minute mile barrier by running a mile in 3:59.4 minutes in 1954, it had been thought of as an impossible feat.

The human body, it had been argued, was simply not capable of a four-minute mile. Bannister, reputedly as part of his training relentlessly visualized the achievement in order to create a sense of certainty in his mind and body. The ability of the power of belief to affect what is possible is something we will look at a little more closely later in this chapter as we search for a possible mechanism that allows us to supersede our limits, but right now what is important is to recognize that without the mind the body is not capable of delivering anything beyond an average performance.

Two months after Bannister's record-breaking feat, during the 1954 British Empire and Commonwealth Games hosted in Vancouver, British Columbia, in Canada, two competing runners, Australia's John Landy and Bannister, ran the distance of one mile in under four minutes. Then some more did a little later in the year. Today there are strong high school runners who can run a mile in under four minutes. No one thinks it can't be done.

It appears that once the seemingly impossible is breached, a magical barrier is lifted. Repeating it then becomes easier. Although it is bodies performing the feat, it is actually minds that first have to believe it can be done. To say that a sniper somehow thinks his bullet to the target sounds delusional. Reality is not a thought experiment some would argue. It has concrete existence. There is a gun involved. There are gun sights, bullets and bullet loads, trajectory tables. It's mathematics at play that make things happen, not magic.

Logically, a computer then ought to do way better than a flesh and blood sniper.

In Austin, Texas, there's a company called TrackingPoint. Its Web site says that the company is "a group of technologists, ex-military, shooters, and hunters" with a mission to deliver a one-hundred-year leap in small arms capability. The aim of the company is to build a gun around a computer that is intelligent enough to make long-range shooting easy. By creating a smart gun, the company aims to make the human sniper redundant, transforming his role to simply someone who will move the gun around and point it in the right direction.

The company's catalog shows that $22,000 will buy you a Wi-Fi enabled rifle with a password-coded, laser-guided smart scope that will not only calculate all the variables necessary to make a long-distance shot but will also record everything for you and share it in your social media accounts including notifying your family and friends on Facebook about the shot you took. Obviously its manufacturers are not thinking about the weapon being used in covert ops behind enemy lines. Or at least I hope they're not.

The on-board weather system of the smart rifle takes into account environmental factors that may affect the accuracy of the shot. There is a lot of mathematics involved in calculating shooting variables, and to do it right the smart rifle has a lot of on-board circuitry that brings the total weight of it to over twenty pounds when fully loaded. Again, its designers did not intend it for any kind of "running and gunning" scenario, otherwise we'd have to seriously start thinking about building supersoldiers.

Its Web site states, "Shooters of any skill level can now shoot better than the best shooters who ever lived." It's a bold claim. There is a catch to it. Despite the impressive circuitry, the weight, and the social-media-sharing aspect of each shot taken, the "team of seventy people [who] spent three years creating the technology" that powers the smart rifle only managed to give it an

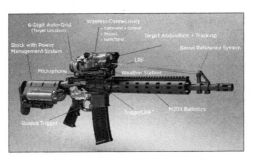

Fig 1.2 The TrackingPoint smart rifle looks more like an enhanced computer system built around a gun barrel and some ammunition than a rifle.

effective range of 1,400 feet (426 meters). That's just over a quarter of a mile. Craig Harrison's manually calculated shots on that November day in Musa Qala were aimed at a target more than five and a half times that distance.

Instead of showing us how human snipers can be made redundant, the smart rifle manages to make the limitations of technology in this area appear obvious. In order to calculate all the variables it needs, the smart rifle has to have sensors not just on the rifle itself but in the world around it. It has to be able to translate what it sees into weather data for its projected target and the environment the bullet will pass through on its way to it. It needs to be able to create inferences from the data it sees, linking up all the relative readings into a complex web of interwoven relationships. It needs, in other words, to have not just data but real-world knowledge. And it must be not just knowledge about one set of data but knowledge that is transportable, inferential, and capable of mutating according to context. What the smart rifle really needs to have is metaknowledge, knowledge about knowledge so that it knows its weaknesses, strengths, and blind spots, and knows how to compensate for them.

Even if the smart rifle was somehow connected to an equally smart grid that had sensors all over the field of fire and could take readings near and around its targets and transmit them back to the rifle and its intelligent scope, it would still have to understand how all these different readings worked together to form a composite picture of not just one sector of space but also all the other sectors associated with it. And it would have to understand not just space but all space and not just all space but time too.

A human sniper does something that the computer-enabled smart rifle cannot do: He visualizes the present well enough to understand how all the different parts in it move together in rela-tion to each other. He understands the relationships that govern things. This allows him to calculate how every element behaves and where they will be next.

Bullets, moving through the air, buffered by updrafts and crosswinds, traveling across terrains which move under them toward targets that themselves may be in motion, become a tap-estry of intersecting puzzles the sniper's mind is trained to solve.

It is tempting to think that this complex juggling of shifting variables is a sniper-specific skill. It's not, however.

The overused, clichéd, and yet still immortal words of Walter Gretzky, passed on to the world through his son Wayne, tell us so: "Skate to where the puck is going, not where it has been." Wayne credited his legendary success to his dad's advice to look into the future, rather than chase the present, and work to meet the puck there. Instead of being a fast reactive player he became an excellent positional one, capable of reading a situation and pre-dicting its development.

As we shall see, baseball players routinely engage in a similar sort of activity, swinging the bat long before they can see the ball flying toward them and scoring home runs through that exact same projection of their inner vision into the future.

It's not often that carbon-based life forms can outperform silicon-based hardware. After all, Google's artificial intelligence algorithm, AlphaGo, beat the odds and defeated Korea's Lee Sedol, considered to be the best Go player in the world, over a five-game set in March 2016. From a combinatorial point of view shooting a rifle appears to be a lot easier. Go's nineteen-by-nineteen grid generates more possible move combinations than there are atoms in the known universe. Shooting a rifle is a

Fig 1.3 The TrackingPoint smart rifle looks pretty impressive, but at twenty pounds plus when fully loaded, it remains a slightly unwieldy novelty. Its $22,000 price tag also puts it out of reach for most gun buyers and the military.

simpler task. And yet, it's not so much the technical difficulty of the task that defeats machines in this regard, but more the deep cognitive skills it requires.

Inside our heads a certain magic takes place, and if we could understand it well enough to replicate it we could guarantee to achieve better outcomes from the decisions made in a business or personal context for anyone. It sounds almost like a pipe dream. Learning to be as precision guided in our judgments as a sniper and as mentally disciplined as an elite soldier, without undergoing the physically crashing training they do, is right up there in geek dreaming with hoping to learn martial arts by borrowing a book from the campus library.

But that's just the point of this book. The power of belief suggests that there are threads that connect what happens inside our heads with outcomes we experience in the world around us. "There is nothing impossible to him who will try," said Alexander the Great, the military genius who sprang out of Greek Macedonia in 334 BC to conquer most of the then known world. "I think only of making that shot. I become my rifle," says Ghost Dog. There are tenuous yet important connections between our thoughts and our reality, and they have become the subject of many different studies.

> **THE SCIENCE:** When we believe in ourselves our brains operate differently. Paradoxically, self-belief works when the "I" disappears and is replaced by a "you" we can talk to kindly or a greater "we" we can truly feel part of. Self-belief is critical to achieving consistently high performance and reprogramming the physiology of perception in order to influence an outcome.

I THINK, THEREFORE I BECOME

Theodore Roosevelt, who seemed to have a quote for just about every occasion, gave us one on belief that has always had broad appeal at a base instinct level: "Believe you can and you're half-way there." It's the kind of thing that looks good on college dorm walls as students battle sleep and fatigue, pulling all-nighters. In the real world, we tell ourselves, such platitudes perish before the light of harsh reality.

The thing is that secretly we want to believe. Control over ourselves is the one thing we all crave. We all know that in a fluid world where everything changes all the time the one thing which perhaps we can be guaranteed to control is us: our minds and our bodies, our thoughts and our instincts. So what if there is a pathway that leads from the internal world of the mind to the external world outside it? A thread that links our hopes with our actions which can then lead to the realization of our desires?

The sentiment expressed by Roosevelt's quote, the idea that by believing in ourselves we somehow seed the outcomes we expect to see is not new. *Yad bhavam tad bhavati* is a yogic teaching right out of the Vedic Sanskrit literature. It can be translated as "You become, as you think," and it's over three thousand years old, dating back to the Iron Age. It is probably one of the first and oldest recorded instances of the idea that belief in oneself has transformative power over one's reality. In a way, this idea keeps on popping up again and again, slightly restated. Kept alive in India in the Vedas, it would resurface independently about one thousand years later, in Chinese this time, in one of the four books of Confucianism called *The Great Learning*, where it would be restated as, "What is within will be manifested without." Roosevelt's less cryptic, populist exhortation would come about two and a half thousand years after that in the timeline, and it would be aimed at a Western, modern audience.

The evidence I was seeking of the thread that leads from deep inside our heads to the world at large, however, came from something a little more modern than the Vedic scriptures: social media.

In the Department of Psychology, Psychiatry and Biobehavioral Sciences at the University of California's Social Cognitive Neuroscience Lab there is a team of five researchers who've been looking at an interlaced pattern of interactions and outcomes of social media posts shared on the Web. Their thesis is that social media posts go viral when those who created them believe they will. Their study shows that the ideas that are destined to spread have a characteristic signature at their origin, one which is, quite literally, within the brain of the idea's creator. The pathway that links what happens outside our heads to what is happening inside them is formed by key regions in two circuits in the brain that are activated in the sender: the "reward" circuit, which registers the value of the message to the sender, and the "mentalizing" circuit, which activates when we see things from the point of view of the person who receives the message. The researchers found that from the moment we first formulate a message, these two factors play a key role in whether or not the message will go viral.

What is profound here is that, because the research can predict which social media posts will go viral and which ones will vanish with barely a trace by looking at these two factors which form the signature of the message itself, we now have the means to optimize social media posts so that they become incredibly shareable. All we have to do is work on the message so that it is of value to both the sender (us) and the receiver (our audience).

It sounds simple but not everybody can work like this. Creating a social media post takes time and effort, and frequently the motivation that becomes the seed that starts it all, is of direct value only to the sender. The focus tends to be there rather than on the receiver, which means that the message itself will be unilateral, and the post will not be optimized sufficiently for it to go viral.

From the Sanskrit and Confucius's teachings to Roosevelt and social media, the mind finds ways to impose its will upon the outside world by "signing" its actions, creating combinations of focus and intent that directly affect the outcome. The battlefield, however, is not the same as a social media network. If snipers and social media post creators use the same mental pathways to project what is inside their heads onto the world and make it real, it is difficult to see the similarities. In a battlefield the "message" sent by the sender is made of lead and more than likely intended to kill the receiver. It is hard to see how the concept of mutual value can be applied in that situation so it can affect the outcome. Some other mechanism must clearly be at play in that context.

To see what it may be, we need to look not just at the conscious mind of a social media maven or the disciplined mind of a sniper, but at the unconscious mind of some ordinary folks, people whose brains are largely untrained by social media marketing tropes and are not battle-hardened by war. The idea is that if there is a pathway through which the mind imposes its will on the world via the actions it takes, then the competitive advantage which it provides must be replicable by any mind, not just ones trained in e-commerce or war.

Psychologists Ulrich Weger of the University of Witten/Herdecke in Germany and Stephen Loughnan of the University of Melbourne in Australia looked into just that when very recently they asked two groups of people to answer some test questions.

People in one group were told that before each question, the answer would be briefly flashed on their screens, it would be too quick for them to consciously perceive, but slow enough for their unconscious to take it in. The other group was told that the flashes simply signaled the next question.

In fact, for both groups, a random string of letters, not the answers, was flashed. But, remarkably, the people who thought the answers were flashed did better on the test anyway. What happened was that expecting to know the answers made people more likely to get the answers right. The experiment showed that if there is belief in the ability to do something, even if that belief is founded on a completely false premise and has a foundation that's built on sand, the brain still has the ability to deliver results that defy the odds by altering the signature of its decision-making inside the head and then affecting the outcome in the world outside it.

It's good news that belief in one's self is tied to a "signature," which is then expressed through words and actions. It gives us the opportunity to mine the data and capture what in the past would have been impossible to capture. It allows us to link the dots, as it were, that take us from thought to action, self-belief to victory over adversity. Snipers are trained to a high degree. Self-belief is drilled into them. In the hit Hollywood film *Black Hawk Down*, actor Ewan McGregor, who along with the rest of the cast went to boot camp to be trained by the same Ranger unit that took part in the real-life events depicted in the movie, gave an interview describing a civilian's perspective of the physical and mental presence drilled into Rangers. "They teach them to act in a manner that projects violence," he said. "There is a knowing mental and physical component to the way they act that lets them know they are in control. As a civilian it's an idea that occupied my mind for some time afterward."

These mental and physical components of self-belief are closely interlinked. They are used to slowly interweave the personal narratives that very effectively create a powerful sense of identity. It is this sense of identity which, in turn, creates a deep level of confidence in a person's abilities. Confidence, even when under pressure, has a way of turning an impossible situation into just another challenge to be met.

THE BUSINESS CASE

We all know the familiar feeling before an important presentation, a public speech before a large audience, a critical business meeting, or a career-defining interview. There is a voice in our head that tells us, quietly, just how high the odds are, how bad we are at everything, and how we will most probably crash and burn.

"We all have demons inside us." We commonly use this relatively medieval superstitious belief to explain the apparent illogicality of getting in our own way and self-sabotaging our efforts. The phrase also conveniently distances our self-destructive tendencies from us, a little. It's not us, it's something *in* us that's telling us that we're no good. It's almost like an independent entity, which means it's outside our control—most times.

We all want to win at what we do. Yet, faced with odds, difficulties, and problems we seem to run out of steam. When we are all highly motivated and focused on the outcomes we want and yet so few of us actually accomplish them, the question that's asked is, why? Why doesn't success, in the critical situations we face in life and business, come easy? Why are we more likely to make the wrong decision than the right one? Why do we fail more often than we succeed?

Although there are many contexts in which failure can occur, the question of why someone has failed usually has the same answer: they didn't believe they could succeed. Whether you're a sniper stationed in Fallujah or an entrepreneur leading a start-up and burning the midnight oil in San Francisco you have the same basic tools at your disposal: a brain that thinks and the desire to succeed at your task. The difference between the sniper and the entrepreneur lies in a mind that's trained to clarify what's at stake.

In a revealing article, online media brand *Fast Company* provided a list of reasons why companies fail based on the results of a quiz given to one hundred start-up owners. Their combined experience distilled different scenarios into ten reasons which cover the broad spectrum of problems and which can succinctly be summarized as being in the wrong place, at the wrong time, with the wrong mind-set.

All of these, or a combination of them, are present in the list of ten reasons they presented for start-ups failing:

- Building a wrong product
- Not being able to build the right team
- Lack of unique value propositions
- Lack of persistence
- Failing to pivot/change direction
- No mentors or advisers
- Slowness to launch
- CEO/founder(s) unable to make decisions
- No business plan
- Unaware of competitors and changing market conditions

When you have a combination of three (or more) random variables, two of which are usually controlled by outside factors and only one of which is controlled by you, you face two stark choices: Give up or use what you have to make things work. But is that enough?

When Ghost Dog, my anonymous sniper, said, "I think only of making that shot. I become my rifle," he was providing the critical clue we need. Under stress, in a critical situation, he became self-effacing. In effect, his ego disappeared and everything he was, everything we commonly understand as consciousness became part of the process of determining if a particular target was viable and then the necessary steps to acquire it.

Egos, however, are important. Personalities are what make a business work. So how do we turn them off when the moment requires it so that our decision-making process becomes better? What should we do to help our focus turn from a broad beam to a laser point?

Snipers have brains that have been trained to resist the ravages of stress. The mind-set they employ can be broken down into three actionable steps that are of direct use to anyone in either a business or a personal situation:

- Control
- Analysis
- Action

Imagine a high-pressure situation with a fluid dynamic and high stakes where decisions have to be made fast. Now, anyone who knows what they want, why they want it, and what they have to do to get it and clearly understands the obstacles in their way and what it will take to overcome them enjoys a competitive advantage over everyone else who turns up and tries to muddle their way through without having any of the mental tools required. This is a classic case of Rudyard Kipling's "If—" again: keeping one's head. A sentiment which snipers have evolved into an exact science through these three steps.

In order to achieve the three-step sequence of control, analysis, and action they need to establish a bedrock of self-belief, and to do that they use three mental pillars known as the Three Ps.

They are:

- Passion
- Purpose
- Persistence

The key here is identity. Without it, self-belief, the knowledge that despite the odds you can succeed, becomes impossible. Forging an identity is a very, very old practice as we shall see, but we shall start with self-belief.

THE THREE PILLARS OF SELF-BELIEF

There are two critical things that separate us, ordinary folk, from a sniper. First, no matter how much we may call ourselves warriors and borrow heavily from the military jargon handbook as we run our start-ups and manage our businesses, our lives are never in danger. Second, even the best trained of us, the most intelligent and expensively educated, go into a business unrehearsed. We simply have not run a dummy business beforehand, going through each meticulous detail in a scenario prepared by a veteran entrepreneur who has experienced both success and failure. We haven't had to be graded for achieving real results and overcoming adversity. Unlike a sniper we go into business feeling safe, unaware of the things we need to know and ignorant of the things we don't know. Yet we are confident that our skills and knowledge are sufficient to get us through what difficulties lie ahead of us. The disparity that is created by this approach serves to further undermine our self-belief at the first stumble, where our apparent ignorance and lack of critical skills become apparent and the unshakable confidence we so badly need is further undercut.

Snipers spend up to two years learning their craft, perfecting their skills, being graded and taking part in mock scenarios that demand they use everything they know. They learn how to overcome incredibly challenging conditions in order to achieve their assignments. In addition they train to be interrogation-hardened, which helps them better understand the deep core of who they are and what they are prepared to do.

Snipers emerge from their training with their core strengthened, the additional layers they acquired as a result of what they'd been put through insulating them further, making them stronger, better.

By comparison most people in the business world run on optimism, ambition, caffeine, and hope.

Global statistics are hard to come by in a meaningful manner, but a nation-by-nation comparison among the world's leading economies compiled from figures released by the US Bureau of Labor Statistics and the Office of National Statistics in the UK shows that new businesses fail at a rate between 50 and 70 percent. In a ten-year horizon, the survival rate of new businesses is between just 4 and 9 percent.

Theo Paphitis is a Cyprus-born British retail magnate known for his appearances on the hit BBC TV show *Dragon's Den*. In open acknowledgment of the need to develop the right mind-set (just like snipers), he has called for entrepreneurship to be part of the British school curriculum for children beginning at the age of eleven. The world has changed, he argues. Academic abilities alone are no longer enough. What is required is the development of a specific type of thinking. It is the mind-set perhaps that makes the difference, that gets you through things when your business idea finds itself "in the wrong place, at the wrong time."

"Entrepreneurship can be taught to people with average academic abilities—the proof of that is everywhere you look," Paphitis said in a 2014 interview with *The Guardian*. "If young people were better equipped with enterprise skills, more start-ups would succeed, and the impact on the economy could potentially be huge." It's a point that's missed by many who look at businesses that fail.

It would be facile to believe that something as complex as running a new business could be saved by a simple mental trick. This is no more true than the suggestion that all a sniper has to do is believe in himself and his abilities and the rigors and dangers of the battlefield will then somehow be wished away and his job will become easier.

Surviving and succeeding in some of the most hostile theaters of war requires a lot more skills than just unquestioning self-belief that stems from a quiet awareness of one's purpose in a given task. But this kind of unwavering self-belief builds a sound foundation upon which a lot of other skills can be placed. It becomes the primary springboard that links the all-important internal world within our heads to the external world we function in as human beings.

The first stage then of building a sniper, of developing the kind of clear identity that helps him define who he is, lies in those three pillars of sniper training: passion, purpose, and persistence. Here is how they translate into civilian attributes:

Passion—Arguably one of the most misused words when it comes to businesses, it has to stem from a deep identification with the job of the person. If what you do is not a direct and involved expression of who you are it will be difficult to be passionate about your work. People who are passionate about their business see work as a reward in itself. This doesn't take away the need for careful planning, a decent business plan, and logical, risk-averse behavior, but it does make the enormous amount of thinking time and energy that is required to raise an individual's performance to exceptional heights seem like a hobby instead of a job.

Purpose—No job is just a job. Everything we do is part of a complex pattern of interwoven relationships which mix personal and professional life. We need to earn enough money to make a living while building the wider world we want to live in. Provided we have some clarity on how everything we do fits into this mental picture, thinking about the first of these tasks should not distract from the other, and vice versa. Purpose is never something that's just given to us. We have to work hard to understand how it applies to what we do. But it provides the kind of clarity of thinking that then leads to the third step.

Persistence—Never stop doing what you are doing. If it is part of who you are and what you do then every obstacle placed in your path is just another challenge to overcome. Challenges have a way of presenting solutions to the dilemmas posed if we are willing to attack them long enough from a sufficient number of angles.

There are countless real-life examples of these three elements at work.

There is inherent irony in the idea that the lightbulb, the symbol most often associated with having an idea, was invented by a man whose teachers said he was "too stupid to learn anything."

Thomas Edison was fired from his first two jobs for being "non-productive." Yet he made a thousand unsuccessful attempts at inventing the lightbulb. Similarly, Walt Disney was fired by a newspaper editor because "he lacked imagination and had no good ideas." He went bankrupt several times before he built Disneyland. In fact, his proposed theme park was rejected by the city of Anaheim on the grounds that it would only attract riffraff. And, Henry Ford failed and went broke five times before he succeeded.

Just as a tripod needs all three legs to stand, possessing just one or two of the Three Ps will not give us a finished product. True passion requires purpose; both passion and purpose create persistence. You want to take the first step into building a mind-set of excellence? Learn who you are. Understand what drives you. Discover what you really deeply care about. It's a solid foundation to build on.

DEFINE YOUR OWN MENTAL STATE

Temet nosce, Latin for "know thyself," has its origins in an inscription over the forecourt of the temple of Apollo in Delphi, Ancient Greece. In Greek it is written as γνῶθι σεαυτὸν, which is loosely translated as "self-knowledge." The temple housed the Oracle of Delphi and it was a special place in Ancient Greece. The priestess of the god Apollo was reputed to have special powers, her aphorisms were given to those who sought her advice about their futures. There's a good reason for self-knowledge in such context.

Without knowing who you are and why you do what you do, you can't hope to control your present or choose your future. Picture Craig Harrison, lying prone on a dusty, hot, and dry plain miles away from home battling fatigue, stress, intense mental pressure, and huge technical limitations, when he made his record-making shots. Given what he was fighting against, no one would have faulted him for folding that day. For cursing the limitations of his equipment and blaming the Ministry of Defense, the body which in the United Kingdom decides, through a labyrinthine process of bureaucratic endeavor, what equipment the British Army will get, for his failure. No one in their right mind would have argued that a target that was so far beyond the effective range of the sniper rifle Harrison was firing as to render the calibrations on his scope useless could have been reached.

Harrison did not fold that day. Amazing as his feat was, what is of direct interest to us here are two obvious questions: How exactly did he manage to overcome all his doubts and the perceived limitations of his situation? And, can anyone learn to do it? A sniper is an incredibly formidable, highly effective presence. The statistics from major military conflicts are a testament to just how formidable and how really effective the average sniper is. While full-scale war produces large numbers of casualties, human beings are hard to kill. A combination of the fear of being killed and an aversion to killing produces a culture of poorly aimed, indiscriminate fire that's pointed toward the general direction of the enemy. In battlefield parlance this is called "spray and pray."

In his book *On Killing: The Psychological Cost of Learning to Kill in War and Society*, US Army Lieutenant Colonel Dave Grossman discusses how in World War I, for every combat casualty there were around 10,000 rounds fired. By World War II, this figure had risen to about 25,000 rounds. In the Vietnam War, it was about 50,000 rounds.

A General Accounting Office (GAO) report from the Depart-

Fig 1.4 Memento mori mosaic from excavations in the convent of San Gregorio, Via Appia, Rome, Italy. Now in the National Roman Museum, Rome, Italy. The Greek motto *gnōthi sauton* (know thyself; in Latin, *nosce te ipsum*) combines with the image to convey the famous warning: *Respice post te; hominem te esse memento; memento mori.* ("Look behind; remember that you are mortal; remember death.")

ment of Defense cites how the US Army has fired 250,000 rounds for every insurgent killed in Afghanistan. Compare this to the 1.39 rounds per kill ratio snipers have been averaging since Vietnam.

Sniper rifles have changed radically since Vietnam. The average kill ratio, however, has hardly moved. Clearly there is a consistency in the approach that has little to do with the weaponry. The secret we are seeking lies in the person that holds the gun.

The best way to view a sniper is to think of him like an onion. There are layers upon layers that go into making him what he is. His lifestyle, his youth, his aspirations, his ambitions, his training, his faith. The list goes on. Every time something happens in a sniper's life it becomes another layer, refining him, augmenting him, cementing his presence. Each sniper is different. Yet peel off all the layers one by one and at the very core you find the same thing in every sniper: a conviction of who they are and what they do that's unshakable. That's their core identity. The part of themselves that keeps them together when they are no longer on a mission or no longer in a war zone and the memories of what they have experienced bubble up in their minds.

In his book, Craig Harrison called this the essence of being a person. Every one of us needs to work it out at some point. Snipers have to do it in order to survive their training and be effective at their job. They get to know themselves well. In order to do that, they look deep inside the person they are and ask the difficult question of why they are the way they are.

In looking for the practical aspects of this identity formation we can apply to business I asked the real-life snipers I had access to the question of why they are the way they are. Surprisingly, I got back few replies. Most of them didn't want to say, or couldn't. Special as they may appear to us, articulating what makes you special requires a very precise awareness of your existence, and that's hard to come by. It needs the context of where you fit on a planet that houses seven billion plus souls. It's not that it is uncomfortable to think like that, it's just that in most cases it is not necessary. Snipers feel their identity and find comfort in their capabilities, articulating the core of the onion they have become to themselves through belief and attitude.

But attitude and belief are a filter. I dug deeper.

I persisted with Ghost Dog and in the end he sent me this: "I feel I matter." Had he been alive in the times of the Oracle of Delphi, the priestess there would have loved to have him as an acolyte. I thought of what he said for some time, playing his pithy words against the unarticulated ones of those others who either would not directly answer my question or would choose to describe other things, thinking perhaps that I would see what they meant by them. It was like a puzzle.

The pieces fell into place gradually. Self-knowledge is not so much about articulation of who you are to yourself or even the ability to explain why you do what you do to a virtual stranger. It is all about being aware of yourself, truly sensing your own mind. It's the kind of awareness that makes passion evident and purpose clear. It allows us to define who we are and understand why we do what we do. Purpose alone, however, is not enough. We also need persistence. Without persistence the hurdles we face become insurmountable. Without it any sense of purpose we feel soon evaporates. Purpose and control go hand in hand. They tie into our sense of identity in ways that go beyond the visible aspects of who we are.

In my notes I broke down the stages a sniper needs to go through to make the impossible happen:

- Control—Understand yourself well enough to be able to edit out discomfort when it appears. Fathom your motivation so that you understand what you are prepared to do and why. Take pride in your identity so that it becomes a bedrock of strength against the negative voices in your head. Control is about creating that inner dialogue which makes those negative voices fall silent.
- Analysis—Break things down into tiny steps. Look at your feelings. Understand why you feel the way you do. This helps you overcome things like uncertainty, anger, fear. Analyze the problems you face. Don't look at them as a whole.

Break them down into chunks. Look at what you need in order to solve each tiny part of them. Even if you are looking at a dead end from a distance, apply the bit-by-bit approach. Solutions frequently present themselves through action.

- **Action**—Don't do too much at once. Don't hurry when you are under pressure. Be precise, methodical, meticulous. Every detail actually does matter, and to say it doesn't is to deprecate the value of what you do. Details keep you anchored and thinking, analyzing, and controlling. Everything ties into everything else.

A sniper who applies these stages in his head enjoys an instant competitive advantage over any adversary. The process rather than talent allows him to "keep his head." Craig Harrison was using his training in Fallujah when he made his impossible shot and secured his name in the record books.

He solved each problem one at a time. Every action he took gave him the data he needed to take the next one. The overall massive problem of his task and the impossibility of the shots he had to take did not factor in this process. His ego disappeared. The negative voices in his head fell silent. He became his rifle.

Self-belief, a clear sense of identity, a carefully articulated and established purpose give us a kind of super-human control which leads to a sense of focus that is truly empowering, liberating, and usually exceptional.

How can we transfer this kind of control to civilian life? The checklist becomes clear:

- At all times in your working life know what you can control. Know what you can't.

- Understand what you can do. Know what you cannot do.
- Have clear guidelines on all actions you are empowered to take.
- Use your passion and sense of self to drive yourself forward, but do not make work about you.
- Learn how what you do helps others.
- Take deep comfort from the results of your work.
- Cultivate a deep professional interest in what you do.
- Learn from your every action.
- Do not neglect your inner self.
- Strive to constantly develop your skills.

THE SNIPER SKILL ACQUISITION LIST

In this chapter you learned:

- Self-belief can deliver positive outcomes even in the most difficult of circumstances.
- The brain can be programmed to perform better under pressure by distancing ourselves in our self-analysis and seeing what we experience more objectively.
- Our identity and personal belief system are key to our being able to sustain our performance in difficult circumstances.
- A clear head in the most stressful of circumstances is possible when we have clarity on what our "mission" is and we understand our capabilities.
- A clear vision, determination, passion, and perseverance can deliver a competitive advantage even in situations that on paper appear to be quite hopeless.

He who controls the battlefield, controls history.

—SOLID SNAKE, PROTAGONIST OF THE *METAL GEAR* SERIES

2

Choosing the Battlefield: Control the Variables in Your "Area of Conflict" by Defining the Elements That Determine the Outcome

SIMON MENNER IS A GERMAN artist who is obsessed with the power of images. He knows that they can affect our perceptions, and our perceptions then go on to shape our thoughts. His photography and visual art projects are commentaries on modern life. Through his work he talks about modern society, the lives we lead, the consumerist trends we subscribe to and the marketing tropes we accept. He gives his projects names like "Top Secret," "Stasi," and "Metacity."

In 2010 he conceived a bold experiment which he appropriately called "The Perception Complex." He reached out to the German Army to see if they were interested in letting him photograph trained snipers with many years' experience as well as newer recruits. He stipulated they should all be camouflaged, hidden in their environment, and aiming their deadly rifles directly at him. He wasn't sure what he would find exactly, but knowing the reputation snipers have for blending in to their surroundings, he knew that what he recorded with his camera would open up new vistas of conversation on their skill and, by association, the perception of the visual image.

Menner's initial idea was to use the photographs as a powerful statement about the hidden elements in modern imagery, a metaphor for things that hide in plain sight and that we are unaware of even though our brains process the images completely. As it turned out, it was the idea of a hidden sniper aiming a gun directly at the camera that really took off with his audience. The result was a series of landscape photographs that ranged from fields and forests to the stark, rocky terrain of the Bavarian Alps.

In what quickly became a game of "spot the sniper," Menner's work appeared in magazines and newspapers across Europe.

Fig 2.1 It seems inconceivable that a sniper could be hiding in open, rocky ground, his weapon aimed directly at the camera. Yet, this is exactly what is happening in this picture. Simon Menner photographed it not knowing where the sniper was hiding.

Wired interviewed him. *The Daily Mail*, in the UK, ran some of his pictures. Online magazine *Slate* ran a story on his work and illustrated it with the pictures he took of hidden snipers. The images went viral on the Internet and sparked a lively public discussion on whether they were even real and if the snipers that Menner claimed were in the pictures were the results of skillful image manipulation techniques.

Menner found the online conversation amusing. "First of all, it is real," he wrote as a response to the many questions that were being posed, "whoever has doubts about that should contact the German Army. There were snipers present in every single shot and they were in fact, ordered to aim at the camera, so they could

Fig 2.2 Even when circled the sniper is not immediately visible. He becomes detectable only by the barrel of his rifle which does point at the camera and the viewer.

see me, even though I was almost never able to see them. The professional training they have received means that in some of the images, no trace of them can be seen, even if you look at the image pixel by pixel."

Menner's work is a metaphor. "The key question for me and my work at the moment is, how images are used to influence people and their decisions," Menner wrote. "At the core, hiding snipers and ads for Apple have something in common, since both try to infect us with ideas about things we are not able to see. But I think that this is easier to detect while 'looking' at hidden snipers than by looking at Apple ads."

Simon has since expanded his work to cover snipers from the armies of Latvia and Lithuania. The landscapes he has shot as part of his project are haunting and beautiful. The light makes them look like works of art, the colors reminiscent of a Rembrandt. But it's the knowledge of what's hidden in them that makes them such a draw.

The first thing a sniper learns is the importance of carefully choosing his place and time of engagement. "Choosing a good vantage point is crucial in being effective and staying alive. Your position could either get you killed and obscure your vision or it could cover you and provide clear shots," says one instruction manual that's conveniently labeled "Sniper 101." The advice is so good that you'd be forgiven for thinking that it's been written for army training. In fact it's the instruction manual for sniping in *DUST 514*, a free-to-play first-person-shooter game developed by CCP Games for the PlayStation 3 console. Fascination with a sniper's field craft techniques permeates every culture, even the online gaming industry, but it's what we actually learn from it that's important.

The late Muhammad Ali famously said, "The hands can't hit what the eyes can't see." But it's also patently clear that the brain can't process what the eyes can't see. When we are looking for something that's hidden from us, prior knowledge of context becomes an advantage. There is an easy test we can do to prove this. Take a coin and throw it over your shoulder so that it lands somewhere on the ground behind you. Then turn around and try to pick it out on the ground, quickly by looking at the area where you think it has landed. It is really hard to find. It usually requires an inch-by-inch methodical search before the coin, often lying in plain sight, finally reveals itself to our sight and then it becomes rather obvious. And the more information we have coming at us, textures, patches of light and shade, objects that are lying around, the harder it becomes to find the coin.

However, there is a way to make the task easier and faster. Drop a similar coin on the ground, but now do it directly in front of you so you can see where it is. Look at it, taking in as much of the surrounding area as possible. Then look for the other coin you tried to find before but couldn't. Usually, as you scan the ground, its location leaps out at you. Scientists call this visual precuing. By dropping a similar coin on the ground and looking at it we are creating both object-specific and location-specific data that is fed into the brain which then uses it to better understand the visual information captured by our eyes.

The mechanism that allows us to more rapidly discover a coin we threw on the ground by looking at another coin in a similar setting also allows snipers to hide so effectively even when there is little cover. They do it by cleverly anticipating what someone will see and either feeding the brain of the observer the information it is expecting to see or disrupting the flow of information so that the brain does not see what it should. How this works has very little to do with our eyes and a whole lot to do with how our brains process the flow of data that allows vision to happen.

> **THE SCIENCE:** Visual information is used by the brain to create a detailed construct of the world. That construct becomes the model which allows pattern recognition to take place. An understanding of patterns is key to success because they guide perception. Perception, in turn, shapes reality.

HIDING IS A MIND GAME

Every time you look at the world this has to happen: the eyes have to open so visual information can flow from the retina through the optic nerve and into the brain, which then assembles this raw information into objects and scenes.

The work of recognizing different objects and scenes takes place in the brain and it's an exercise in complex neural network structuring. The processing of visual data happens in the ventral visual stream (known as the "what" pathway). It's involved in object visual identification and recognition and it feeds information into the inferior temporal (IT) cortex. Object recognition requires the participation of several hierarchies of the brain, in which many parts work seamlessly and frictionlessly together.

Because we are so adept at recognizing different sized objects we barely register the work that goes on to make it possible, but that does not make it easy. Humans can easily recognize different sized objects and put them in the same category because of one particular skill of the brain that pattern analysts call edge analysis. Simply put, every object, in order to have an existence that is classified as real, needs to have some immutable quality, something that does not change depending on the time of the day, its temperature, the shape it is in, or any other changes in its outward appearance. These constant attributes are called invariances in mathematics.

So, a squirrel hanging upside down from a tree does not look the same as a squirrel that's sitting on the ground eating a nut, but we have no difficulty recognizing that both are squirrels. The shape and inherent features of an object become an inseparable part of its visual identity. It doesn't matter how the object is placed, how big or small it is or what side is visible to us. There is a hierarchical build-up of invariances, first to position and scale and then to viewpoint and more complex transformations requiring the interpolation between several different object views.

Brand marketers understand this ability so well that they work hard to create brand logos that are recognizable in an instant. The Coca-Cola Company's now-famous contour bottle which, according to its Web site, is so distinctive it "could be recognized in the dark or lying broken on the ground," was patented in 1915 by the Root Glass Company in Terre Haute, Indiana, for that exact same reason.

Here's how the brain achieves this marvel. We have cells in our visual cortex that respond to simple shapes like lines and curves. As visual cues flow into the ventral stream, the "what" pathway, they activate more complex cells in our brain which respond to more complex objects like faces, cars, mountains, and so on. Neurons found deeper along the ventral stream pathway show an increase in receptive field size as well as in the complexity of their preferred stimuli. Humans take remarkably little time to recognize and categorize objects. For all intents and purposes in everyday life the processing speed is so fast that the act of recognition appears to be almost instantaneous. Neurophysiologists working in this area explain that the brain's ability to almost instantly recognize a shape suggests that there is some form of feedforward processing of information going on. Information processed by the cells in one level in the ventral stream hierarchy which determines, for example, shapes, is likely used by the next level which determines texture and so on.

This internal chain of command inside our heads is set up in such a way that there is a high degree of implicit trust. The levels above it do not normally question the processed results of the levels below. As we look for shapes and textures and try to identify a particular object we do not question whether the colors our brain has reported are correct, for instance. There is good reason for that internal trust score in the analytical process. It makes the task of visual recognition of objects incredibly fast and, in most cases, accurate.

But it also means that information needs to be processed by the brain before vision can occur. It is vision that gives us the gift of sight, not our eyes. They are just the instruments through which information is captured and then channeled. Snipers grasp the intricacies of the process of vision even if they do not understand its scientific breakdown in quite the way I've described it here. It is their understanding of it that makes the act of becoming invisible possible.

In what is a lesson to both camouflage experts and marketers (who want the logos of the companies they promote to be as visible and recognizable as possible), the history of camouflage is one of experimentation with competing theories rather than common sense.

2-D OR NOT 2-D

Our eyes see the world in two-dimensional images, not unlike a photograph. Through the optic nerve, they channel all the visual information they gather to our brains where a hierarchy comprised of as many as twelve separate layers processes it into three-dimensional representations of the world.

Stereoscopic vision, the ability to see the same 2-D image from two slightly different perspectives (that is, from our left and right eyes) is only one of the methods the brain uses to stitch together the three-dimensional models of the world we see. We also use shading and contour, reflections, movement cues, distance, depth and 3-D shape cues, size, occlusion, patterns, texture, and linear perspective. The more of these elements that are disrupted, the harder it becomes for the brain to see and then recognize an object.

The art of camouflage falls under two broad categories: concealing an object so that it blends with its surroundings, and disrupting the information it conveys visually so that it misleads the observer into processing it wrong.

During the First World War, the British Admiralty realized that it was impossible to conceal a ship in open water in many different conditions. It then adopted the suggestion of British zoologist John Graham Kerr who, inspired by nature, proposed a camouflage of contrasting black and white stripes not unlike those of a zebra or a giraffe.

What would come to be known as dazzle camouflage or

razzle dazzle was explained by Kerr to First Lord of the Admiralty, Winston Churchill, in a letter. Disrupting a ship's outline this way, Kerr wrote, would confuse the enemy about its shape, size, and direction, making it difficult to target it accurately. In the same letter, somewhat confusedly perhaps, Kerr also outlined the theory of parti-coloring whereby a ship would be painted in alternating gradations of shades of gray and white to blend with its background and make it difficult to see through a targeting viewfinder.

Kerr was a scientist. His explanations of parti-coloring and countershading was detailed and backed by many examples. Dazzle, on the other hand, was a method that would find a champion in marine artist and Royal Naval Volunteer Reserve officer, Norman Wilkinson, and popular backing by artists such as Pablo Picasso, who claimed that Cubists like himself had invented it.

Without any scientific evidence or trials of any kind, the British Admiralty, swayed by the social connections and strong convictions of the well-connected Wilkinson adopted dazzle over countershading. Before too long the US Navy had followed suit. To make matters even worse the Admiralty's unscientific approach to what should have been a science-driven endeavor was compounded when dazzle camouflage was applied on ships without any protocol. The patterns applied went through so many iterations that, like modern software versions, they became known by their measure and design numbers. Dazzle camouflage was to be kept in use until 1945 with iteration numbers going as high as thirty-three.

The experience gained by the navy from using dazzle camouflage however created a natural progression that, many years

Fig 2.3 The US Navy aircraft carrier USS *Saratoga* (CV-3) in Puget Sound, Washington, making twelve knots, September 7, 1944. *Saratoga* wears her single camouflage measure 32 design 11A.

Fig 2.4 HMT *Olympic*, RMS *Titanic*'s sister ship, in dazzle camouflage while in service as a World War I troopship, from September 1915.

later, would entirely justify Kerr's suggestion for gradient colors and countershading, and would advance the understanding of how camouflage disrupted, impeded, or subverted an observer's system of perception.

Ironically, the lessons regarding the effectiveness of camouflage, so tortuously learned by the British Navy, had already been learned by the British Army during the Second Boer War in South Africa in 1899. This is where the sniper's ghillie suit also makes its first official appearance.

Before the Boer Wars the ghillie suit was a form of portable hunting hideaway, developed by Scottish gamekeepers. The word *ghillie* comes from the Scottish Ghillie Dhu, itself derived from *gille*, the Scottish Gaelic for "servant" or "lad." It was not unusual in those times for a lord or landed gentry to be assisted in deer hunting, deer stalking, or fly fishing expeditions in the Scottish Highlands.

During the Second Boer War, a Scottish Highland regiment formed by the British Army called Lovat Scouts went on to become the British Army's first sniper unit and make the first known military use of a ghillie suit.

A modern ghillie suit is part of the sniper's camouflage gear. It is a five- or six-part overall typically made of net or burlap with loose strips everywhere and the ability to insert local foliage or twigs when hiding in nature. Its camouflage value lies in its three-dimensional capacity to blend into the background in a way that dissolves the usually angular shape of an individual. Our brains are designed to see patterns in order to recognize a person or an object. By removing the pattern associated with a person in the brain's visual library from a scene, the ghillie suit gives nothing

Fig 2.5 A British sniper from 5 SCOTS (center) and French snipers of the 8th Marine Infantry Parachute Regiment train together at Exercise Boar's Head, Otterburn Training Area, Northumberland, in England. Exercise Boar's Head was a company level live firing exercise which took place at Otterburn Training Area involving a British Army infantry company from 5 SCOTS, a unit of the British 16 Air Assault Brigade and a company from the 8th Marine Infantry Parachute Regiment, a unit of the French 11th Parachute Brigade. The fancy scope of the left-most sniper is a Sagem Sword Sniper three-in-one sight.

for the eyes to focus on. The visual information the eyes convey to the brain is insufficient for it to recognize any outlines which can be used to identify a person.

In this way the ghillie suit appears to turn its wearer invisible to the naked eye (infrared spectrography would still pick up a heat signature). I say appears because that's not really true.

Richard Boucher spent ten years as a Special Forces team sergeant and sniper. Now retired, he still instructs new snipers in both range and classroom. The skills he teaches them include marksmanship, field craft, ballistics, photography, and reporting. In his manual, titled *Camouflage and Concealment*, he has two paragraphs that immediately focus the mind.

Camouflage construction consists of hiding, disguising and blending. Hiding means completely concealing the body from observation by lying or moving behind or in an object or thick vegetation. The sniper cannot use hiding when he is in position because if the enemy can't see the sniper then the sniper cannot see the enemy. Once the sniper can see the enemy then the enemy can see the sniper as well. The sniper must keep that in mind at all times! The sniper can use hiding while in movement to his objective. The sniper does want to keep something between him and the enemy as much as possible. The ghillie suit does not hide!

Deception through disguising. Deceiving is a technique used to trick the enemy into false conclusions about the location or identity of the sniper. In some theaters of operations, or during long overland movements, deception may include the use of disguises, such as simply adopting native dress and moving during hours of limited visibility so as to fool observers. A more elaborate plan, requiring more practice and familiarity with the area, would include walking, sitting, dressing and behaving as the local populace. The sniper must understand that disguising is a very difficult technique and is usually not worth the effort. The ghillie suit does not disguise!

If the ghillie suit does not disguise and does not hide, what is it exactly that it does? The answer has to be worked for a little before it becomes apparent. The ghillie suit, just like the black and white, contrasting zebra stripes on naval warships and the subsequent gradient tones that were adopted, is a tool. It either subverts or disrupts the flow of information from the eyes to the brain.

It creates a two-dimensional image from which a three-dimensional picture of the world takes shape. If the sniper knows what he is doing, if he understands his craft and has the skills required to play games with information, he helps create a three-dimensional picture in the minds of those who look toward him from which he is absent.

A sniper, like a great businessman, is an illusionist.

Snipers then aren't so much extraordinary people as much as they are people who are extraordinarily capable of patiently and diligently applying a set of practical steps to a given situation. They are master methodologists. And methodology is something any of us can learn to apply.

BREAKING DOWN THE FORMULA

Sniper skills are next to useless to us, of course, unless we can metaphorically bottle them and transfer them elsewhere. Studying snipers is not of much use if the Zen-like calm of a sniper's seemingly perfect mind cannot be understood well enough to be replicated at will, almost. Luckily for us both of these things are possible and cognitive neuroscience, an academic field concerned with the scientific study of the biological processes that underlie cognition, is helping us out.

We all possess brains that are remarkably similar in their capabilities, their plasticity, and their potential for development.

In the eyes of neuroscience we are all works in progress, eminently trainable and highly adaptable.

Despite the many articles in the popular press decrying our short attention spans, we are natural multitaskers, capable of handling several things at once. What we do not do so well is multitask without some mental training first.

The reason for that lies in resources, or rather in the way the brain allocates resources when it is asked to perform more than one task at once. *The Oxford Handbook of Cognitive Science* refers to the problem like this:

> *Multitasking is a complex cognitive process that usually results in at least one of the concurrent tasks being performed more poorly than when it is performed alone. Effective multitasking requires that two complex cognitive processes co-occur gracefully while sharing at least some common infrastructure. The scientific questions concern the nature of the co-occurrence: How is competition between the two thought processes for shared resources resolved?*

Our brains, magnificent as they may be, require guidelines and experience to know how to deal with the allocation of resources problem. Even those among us who already have some ability only become better at multitasking over time and with training. It is brain function, the innards of what's inside our heads, the metaphorical tubes and belts and whistles that underpin the cognitive tasks we perform. And brains, in that regard, are just like muscles: they can be developed to perform better.

A sniper, appearing to be super cool under pressure, is capable of controlling his anxiety and fear so that his heart rate and breathing don't interfere with his targeting. His eyes are focused on the task, his brain is so fully engaged that multiple tasks that happen almost simultaneously appear to be just steps in a sequence being taken one after another. In that mode he is a superbly trained cognitive machine. His neural functions are honed to a fine edge.

One study carried out by the Center for Cognitive Brain Imaging in the Department of Psychology at Carnegie Mellon University showed just how the brain works when multitasking. It used functional magnetic resonance imaging (fMRI) technology to take snapshots of the multitasking brain in action. Its subjects were another group of people who have to perform efficiently under pressure, juggle multiple tasks at once, face shifting variables and unexpected events and still perform efficiently every time: Gamers who must process multiple streams of visual information while commanding a first-person POV character in a virtual battle environment, all the while conversing with team members and/or adversaries.

The games require rapid high-level processing of multiple streams of visuospatial information, culminating in rapid and accurate motor responses and enhanced visual processing abilities. Studies of people with a great deal of videogame experience show that experienced gamers develop enhanced visual attention abilities.

The study found that exceptional gamers exhibited six characteristics that were the same across the group being studied even if they happened to be of different ages, sexes, or gaming habits. These characteristics can be loosely summarized in three primary points which apply equally to businesses and businesspeople:

- **The brain works as a network.** There is no particular center in the brain that is reserved for successful multitasking. It requires the connection of many different parts of the brain which suggests that the person multitasking is recruiting many different skills at once and is calling upon both experience and knowledge in order to do so. Snipers, in the execution of their craft, bring to bear an incredible wealth of knowledge and information.
- **Senses and movement are tightly integrated in cognitive processes.** There is no real dividing line separating mind and body. They are truly one. Snipers take time to physically hone themselves. They turn their bodies into additional sources of information. They become embedded in their environments.
- **The more demanding a task, the more resources the brain will allocate to it.** Snipers use everything they have. Each shot, each mission may be unique but it builds on every previous shot and every previous mission. The sniper's superpowers may be his observation skills and his patience but it is his ability to learn and remember that makes him almost superhuman.

These three primary points mean that we can go deep into the sniper mind and pull out the formula a sniper uses as he finds himself in a pressured situation, see what mantra keeps him zeroed in when he should logically be going to pieces, his mind overwhelmed by competing processes, his attention distracted by all the items clamoring to be processed, his will paralyzed with the anxiety of a high-stakes moment.

The formality of sniper training devolves the tasks a sniper faces by breaking everything down into three distinct stages, each with specific steps of its own:

- Observation
- Situation Assessment
- Outcome Calculation

These three stages provide an operational framework that holds equally true in the battlefield and the boardroom. Work and life.

Snipers translate these three stages into less formal language:

- Observation
- Invisibility
- Control

Observation requires patience. The careful collection of facts and their verification so that all the variables are gathered and itemized. Even the ones that are mutable and therefore can create surprises. Observation requires detachment when each element that is noted is factored in, weighed carefully even if the weighing has to happen fast, on the fly. Observation creates a sense of detachment because it negates the need for immediate action. In that moment the sniper feels, like a fly on the wall, a watcher of his own activities. Observation takes time and is instrumental to revealing the dynamic patterns that underlie each situation; it is critical therefore to the building up of a plan of action.

There is a lot to be learned from this approach. In business life, observation is not usually considered a huge advantage.

Watching and waiting is considered procrastination. Decisiveness is equated with swift action. But these are traps that can suck us into actionable steps long before a situation has been appraised correctly. Observation adds a detailed, methodical approach to data gathering that allows a more granular picture to emerge. This then leads to greater clarity, better understanding, and choices that one can truly commit to.

Invisibility, obviously, is not real invisibility. We've seen already that snipers possess a richly detailed awareness of the processes that govern perception and how to trick them. The ability to blend into one's surroundings without drawing attention is not so much about becoming invisible but rather becoming unnoticeable, which is a fine but critical distinction. It is looking at the world with eyes that miss little and a mind that thinks of everything.

THE BUSINESS CASE

Let's face facts now. Few of us consistently apply methodology to anything in our lives. Our business and personal lives seem to be mired in some kind of perpetual treadmill where the things we learn have a half-life that's shorter than what we expect it to be. We forget the things we ought to know and have to relearn them again, much later. Unlike snipers we seem to learn imperfectly. We require quotes framed on our office and bedroom walls to inspire us and motivational posters to make us find the depths inside us that we know ought to be there. Most times, we end up teaching ourselves the same lessons in different contexts, again and again.

Why?

Extraordinary as they may appear snipers are still flesh and blood. Their skill sets and knowledge are subject to the same degradation of time and attention as ours are. Their mental processes exploit the same neural pathways that we each have access to. To be able to sustain their focus and dedication consistently at such high levels for prolonged periods of time, they must be able to access something most of us cannot. They must have some kind of structured support. Something that allows them to ignore the pressures that force the rest of us to lose focus.

The obvious answer here is discipline. But that's not it. Discipline itself takes effort to apply. In the army discipline is applied, imposed almost, by the collective. A soldier is part of a unit. His unit is part of an army. An army is guided by training and traditions, everything is reinforced by a chain of command, clear guidelines, and perfectly defined relationships between those who command and those who obey. There is a robust, detailed structure that keeps everything in place and works to remove ambiguities.

Although they are a part of it all, snipers also stand apart from it. Whatever task a soldier is given to perform it is highly unlikely that he will have to perform it alone.

Snipers on the other hand operate on their own. Even where they are deployed in small, two-men teams, they are relatively alone when compared to the numbers found in other army units.

Yet, no man is an island. No one can function alone for very long, without beginning to exhibit aberrations in their behavior. Errors accumulate easily in the operating system we run as human beings and they prevent us from functioning efficiently. Increase the mental pressure a person experiences in a particular situation and the stress level rises. Stress can incapacitate at both a mental and physical level. Snipers are extraordinary in their ability to sustain their efficiency and effectiveness in circumstances the rest of us would find intolerable. And discipline is a poor explanation of how they do it. Since discipline itself usually requires extra effort to maintain it appears an overly complicated process to apply. So, what helps a sniper maintain his focus? What is it that makes him unique among equals?

To answer that I went hunting for the personal mythologies of my sniper contacts.

When it comes to identity, we are all constructs. Who we think we are is the result of our upbringing, memories, skill set, knowledge, experiences, and personal belief system. Of all the onion layers that make us who we are, our belief system is what powers our core. It's what creates the essence of a human being and makes it possible for each of us to exceed our limits, confound expectations, and do the impossible.

In the 1998 Steven Spielberg hit *Saving Private Ryan*, Private Jackson, the company's resident sniper, quotes verses from the Bible (Psalms 144:1–2) before lining up a shot: "Blessed be the Lord my strength which teacheth my hands to war, and my fingers to fight: My goodness, and my fortress; my high tower, and my deliverer; my shield, and he in whom I trust; who subdueth my people under me."

Religion is the default core belief system for many people, particularly those who find themselves in active service in war zones. The late Chris Kyle, the former Navy SEAL who was the subject for the movie *American Sniper*, used his belief in God to cultivate a deep sense of righteousness to help him navigate the psychological and mental minefields of successive tours of duty in Iraq.

"You need to know why you wake up each morning. Why you keep on breathing day after day." This from Bobby B. He answered all my questions on the technicalities of being a sniper: "You create your own record-keeping system. Every shot, every variable, every condition, every mission. You go over each one again and again and again. You play 'What if' in your head until it feels like you're going mental. And then, if you can you try out some of the shots again, changing some of the parameters, it then begins to make sense. You see just how you can make incremental gains that help you go past the limits of what is possible on paper."

He explained his incremental gains strategy. No one shot depends on a single variable or even a set of variables. It is never about things working for or against you. There are always factors doing both. So it is important to know what works well for you and boost that so that you make incremental improvements on all the things you can control: elevation, ammunition temperature, settings that took into account updrafts and downdrafts, position, routes in and out of the zone you're in. It all plays a part.

Bobby's strategy could help struggling start-ups get public relations capital, new businesses make inroads against entrenched competitors, established businesses begin to move a needle that has plateaued for them. Reading his words I could see the sense they made. How everything suddenly became simple: Have a plan. Then work it.

The trick to this, of course, is making sure the plan you have is the plan you need to have. Bobby wouldn't be drawn out on his stance on religion. Each time I asked he'd either ignore the question completely or talk about the way training teaches you to go through a mental checklist. You break down each step into actionables and then focus on executing them. Obstacles you come up against need to be either removed or circumvented.

Richard Boucher's manual on camouflage perfectly summarizes the difficulty of the task snipers face in training: In addition to the need to remain hidden at all times and be able to engage a subject while remaining undetected a sniper also had to

> ... *move within 200 meters of a trained observer, fire two shots, one with a walker within 3 meters, and egress the area without detection. This demonstrates the sniper's ability to move to within 200 meters of an observation post, which would be placed from 150 to 200 meters from the perimeter. The actual target would be inside the perimeter and this would account for the 400 to 600 meter shot. These requirements test the sniper's ability not only to move stealthily, but his skill in the art, and science, of camouflage. Remember that the sniper's mission is not suicide, thus he must now leave the area without detection while the enemy is fully alert and has an attitude problem.*

If that is the basic standard snipers needed to attain before graduating, their ability to focus borders on the superhuman. To achieve it they slip into character: their self-defined identity. Bobby knew who he was when he woke up in the morning. He knew it with a certainty that burned away the clouds of doubt that most people face.

In learning to hide as they do snipers understand how we see. Their skill in camouflage is the ultimate test of deception versus perception.

If staying hidden is such a necessity, the ability to choose the battlefield must be critical. Not all areas are the same and not every field of action will provide the same degree of difficulty when it comes to camouflage. David Reed is a former Ranger sniper and army instructor who now edits *Sniper Country*, a Web site dedicated to helping snipers and would-be snipers learn more about and perfect their craft. He has this to say on the subject of picking your battlefield: "The area you select should make success likely." His instructions are based upon the US Army's sniper training programs at Fort Benning Sniper School and Fort Bragg Special Operations Target Interdiction Course. His advice is intended to provide a helping hand, a means through which the odds that are usually stacked against a sniper, operating at the very limits of his capabilities, can be tipped to his favor.

Researching this book, trying to understand how snipers can do the incredible things they do, I began to see how the men and women who train as snipers undergo a transformative process, the "reengineering" that Craig Harrison talked about when he related his experience of becoming a sniper.

There were pieces of a greater puzzle that were beginning to fall together. All I needed was to find the edges, understand the logic of the patterns I was uncovering and apply it to business. Simon Menner's art project was key. Snipers don't hide in the environment they are in, they hide from the minds that observe that environment. They seem to be aware of how the world works, in depth. How the different elements of the environment synthesize a picture. How light and shadow work together. How different textures work with each other to produce the invariances that allow us to recognize an object.

Without prior awareness of a sniper in hiding we may never

be able to see one who is actually hidden. Our brains need visual pre-cuing, knowledge of the context, and prior experience, much like they need to see one coin on the ground in order to find another. But that's not all. Not by a long shot.

Monty B. is the nickname of a forty-three-year-old lance corporal who served with the Coldstream Guards in Afghanistan as part of the British contingency there. He holds the honor of having the highest number of sniper kills with a single shot in recent memory. Using a weapon identical to the one fired by Craig Harrison, from a distance of 930 yards (just over half a mile) he hit the suicide vest of a Taliban fighter, detonating it and killing him and his five armed companions instantly.

"I can't emphasize enough that sniping is not about shooting every day. It's about hours and hours of observation," Monty said in a newspaper interview where he talked about his training. "You hide things in different areas, camouflage them. And then lie observing those who observe them or go past them. You need to understand the reasons people might have spotted some and not others."

Snipers, it occurred to me, are like the aloof, vigilant, superheroes depicted in *Watchmen*, the alternate-reality comic book series in which the silent, distant observers of humanity see things in the actions and decisions of their fellow men that no others see. Snipers are not just tasked with taking action, they have to justify it to their superiors. With every kill shot subject to oversight they have to be certain of their choices. Their real superpower then is the ability to observe and think about what they see. This explains why they appear to be loners, why they have been traditionally mistrusted. Observing others is not something you can switch off. Human nature is in constant flux. Like actors and writers are never off the job, snipers are constantly working, their minds observing, itemizing, and cataloging. This creates a sense of distance from others that those around them respond to.

If businesses had the equivalent of a sniper team working for them, constantly observing, itemizing, cataloging, they'd suddenly have an incredible competitive advantage. They'd be able to see themselves as others saw them. They'd be able to identify obstacles in the ways they connected with their audience, found their potential clients, and communicated their marketing message and remove them before they became a problem. They would be able to visualize their competitors looking at them and act in ways that would fool them. They'd be able to understand exactly what a customer saw when she was looking at them and create a frictionless way of doing business.

Such a powerful mind-set is not easy to manufacture. Most of the times snipers, caught up in the task at hand, don't even realize they possess it. One of my respondents, under the condition of anonymity, showed me just how powerful a weapon it could be. "I just meet all conditions, before shooting," he said cryptically.

He went by the name of Mr. T. A Frenchman. He'd been in the 19th Fighter Group, 2nd Armored Division, in Villingen, Germany, before transferring to the 23rd Infantry Regiment Commando Force Training Center at Les Rousses, Jura, in France. He'd seen action as a sniper more than a few times, been in hot water more than he would say, and was not always willing to be open about it.

"I started a new business a year ago with a great partner," he finally told me on video call via a Google Hangout on the promise that I would not reveal his name. "I am president of a smartphone, tablets, and connected objects repair start-up in the form of a network of partners, franchisees, and master franchisees." He said the company's aim was to grow internationally.

His sniper's mind is his greatest asset. "Business intelligence carried out by me, allowed me to find a complementary concept in our market and to define a strategy where nobody expects us to compete with companies that rushed to this emerging market. [As a result] I see them while they do not see me yet, and they may one day ask, 'But how did they do this?'"

Talking to him, I realized that while snipers cannot always "choose" the battles they fight, nor can they always choose the battlefield, they make a whole host of other choices, each of which affects the reality, the experience, and the outcomes they achieve. In that sense the "battlefield" is always of their choice because it is created by what they have done on the lead-up prior to it. As Mr. T said, "I see them while they do not see me yet."

In business, a lack of observational skills means that you are always in reactive mode, never able to stop and plan, which also means that you are not in control.

So how do we turn this around and use the sniper skill set to our advantage in a business setting?

- **Do your homework**—Understand what it is that makes your business tick. What is its lifeblood? What is a frilly extra? Understand what makes your niche of the market go round. Beyond money, which everyone needs, what is the primary supply of fuel? Is it reliability? Reputation? A high profile? The need to experience what you do before someone buys? Is it engineering? Design? A high-end concept? These are the things you need to isolate. The moment you do you can then also see who your real competitors are.

Then you can see what it is they are doing. This allows you to quantify your data and plan your actions better.

- **Manage your presence**—When you understand the dynamic principles that guide your business you are better positioned to stave off being disrupted by developments which you could not see before. Uber, disrupting the global taxi industry, CrossFit and SoulCycle disrupting the $21 billion gym industry, and Simple catching the banking behemoths by surprise are just a few examples of what happens when all you can see is what you do. When it comes to business practices and business decisions, invisibility is translated into actions that power fundamental differences but which remain largely unobserved.

- **Have clear goals**—Business life is notorious for scope creep, the incremental broadening of targets and mission statements that diffuses focus, and this includes when goals are set. When there are no clear, feasible goals that can demonstrably tie into a greater, overall strategy energy is wasted achieving very little. As a result it is easy to become demoralized. Clarity in approach helps create clarity in thinking. Clear thinking leads to greater, overall confidence.

For business leaders and strategic thinkers, these three steps are used to give a sense of control. When there is "conflict"—the account-clinching presentation, the sales day that captures a lot of attention, the product launch that expands market share, and the company announcements that drive brand equity—the ability to control outcomes is determined by the choices that are made.

There is a risk here of becoming lost in the details. When we amass data in order to make a decision, anxiety sets in. It becomes difficult sometimes to decide when enough is enough. The best help in these situations comes from another Rudyard Kipling poem titled "I Keep Six Honest Serving Men . . ." In the poem Kipling details them as: what, where, when, why, who, and how, and many an investigative journalist has used them to determine just when there is enough information and an article can be written in a way that has real value.

In chapter 3 we shall see some of the secrets snipers' minds reveal as they make difficult decisions or perform critical tasks, and we shall learn to think more like them. In the meantime, for those moments when the list of tasks which need to be performed in tandem gets to be too much, prioritizing is always a matter of taking a step back, taking stock, and assessing using the six steps below:

- Collect a list of all the tasks you need to perform.
- Split the tasks into "Urgent" and "Important."
- Ascribe a numerical value of importance to each one from one to three, with one being most important and three the least.
- Determine the amount of effort each task will require to complete and assess it in terms of urgency or importance.
- Be willing to be flexible and adaptable as some tasks may change or prove to be harder than expected.
- Know when to cut; not everything should be on your list.

This is an approach that produces a very specific sense of certainty. Success is a mind-set. Confidence cannot be manufactured. When the right mind-set is achieved, confidence is the by-product. Everything really is in the mind because we can never become something we are unable to consider.

THE SNIPER SKILL ACQUISITION LIST

In this chapter you learned:

- You can stack the odds of success in your favor by believing in yourself.
- Mental tricks such as talking about yourself in the third person help create sufficient distance to get rid of the ego and create a broader perspective.
- The sniper's skills of observation, situation assessment, and outcome calculation are a good fit for businesses of all kinds.
- Understanding how your business looks from the outside is a very good way to understand its position in the marketplace and your brand's real power.
- The secret to being decisive lies in knowing when to say "enough" to the data collection process.

Any man could, if he were so inclined, be the sculptor
of his own brain.

—SANTIAGO RAMÓN Y CAJAL, ADVICE FOR
A YOUNG INVESTIGATOR

3

The Right Tools for the Job: Learn What You Need to Use, When, Where

A TRIANGULARLY SHAPED AREA JUST south of Baghdad was an unfriendly one for soldiers in 2004. The Mahdi Army, Shia militants, were on the rise and the Iraqi insurgency had begun to target US and Coalition forces stationed in the area. For 14 Fox Company of Marines, on a routine sweep mission through Latifiya, which would—a little later—be dubbed the "triangle of death," things were going to get very interesting, very quickly.

It was April 9, the day when, in Baghdad itself, a civilian fuel convoy operated by private contractors Halliburton and Kellogg, Brown & Root would be ambushed en route to Baghdad International Airport by the Mahdi Army and several US Army soldiers would be killed.

As was routine by then, marine companies out on patrol had a sniper overwatch. This time it was provided by Staff Sergeant Steve Reichert, just twenty-five years old at the time, and his spotter Corporal Winston Tucker. The patrol's mission that day was to look for insurgents in the area and protect Arba'een pilgrims moving through. Reichert and Tucker had taken position on top of an oil storage tank outside the town despite knowing that the position had come under attack from small arms fire the day before.

"We had little choice on the matter," Reichert would say in a History Channel interview years later, recalling the event. "It was not the best spot in the world, but we needed to be there."

The need for their presence soon became apparent. After spotting what appeared to be an improvised explosive device (IED) put into a dead animal left by the roadside and alerting the marine patrol, Reichert and Tucker watched the town around them erupt into an ambush.

The engagement would soon turn into a thirteen-hour-long firefight that would claim the lives of several marines. About halfway through that engagement and while taking fire directed toward them, Tucker spotted a group of three men armed with belt-fed machine guns running on a rooftop and ducking out of sight, behind a brick wall.

Knowing that from their vantage point the three men could do significant damage to the marine patrol below them if they could bring their firepower to bear, Reichert realized he had to do something about it, fast. From where he was he could not see the three men behind the brick wall. But he was not about to hesitate either. The gun he was firing that day was the M82A3, also known as Barrett M82, probably the most powerful sniper rifle in the world. Its .50 caliber bullets with a specialized tungsten core that packs both an explosive and incendiary component explain

Fig 3.1 The Barrett M82, standardized by the US military as the M107, is a recoil-operated, semiautomatic, anti-material rifle developed by the American Barrett Firearms Manufacturing company. It is used by many units and armies around the world.

why the rifle's designation is: anti-material. Properly handled it can bring down a helicopter or light aircraft, stop a truck or take out a light armored vehicle.

Reichert's account of the moment sounds dispassionate: "Taking this team out became our priority. The first round we sent out was off by a few mils. Corporal Tucker picked up the splash and gave me a correction. The second round was also off, but a lot closer than the first. The third round landed on the stairway wall they were crouched behind. The backside of the wall turned red and we didn't see any activity from that point on."

Reichert's shot from a mile away, a distance equivalent to seventeen and a half football fields, set a record for one shot with three kills, landing him a career training future snipers when he retired from the US Army for medical reasons.

As he admits himself, having the right tools for the job was critical. While he also carried the M40 sniper rifle with him and had to use it when he ran out of ammunition for the M82, it was the heavier weapon that was instrumental in saving the lives of the people he was protecting that day.

THE SCIENCE: The neurobiology of peak human performance shows that perfect form and incredible output always come down to the priority in which the brain recruits the different centers required to perform and the degree to which the ego is suppressed so that the performance can take center stage.

LOOKING INSIDE PEOPLE'S HEADS

In New York City, Jordan Muraskin was staring at his laptop to see what the brain of a baseball player looked like the moment he was making the decision to swing or not at a curveball approaching him at 70 miles per hour (mph).

His laptop contained data that was neatly organized into graphs, data tables, and heat maps. Each panel represented the visualization of an abstraction, a reading taken by electrodes of something that could not be normally seen. Presented in this compartmentalized, fragmented, and largely abstracted way was the mind of a baseball player the moment he was making the decision to take a swing. It was invisible thought captured as it was being created.

The baseball players Muraskin was studying had agreed to take part in an experiment using baseballs being fired at them at speeds in excess of 70 mph. The distance from the rear point of the pitcher's mound to home plate where the player is waiting with the bat is exactly 60 feet and 6 inches (18.4 meters). A baseball traveling at 70 miles per hour needs just one second to cover 103 feet (31.3 meters), which means that it is moving some

948 times faster than the speed at which our eyes can blink and it requires just 0.58 seconds to reach home plate.

That's faster than the eyes can see it, never mind the brain can register it. Yet baseball players routinely hit home runs off 70-mph pitches; they even manage to hit balls pitched at 95 mph and even 100 mph. Muraskin could not understand how this was possible.

The data points on Muraskin's laptop were neatly grouped and labeled with names like Neural Discrimination Strength, Decision Position Metrics, and Neural Decoding Performance but hidden in the numbers and the undulating graph lines lay what Muraskin believed was the answer to a deeper question. What was it that made a baseball player who he was? What hidden power, what unseen secret turned one man into an unstoppable home-run hitting machine and another into a has-been whose career was taking a nosedive, his batting average marking him for a quick sale while his club tried to recoup some of its investment?

On the other side of America in Carlsbad, California, some 2,839.3 miles away, or forty-one hours of cross-country driving via the 80 West interstate, if Google Maps is to be believed, Chris Berka, CEO of Advanced Brain Monitoring (ABM for short), was staring at similar graphs and metrics. His labels were different, but his charts and graph panels told a similar story.

Pulled out of the inside of the head of a top army sniper as he was about to make a difficult shot, Berka believed his figures, charts, and numbers showed important aspects of the critical decision-making process. He had a picture of the brain preparing itself to function at its very peak.

Although they did not know it, the two men were looking at a remarkably similar picture for remarkably similar reasons. They were both chasing after the Holy Grail of brain analytics. Using functional magnetic resonance imaging (fMRI for short) they looked at snapshots of how the brain used its structure to think, hoping to see the magic formula, the secret which, once revealed, would allow them to help less gifted brains perform better.

The concept is an old one, applied to a new context. The American engineer Frederick Winslow Taylor pioneered the idea of time and motion studies in 1911, as a way to optimize and standardize industrial plant production. The idea relies on there being only so many ways that are optimal for the performance of a given task. If you can study them all, you can then analyze them and break them down into a formula which can then be applied independently across many different plants.

The principle also works with mental tasks. The brain has a physiology which follows the laws of physics. Blood can only flow at a particular speed, electrical impulses can only jump across synapses at the speed of electricity, and there is only so much blood sugar to go around to power it all. All this suggests that there has to be a mechanism to thought and thinking. Understand how the brain makes critical decisions and you can understand how you can re-create the state of mind that makes exemplary performance possible for everyone. Critical decision-making can then be democratized, its processes broken down into subsets of mental routines that with proper training anyone can activate. It can be made available to the figurative masses instead of being the carefully hoarded secret of the select few.

Muraskin and his research partner Jason Sherwin, both at Columbia University, first combined their skills and interests to analyze ballplayer brains using an EEG in the spring of 2012. At the time, only a handful of other published experiments had related actual neural data to baseball. But, as they examined six random subjects, none with any advanced baseball experience, the Columbia researchers noticed something peculiar. Every time the batter incorrectly identified a pitch, there was a large neuronal current source, like water bubbling up from a spring, in a region of the brain called Brodmann area 10 (BA10), located in the prefrontal cortex, directly behind the forehead.

This time, Muraskin and his partner's lens into the brain was fMRI, which investigates neural activity by measuring changes in blood flow through the brain. Large, expensive machines were their "brain goggles."

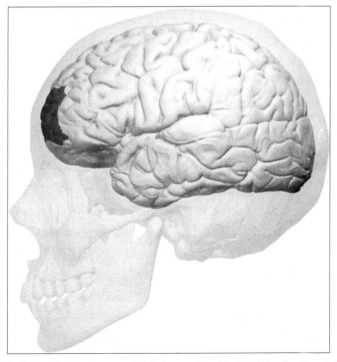

Fig 3.2 The Brodmann area 10 is located just behind the forehead. It gives emphasis to vision and language processing.

Chris Berka was working with snipers, men and women who held metal in their hands. Metal and magnetic scanners do not go well together, so using a large fMRI scanner to test them was out of the question. His "brain goggles" had to be a lot more portable and smaller. Working, initially with a Defense Advanced Research Projects Agency (DARPA), an agency of the US Department of Defense responsible for the development of emerging technologies for use by the military, Berka's team had to use equipment which was unobtrusive enough to be worn by top brass, business leaders, as well as top snipers tasked with taking difficult shots.

If there was to be the equivalent of a time and motion study for brains which made sense, there had to be a way to examine not just the brains of those who were being studied, the subjects who possessed specific knowledge or specific skills, but also the brains of those who hoped to acquire those skills for themselves.

DARPA was really interested in the project. The military needs its leaders to be extremely adaptable, flexible, creative, ethical, and moral, as well as being able to deal with a variety of global environments. It's exactly the same issues that business schools have been studying for decades. The idea that there could be a formula that could somehow be packaged and sort of "injected" into military leaders and business people was exciting to them. It would negate the hit-and-miss approach of finding the right people to join the ranks of the military or the business world. It would guarantee high-quality results out of standardized training programs. It would settle once and for all the nature-versus-nurture debate about just what makes a great leader: birth or training.

The formula, if it could be found, would win wars and help

make millions of dollars for commercial companies that used it in their leadership training. The stakes could not have been higher.

THE MILLION-DOLLAR BRAIN

A thought is made up of chemicals and electricity. Tracing its root and hoping to understand its form is a little like looking at a forest and trying to decide where it started first: with a root or the first rays of the sun that fed the seedlings? There are simply too many parts to be sure, too many variables to ever hope to be precise. But there's no denying the forest nor its impact. Its shape and form are highly visible. Its very presence has measurable, analyzable effects.

Similarly, in the brain, while we may never be able to track a thought from inception to the point where it can be articulated and its impact weighed and examined, we can see all the parts that work together to make it happen. And it is those parts that actually tell the story we need to understand.

That story finds its most receptive audience in three specific arenas of human activity, each of which makes full use of the concept of the force multiplier. They are the world of business, the military, and baseball. Business leaders, snipers, and top baseball players are expected to meet a high standard in their performance under intense pressure, to do so repeatedly, and to deliver value to their respective group or team regardless of their personal conditions or the circumstances they find themselves operating under. They each add greater "value" to the areas they are deployed in by creating the circumstances that allow the machinery around them to shift into high gear and do its job.

I know that superimposing a baseball game, or a product

launch onto a battlefield crisscrossed by sniper bullets appears to be a reach, but the dynamics governing each one are eerily similar. It's only the details of their individual circumstances that differ.

Business leaders, snipers, and baseball players have always been at the center of the key question that asks, why are they what they are? What is it that makes them special? How do they ascend into their particular role? A tremendous amount of effort, philosophizing, soul searching, prodding, testing, and dissecting has taken place over a very long period of time to determine whether those who are deemed to be special are the result of great genes (and are therefore the product of nature) or great training (and can truthfully be called the product of nurture).

But before we even get to the raging debate of nature versus nurture, it is interesting to see how these three distinct and seemingly very different areas of human activity see their ideal prime candidates. This is where they overlap. In each and every example of a successful business leader, sniper, or top baseball player there is a core identity. A sense of knowing who they are and why they are. A center buried deep within the onion layers of their personality. It gives them a sense of inner balance.

The Romans called this "gravitas" and prized it in their leaders. They felt that it gave a person a sense of a rock-solid foundation in who he or she was, which meant they could be relied upon to make better decisions because they were unlikely to be rattled by outside events. The Romans sought to cultivate this quality in both private and public life and made it one of their sought-after virtues.

It is not unfair to say that our ability to manage anything in life hinges upon our ability to manage ourselves. If our own center "cannot hold" we then feel the world is to blame, things spin out of control, and there is nothing left worth fighting for. There is a solid trail of logic we can follow from outstanding performance that is the result of how the brain thinks about itself to the way it deals with the task at hand.

While in the past businesses, armies, and baseball clubs had to scout for candidates with the potential to join their ranks, we can now look at how these top performers think when they do their jobs, map it, and then use specific techniques to teach the way they think to others. In the Disney film *Million Dollar Arm*, based on a real story, a talent scout used the unorthodox approach of a televised contest to try and find aspiring baseball players who could pitch 90-mph fastballs. By replicating the way a brain works at the top-performer level we disrupt the traditional economics of scarcity and create million-dollar minds that can deliver top results.

Think how different the world would be if businesses could have as many star performers as they could absorb. Armies could have their supersoldiers. Baseball clubs could have their star hitters. Excellence is not something one is born with. It is manufactured with a dozen ingredients the key of which is what the Delphic Oracle of Ancient Greece knew all along: Know thyself. Create your core.

Consider this terrifying scenario:

I'm close to tears behind my thin cover of sandbags as twenty screaming, masked men run toward me at full speed, strapped into suicide bomb vests and clutching rifles. For every one I manage to shoot dead, three new assailants pop up from nowhere. I'm clearly not shooting fast enough, and panic and incompetence are making me continually jam my rifle.

Substitute *desk* for *sandbags* and *business decisions* for *suicidal assailants* and you have your average day at the office, where the tasks keep mounting up while customer crises happen one after another, employees rebel, colleagues conspire, your e-mail inbox overflows with items marked as "urgent," and your phone rings because your wife or girlfriend is convinced that you don't love her anymore.

The battle scenario described above is, fortunately, only on video. It's the very simulation that trains US troops to take their first steps with a rifle, and everything about it has been engineered to feel like an overpowering assault. It overloads the brain with sensory input and cognitive analysis tasks. It creates confusion and it's designed to address self-doubt. Its first-time effect on those who experience it is an intense sense of mental shutdown. It makes you want to just stop what you are doing and walk away. It is easy to imagine similar scenarios, in terms of pressure, experienced by trained snipers in the battlefield.

Performing under such conditions requires the obligatory ten thousand hours of practice and the forging of myelin pathways in the brain that mark the seasoned vet from the rookie. But guess what? Most of us don't have those ten thousand hours and snipers themselves certainly don't when they become operational, early in their careers.

What they do share with us (or we do with them) is motivation, drive, and the need to get the job done. And that's where it gets interesting because in order for that to happen under such intense conditions we have to achieve a mental state known as flow. It's a feeling of effortless concentration that characterizes exceptional performance in all kinds of skills.

Snipers can switch it on, seemingly at will. Their minds, conditioned to face complex challenges quickly, know how to harness its power. Top-flight businessmen know how to achieve it so they can perform under pressure, and baseball athletes like Phillies outfielder John Kruk slip effortlessly into it when they need to. Kruk, in particular, makes a notable example as despite not being the trimmest of baseball players he hit .316 in 1993 and became a three-time National League All-Star, with a lifetime average of exactly .300.

In positive psychology, flow (also known as "the zone") is the mental state of operation in which a person performing a particular task is immersed so totally in it that there is no perceived distraction on their part that can stop them from peak performance.

In Asia, with its tradition of meditation and Zen, there is a vast body of literature describing this mental state that borders on the mystical. The teachings of Buddhism and Taoism speak of a state of mind known as the "action of inaction" or "doing without doing" (*wu wei* in Taoism) that greatly resembles the idea of flow. Hindu texts on Advaita philosophy such as Ashtavakra Gita and the yoga of knowledge such as Bhagavad-Gita refer to a similar state.

But there's nothing mystical about the sensation of flow. Flow psychology was pioneered by Mihaly Csikszentmihalyi, a Hungarian who is currently a professor of psychology and management at Claremont Graduate University and has been head of the department of psychology at the University of Chicago and the department of sociology and anthropology at Lake Forest College. His focus was to help flow appear in the workplace.

Csikszentmihalyi spent a long time studying the seemingly mystical, interviewing musicians and dancers, composers and martial artists, painters and writers, entrepreneurs and business leaders. He wanted to understand what it was that made their brains function in such amazing synchronization when they obviously worked under intense pressure, juggling many different priorities. Along with his colleagues Csikszentmihalyi interviewed over eight thousand subjects from all over the world pulling together experiences from people as diverse as Dominican monks and blind nuns, Navajo shepherds and Silicon Valley execs.

The theory he developed to explain the mechanism under which flow happens is centered around what we can call human bandwidth. In a world that is made up of data, everything is information. The ultimate gateway then is fashioned out of the bit rate limits imposed by biology. The capacity of our brains to process information literally determines how much we can understand.

We are the product of a complex network of sensors. Our brains and bodies form an indivisible network along which information is captured and then transmitted. Exactly how we process it is open to interpretation and the subject of a fierce debate taking place in neuroscientific circles. On the one side of the argument are those who think that the brain works like a computer. Their argument goes a little like this:

The brain is a massive parallel processor that stores information in overlapping patterns of neuronal connections. Single neurons can participate in many different memories and processes. This is exactly why our brains are so good at pattern recognition, why one thought or memory reminds you of another, why an odor can trigger a flood of memories.

On the other side, in admittedly smaller numbers, are those who think that the brain is a tightly integrated part of the network of sensors that make us what we are:

Here is what we are not born with: information, data, rules, software, knowledge, lexicons, representations, algorithms, programs, models, memories, images, processors, subroutines, encoders, decoders, symbols, or buffers—design elements that allow digital computers to behave somewhat intelligently. Not only are we not born with such things, we also don't develop them—ever.

On the outcome of the contest between the two camps hinges, perhaps, the secret to immortality and the answer to the questions of whether we shall be able to truly create superintelligent machines that will one day surpass us, and whether we can learn how to download our consciousness to some kind of storage device and therefore live forever.

Despite their competing and mutually exclusive theories of how the brain functions both sides agree on one thing: RAM, or random access memory, and the biological limits imposed upon the brain when dealing with the flow of information. In his 2004 TED Talk, Csikszentmihalyi revealed that he thought that the upper limit of information a brain can process is about 110 bits per second. While this may seem like a lot, it isn't when it is divided among all the different things we have to do at any moment throughout the day.

Conversation, for instance, is a complex, multilayered code that takes up to 60 bits per second for us to keep up with. Which helps explain why when we are actually talking to someone we are not able to concentrate very deeply on anything else. In most cases we can decide what things to focus our attention on and, usually, choose to multitask, spreading our brain's bandwidth capacity among them. However, when one is in the flow state, the brain is completely engrossed with the one task at hand, without making the conscious decision to do so. The individual can then lose awareness of all other things: time, people, distractions, and even basic bodily needs. This occurs because all of the attention of the person in the flow state is on the task at hand; there is no more attention to be allocated.

A sniper's mind then is not necessarily superior to everyone else's in terms of what it can do. It is, however, superior in what it has been trained to do, namely attain that optimal state of performance which allows it to disregard everything but the task at hand. It is now clear that a sniper's mind is not so much born as it is made. And if it is made we can all learn to think better using similar mental optimization techniques.

THE SNIPER'S DECISION TREE

Brandon Webb, a former Navy SEAL sniper, explained in a Newsmax TV interview the pressures a sniper faces as he makes the decision whether to engage a particular target.

> As a sniper you have this massive decision tree in some situations, but Special Operations doesn't work that way. You have autonomy—a sniper needs to be pointed in the right direction, given boundaries, but with the autonomy to make these

decisions because you are fighting an enemy that can make a
decision just like that.

On page nine of the field manual for the Navy SEALs Sniper Training Program, under the section labeled Command and Control there is a description of how a sniper is expected to operate:

Once the decision has been made by the commander to employ the sniper, all command and control of his actions should pass to the sniper team. At no time should the sniper have to fire on someone's command. He should be given clearance to fire and then he and he alone should decide exactly when.

Operating with a small sniper team (usually a sniper and a spotter), making judgment calls, channeling all of the brain's ability to focus on a primary task requires a central precondition that is firmly implied but which we now must articulate: a close correlation between skills and the challenge presented. This is where training comes in. Snipers train to an extremely high degree of physical fitness and mental toughness so that they can actually prove equal to the challenges that they will face irrespective of the magnitude.

Similarly, baseball players spend an enormous amount of time practicing their batting and pitching, their throwing and catching just so their skills become automatic on the diamond. Businessmen train in MBA programs or go through a series of practical experiences and apprenticeships where they have the opportunity to directly witness business models in action.

Skills require personality. A person's character becomes key

- Experience as a hunter or woodsman.
- Experience as a competitive marksman.
- Interest in weapons.
- Ability to make rapid, accurate assessments and mental calculations.
- Ability to maintain an emotionally stable personal life.
- Ability to function effectively under stress.
- Possession of character traits of patience, attention to detail, perseverance, and physical endurance.
- Ability to focus completely.
- Ability to endure solitude.
- Objectivity to the extent that one can stand outside oneself to evaluate a situation.
- Ability to work closely with another individual in confined spaces and under stress.
- Freedom from certain detrimental personal habits such as the use of tobacco products and alcohol. (Use of these is a liability unless the candidate is otherwise highly qualified. These traits, however, should not be the sole disqualifier.)
- First-class APFT scores with a high degree of stamina and, preferably, solid athletic skills and abilities.

Fig 3.3 Field manual FM 3-05.222 titled *Special Forces Sniper Training and Employment*, contains a very comprehensive list of characteristics a sniper has to have in order to make the grade.

to how they use what they learn to become who they want to become.

What Jordan Muraskin in New York City and Chris Berka in Carlsbad, California, saw when they examined the graphs and charts in their laptops was an image of the brain performing in a state of flow. They saw a person's character in action. Both Berka and Muraskin had machines that could read the mental recipe of success. Both were confident that they could find a way to help everyone unlock it inside their heads, not just top performers. The answer to the question that is perennially asked in cases of difficult cognitive processes—"Do you have the right tools for the job?"—is "Yes, always." But not everyone can reach out and grasp them. Not without some help, that is.

When it comes to making their minds work in a fully engaged mode on the task at hand snipers perhaps have a perceived advantage that's obvious only in hindsight. Their conscious, visual presence is divorced from the world around them and projected through their scope:

I learned to go through the preparation routine as I was trained. Take stock of the situation. Spot my targets. Plan my actions. Observe the ground, memorize the layout. Prepare. Breathe in, breathe out. Steady the weapon. Decide who is a threat. Engage. The world for me was in my scope. Everything else vanished. I was just a gun.

These words of the marine sniper known to me simply as Tetris made me realize that snipers, by the very act of looking through their scopes, managed to project a virtually disembodied presence of themselves the same way that someone in a virtual reality environment will lose track of his body as his eyes and mind engage in the virtual world with trolls, orcs, and pixies in a digital fantasy land.

Meditation experts suggest that the route to a hyper-aware state of consciousness can be achieved by developing a complex personal ritual that prepares the person, their environment, and their immediate surroundings, and even requires a set time of day for a heightened state of awareness to take place.

But snipers can't realistically go into such complex mental and psychological preparation routines, nor is it realistic to have an optimum time of the day during which mental focus can be achieved. In a battle zone there is no time to "purify" oneself or set the mood with scented candles and soothing music. Yet, the literature of battle is full of hints that mentally tough warriors do use a routine to help them achieve that exact, focused state. In Ancient Greece, the Special Forces of the day, the Spartans, were famous for the attention they paid to their hair, carefully grooming and braiding it before a battle, an act that went down in history when King Leonidas and his followers were discovered at it by a Persian spy before the battle of Thermopylae.

Routine is key to achieving flow. If flow is the key to success then how do we get there without having to attain a state of mystical grace or engaging in a mutual bout of hair grooming à la Spartans? How do snipers achieve it when there is no time to compose themselves in the sense that meditation gurus suggest?

The answer lies in the three postulates that flow advocates recognize as being key to achieving the desired mental state:

- One must be involved in an activity with a clear set of goals and progress. This adds direction and structure to the task.
- The task at hand must be clear and provide immediate feedback. This helps the person negotiate any changing demands and allows them to adjust their performance to maintain the flow state.
- One must have a good balance between the *perceived* challenges of the task at hand and one's own *perceived* skills. One must have confidence in one's ability to complete the task at hand.

Snipers meet every single one of these requirements. Their deployment happens under the strictest of guidelines. The feedback they receive is clear and immediate. Changing variables within those parameters are challenges that have to be met. They are by definition equal to the task they are presented with. Knowledge transcends immediate experience and corrects some of our intuitions about ourselves. Snipers are aware that they have been remade. Their brains have been conditioned through the physical rigors that turned them into soldiers. A body cannot function without a mind. While this is an equation whose mysteries are far from solved, we only need to know it works to take full advantage of it.

The foundations of the road we are on right now were laid by others some time ago. In his popular book *Incognito*, neuroscientist David Eagleman argued that a lot of what we do (and therefore much of what we become) is governed by the unconscious part of our brain the workings of which we are largely unaware of. We are puppets on a string, he suggested, responding to stimuli we cannot see, much less understand. In the years since publication, neuroscience has made incredible inroads and the picture has changed somewhat. We are no longer seen as the helpless puppets neuroscientists thought we were.

In the fictional *Star Trek* universe, a medical tricorder is a multifunction hand-held device that works much like a functional magnetic resonance imaging (fMRI) scanner. It is used for sensor scanning, data analysis, and data recording. The supposition behind it is that by capturing specific data from body functions it can accurately diagnose the state of health of a person and suggest a remedy, if necessary. As devices go, it's actually pretty nifty and although in *Star Trek* they never use it as such, it must surely come in handy when it comes to looking at people's mental states. The device creates a data map of sorts. Not of who they are, but how they think.

Guess what? This *Star Trek* device is no longer fictional.

In 2002 a former outfielder turned baseball team general manager by the name of Billy Beane, was also trying to discern things. Invisible things. Billy was the manager of the Oakland Athletics. Money talks, and in the world of baseball money talks perhaps louder than anywhere else. Given a budget that was barely a third that of his largest rivals Billy was tasked with making it work. Whereas most other baseball managers would have either given up or consigned themselves to the fact that without the money to sign up big players the task of taking the Oakland Athletics to the playoffs was hopeless, Billy used the opportunity to put his obsession with minutiae to work. Convinced that the metrics baseball managers traditionally used did not really tell the picture of a player's performance in the modern age, Billy used data to empirically analyze baseball statistics that measure in-game activity to reach decisions about players that the more traditional approach of using statistics such as stolen bases, runs batted in, and batting average simply could not answer.

His approach took the Oakland Athletics all the way to the playoffs. His secret, immortalized in a book by Michael Lewis called *Moneyball: The Art of Winning an Unfair Game* was to focus on data that was not usually visible.

Data is often thought to be information, but that isn't quite true. Data is a building block. As raw building material, at its point of acquisition it hasn't yet been shaped, processed, or interpreted. Information, on the other hand requires meaning and context to be useful. Before Billy Beane popularized a data-driven approach to baseball analytics, picking out great players was considered to be an art supported by the popular acceptance of a nineteenth-century view of the game and the statistics available at that time. Putting a great baseball team together was like water dowsing. There was an acceptance that a sort of divination was involved and a "sixth sense" was required. Baseball managers were supposed to be experienced war horses. Their time in

THE RIGHT TOOLS FOR THE JOB • 95

the game was what imbued them with the special sixth sense that helped them pick out raw talent.

Billy Beane broke ranks with tradition, but he wasn't breaking new ground. In employing a rigorous data-driven approach to selecting baseball players for a team he was relying on a method first put together in the 1990s by Bill James, a baseball writer and statistician. Bill coined the term *sabermetrics* in reference to the Society for American Baseball Research (SABR), and his approach scientifically analyzes and studies baseball through the use of statistical data, in an attempt to determine why teams win and lose. James's approach really uses statistics to create a lens. It looks at baseball players and sees their futures because it more clearly than anything else reveals their present.

This is something Billy Beane got. Data leads to information and information leads to knowledge. Armed with better data we can gain more accurate information which then makes us more knowledgeable and able to make better decisions and better predictions. There is a missing leap here we're hoping to get to that takes us from knowledge to wisdom. Wisdom doesn't just let us know whom to pick to do a job but also what it is that makes them great for the job in the first place. With wisdom our data lens doesn't just get clearer, it acquires X-ray vision capabilities.

If we could see all the invisible things we need to see. If we could understand just what it is in a baseball player's mind that makes him great, what enables one entrepreneur to succeed against all odds while another one, facing smaller challenges, fails. If we could detect the mind-set that makes success possible, the mental synthesis that allows great decisions to be made at a moment's notice. If we could see how a sniper thinks while he is balancing fluid variables and incredible odds as he is about to take his shot. Would we then be able to train ourselves to do things better? Be more efficient?

It's a line of thought whose logic revolves around a simple technological capability: possession of the equivalent of a *Star Trek* medical tricorder that allows us to see the mind in action.

We tend to think about data as a thing of substance. Something that's irrefutable, rooted firmly in an underlying reality from the bowels of which it has been successfully mined. The singular form of the word—*datum*—actually means "something given," and though in the modern world we associate a piece of datum (a datum) with an individual piece of information, in truth data is a set of something which can now be used to describe its state of being.

Data is more important than datum, the collective is of greater value than the singular because the former possesses what the latter evidently lacks: associative value that gives it context and relevance. Context and relevance confer importance. Importance is relative. All of this becomes part of a form of identity. In using data we know what we think it is we see. A datum, in contrast, is like the link of a single chain: we have no idea how strong or weak it is, whether the chain is broken or happens to be massively long, free floating, or tethered to some point very far away. A single datum is useless to us because we cannot quantify it, much less identify it for what it is.

Data then is the abstract layer of connections. Connections allow us to see meaning. Two lit lanterns in the Old North Church holds zero value to those who view it, unless they also happen to be part of a secret network of spies named Sons of Liberty. Link this further to a waiting band of patriots and the lights become something else entirely. That single moment, reduced to a datum, acquires value only as it links to the events that precede it, and it acquires meaning only when it links to the events that will follow it.

Data surfaces from deeper connections too. The thoughts we have as a result of what we see, what we know, what we have experienced, and what we can do become data that means something beyond the instant of its occurrence. Data has other qualities too. It is transportable, independent of the moment from which it arose.

A baseball player facing down a straight ball flying at him in excess of 100 miles per hour outwardly has little in common with a sniper hiding in an elevated position, carefully adjusting his sights to shoot at a target that's over a mile away. But that's just the surface. Each one, the baseball player and the sniper, are just single points of hard reality, each one a datum. Go deeper, pluck them out of their individual settings, study them to link them to what's happened before the moment when one decided to swing the bat and the other one decided to take the shot, and you suddenly have something else.

The decision process of each is governed by the same three-pound prisoner encased in a dark box made of the hardest bones in the body, its sensory input restricted and lagging. How the brain works, how it can make decisions under those conditions that impact the outside world in real time, is something we are only now beginning to understand. Only now beginning to see. And our eyes, this time, are more than flesh and blood, more even than lenses of glass. Our eyes are made of copper and plastic and have the same electromagnetic qualities as thought itself.

In the twenty-first century, we have fashioned the *Star Trek* medical tricorder and we're using it to peer deep into the mind at the moment a decision is being made. If we can learn to activate peak-performance thinking, we can then master our own destiny, control our lives, and direct our fate.

And that's just the prize we are aiming for here. The control we crave is something we can already see in action. Snipers have it in bundles. Top-flight businesspeople possess it and top baseball players exhibit it. The ability to control ourselves, to be able to exhibit that quality Kipling was waxing lyrical about: *If you can keep your head when all about you / Are losing theirs . . .*

If others can do it and we can see how they do it, then we can replicate it. This is a new world we live in. We are developing ever more sophisticated techniques of capturing and analyzing data. Data is the building block of everything we see and everything we can perceive. As it turns out data is also the building block of cognition which makes it the connecting link between the invisible realm of thoughts and ideas and the visible plain of our everyday existence.

Snipers, historically, have come ready-made. They were farm boys who grew up shooting rabbits on the family farm, their sniper's brains fashioned out of the unpredictability of live targets, the relatively poor quality of whatever weapon they happened to have at hand, and the real need to hunt for their food. They were hunters who spent their lives taking shots downwind from prey, carefully hidden, mentally working out variables that would affect their hitting the target. Vietnam legendary sniper Carlos Norman Hathcock II, the original "American Sniper" taught himself to shoot, growing up having learned to hunt for food with a single-shot rifle. Vasily Zaytsev, the hero of Stalingrad, grew up hunting deer and wolf in the Urals. Simo Häyhä, the Finn uber-sniper, was a farmer and hunter before the war that turned him into a legend. These were not men who'd been trained as snipers. They were snipers-in-waiting. Men with already honed skills. The army, when it did get them, gave them a bigger, better gun and some extra training and sent them on their way. But it did not make them.

Baseball players were talents to be scouted, not skill-based individuals to be made. Scouts scoured the country, using their horse sense to somehow "pick" winners. Great businesspeople were exceptions, outliers who somehow managed to rise from the rest and claim the top spots of the business world. When we didn't understand what made each individual the exceptional talent that he was, when we had no means of peering into their brain and seeing the data at work, we were left with the imprecise, archaic tools of adulation and emulation, in other words imperfect copying driven by cultural modalities.

This is why, in the past, we needed heroes as role models. Heroes play a strong psychosocial archetypal role designed to create modes of behavior which guide those around them. Hercules, in Ancient Greek mythology, stood for virtue and justice. Superman fought for "truth, justice and the American way." The Green Lantern warned "all those who worship evil's might" every time he charged his power ring, and Batman brought balance to the cosmic order.

Good heroes use the power of transformation not only to change themselves for the better, but also to transform the world they live in. In the classic hero journey, the newly transformed hero eventually transforms society in significant and positive ways. He is changed and so are those along his path and those they touch, in turn.

Heroes were society's answer to the question: How do we become better people? Lacking any other means of seeing data their existence became encoded, handy transmission modes of vital information. They guided the formation of the decision tree that led to ordinary men and women doing the right thing. Stepping up when it was required. Thinking beyond what was self-serving when the moment called for it. As a society, we invested so much in the hero-legend because we had no other way to focus our minds, as individuals, beyond the amoeba response of heading away from discomfort and running toward comfort. We needed heroes to recalibrate our moral compasses and keep them pointing toward the true north of truth and justice.

We don't need heroes anymore. They're nice to have. A reaffirmation that others hold values similar to ours, everywhere. A signal that "truth and justice" are still worth fighting for. But we don't need to be shown, imprecisely, how to think in order to think better and clearer and how to make better decisions. When we can see the data the decision tree that guides us becomes easier to understand and arguably easier to implement.

THE BUSINESS CASE

In the course of writing this book, I spoke to business executives from companies where I gave in-house talks or held presentations. Many of the young executives I spoke to held sentiments which they were prepared to share in private, anonymously, which sounded exactly like this one:

Everything I do centers around my career. I have spent a lot of time getting the skills and knowledge that got me through the door to this job. I have student debt to get rid of and dreams I want to make real. I work so I can get ahead in life. So when I make a decision at work, I always think, "What's in it for me?"

At a time when we know that team building, leadership, and passion at work are requirements for getting ahead in a marketplace that has become very unforgiving the success of employing the techniques that shape a sniper's mind lies in finding a way to bridge the disconnect between the battlefield, where one's life hangs in the balance and the workplace where careers are often founded on a trail of backstabbings.

Given the fluidity of the situations they face and the fact that their lives are often on the line, how do snipers do it? How do they implement their decisions? The answer to that perhaps can best be shown by a poignant instance in the drawn-from-life blockbuster Ridley Scott movie *Black Hawk Down*. There are many factors that go into this decision-making process and two opposing cognitive systems that are employed in its execution. The result is so critical to understanding the operative priorities that lead to crystal-clear thinking under pressure that it deserves our dipping into it, in a little more detail.

THE BLACK HAWK MOMENT OF TRUTH

The battle of Mogadishu (as the events depicted in *Black Hawk Down* are known) has already had one major feature film and a number of books written about it. It turned what was intended to be a one-hour snatch-and-run operation in Somalia into a firefight between American forces and UN support troops and

Somali militia, that raged for thirty hours. The American forces and their supporters fought to save the crews of two downed Black Hawk helicopters while the Somalis battled to capture them. The battle was the bloodiest involving US troops since the Vietnam War and it remained so until the Second Battle of Fallujah in 2004.

The ferocity of the battle is told by the numbers alone: It cost the lives of eighteen American soldiers and there were seventy-three wounded. The American forces were supported by UN troops of which one Malaysian and one Pakistani died, and seven Malaysians and two Pakistanis were wounded. The Somalis suffered anywhere between 1,500 and 3,000 militia and civilian casualties, with the initial newspaper account reporting 312 dead and 815 wounded. Among the dead Americans were Master Sergeant Gary Gordon and Sergeant First Class Randy Shughart and it is their story that merits our attention.

Both elite Delta Force snipers, Gordon and Shughart had initially been assigned to provide precision air-to-ground fire support to the operation. From their own helicopter they had witnessed the downing of the second Black Hawk, designated Super Six-Four, and seen the deteriorating condition of its crew who, trapped inside the downed helicopter, were becoming the center of attention of hundreds of militia running toward them through the city streets of Mogadishu.

Realizing that the downed helicopter would soon be overrun and its pilot, still strapped inside and firing single shots from an MP5 automatic, would die, Sergeant Gordon requested to be placed on the ground so that he and Sergeant Shughart could set up a defensive perimeter and protect the downed helicopter and her crew until extraction was possible.

While the language sounds clinical and sterile, the situation they must have been looking at was anything but. The square where the Black Hawk helicopter had gone down was overlooked by shacks and derelict buildings, which made perfect firing places for the oncoming enemy. Any intelligent person carrying out a situation assessment would know that the odds of survival in a situation like this are minimal. With a wounded pilot and crew unable to run and backup pinned down by enemy fire elsewhere in the city, any attempt to take on the onrushing enemy bordered on the suicidal. Yet the two snipers were showing no hesitation.

The initial request was denied as too dangerous and command did not budge when it was made again a little later. With the enemy closing in, however, and the helicopter crew seemingly doomed the Delta Force snipers urgently repeated their request. Command apparently left it to the discretion of the sniper team leader who reluctantly approved it.

Fig 3.4 The crash site of the Black Hawk helicopter, designated Super Six-Four, in Mogadishu, Somalia.

Sergeant Gordon and Sergeant Shughart fast-roped from their helicopter to within 300 feet (100 meters) of the downed Black Hawk and its wounded crew, and started working their way toward them, firing as they went, clearing the way to the helicopter. Talking about it much later, Chief Warrant Officer Mike Durant, the helicopter's wounded pilot, would say:

> I never saw where they came from, but they had to come from the rear, otherwise I would have seen them approach. It was a surreal feeling. I mean it was like this awful situation that you just realized you're in is now suddenly over.

The two Delta Force snipers quickly took stock of the situation, moved the incapacitated crew and wounded pilot to cover, and started the process of securing the perimeter, laying down a murderous hail of frighteningly accurate gunfire.

Durant remembers:

> Their actions were professional and deliberate to the point that they looked like they were planning a parking lot. They didn't seem alarmed by the situation that we were in.
>
> It was just focused on the task, doing what they needed to do to improve our situation, and get through it, get us rescued. Whatever it is they needed to do.

Their professionalism did not make them bulletproof. The two snipers, starting to run low on ammunition, were drawing a tremendous amount of fire from the advancing Somali mob. When Shughart was killed by a shot, Gordon retrieved his weapon, gave it to Mike Durant, and then went out to use the downed helicopter for cover as he attempted, on his own, to stem the armed human tide coming toward him.

By all accounts he lasted maybe ten minutes before his position was overrun and he was killed in a hail of bullets. Mike Durant was taken captive, his crew dispatched swiftly. He was released some eleven days later.

When he talks about that day, he recounts the events clearly, his speech steady, his tone unwavering like he is recounting the memory of a hunting trip or a picnic.

> *Without a doubt, I owe my life to these two men and their bravery.*
> *Those guys came in when they had to know it was a losing battle.*
> *There was nobody else left to back them up.*
> *If they had not come in, I wouldn't have survived.*

As a result of their actions, both Sergeant Gordon and Sergeant Shughart received the Medal of Honor, the only ones to receive it from all the soldiers who took part in the action that day.

This is such an incredible act of bravery that even thinking about challenging its logic feels like treason. But challenge it we must in order to understand something really important. Why did they act as they did? What was it that made them decide to take on the odds, stacked as they were, against them and try to save a doomed crew from an impossible situation?

Mike Durant's account provides the necessary clues. Imagine the fractal chaos of the scene. A carefully planned operation gone awry. A wrecked city coming alive with confusion and danger. Two helicopters unexpectedly downed. Incoming small arms fire

Fig 3.5 Delta Force snipers, Master Sergeant Gary Gordon (left) and Sergeant First Class Randy Shughart.

and rocket-propelled grenade (RPG) trails everywhere as the ruined city of Mogadishu became a hotbed of hostile activity. The helicopter Gary Gordon and Randy Shughart were in taking so much fire that the door gunner manning the machine gun was severely injured along with other members of the crew. The city swarming with badly trained but heavily armed Somali militia. A wounded crew's life hanging by a thread, about to be snuffed out.

What imperative activated the decision tree that led to two men walking into what they most probably knew were their deaths and yet doing so with the kind of calmness and professionalism that impressed even a battle-hardened helicopter pilot?

The answer is not duty or patriotism, or a sense of pride or a sense of the righteousness of their mission, or a love of fighting, or even a love of their country. The Black Hawk moment of truth came down to a simple thing—the use of empathy. The inability to look away and let things take their course when they were tasked with the saving of fellow lives. Empathic and analytic thinking are mutually exclusive. Research carried out at Case Western Reserve University in Cleveland, Ohio, shows that when one type of thinking is engaged it represses the neural network that carries out the other.

It is, perhaps, the reason why CEOs can carry out a cost-cutting exercise that produces a heavy human cost but delivers a balance sheet win without even considering the public relations nightmare their actions will bring about. Had Gary Gordon and Randy Shughart acted in a cold, calculating manner, then on paper their actions would have looked like an expensive waste of resources that was unlikely to produce a positive outcome. It would have made more sense if they had stayed inside their heli-copter, doing their best to provide covering fire from the air and hoping that ground forces could reach the downed pilots in time.

But that is not how the brain works when empathy kicks in.

Empathy is such a decisive game changer that it resets a per-son's moral compass toward what is right as opposed to what is expedient. Gary Gordon and Randy Shughart thought like he-roes. They acted with a clarity of purpose that came from the overriding belief of the details of their mission. Despite their ask-ing to be let down into what can only be charitably described as hell on Earth, they had no doubt about what was the right thing to do.

While not heroes in the traditional, mythological, larger-than-life sense perhaps, their actions were nothing less than heroic. Community centers all over the United States today have been renamed for them, and the badassoftheweek.com Web site car-ries a breathless account of their stand. They're mentioned on hundreds of Web sites including snipercentral.com and real-cleardefense.com and their names are proudly remembered by vets in the Rangers and Delta Force.

Tasked with protecting life, they allowed their training and focus to fully engage them, becoming what to the enemy must have looked like two highly efficient, human killing machines, until their ammunition and luck ran out. One could even say that, within the parameters of their actions, their equanimity arose out of a sense of happiness. Not joy, in the conventional sense, but the serene and almost metaphysical happiness a human brain feels when it is fully engaged in a task, performing at the very peak of human capacity.

Were the two Delta Force snipers in flow? Mike Durant's account of their deportment certainly sounds like they were. There is a neural signature to happiness and according to fMRI studies carried out by the Department of Neuroscience and Biomedical Engineering at Aalto University in Finland, that neural signature displays a pattern of engagement of specific areas of the brain which is not dissimilar to the experience of a state of flow.

In language not dissimilar to that of positive psychologists, the Finnish study published a report that concluded that emotions arise out of neural states and have a common neural signature that is recognizable for that emotion across different individuals. The study found that emotions are not encoded in a specific region of the brain. Instead they are represented by a distinct activation pattern that recruits a large number of networked brain regions. It concluded with:

> *We propose that the momentary subjective emotional state is the*
> *result of simultaneous activation of multiple cortico-subcortical*

systems, including regions processing somatosensory, motor, and self-relevant information, but also perceptual, language, memory, and executive control functions. The activation of these subcircuits is integrated in the midline frontal and parietal regions, linking emotion-driven neural and physiological changes to self-awareness.

In "The Neuroscience of Happiness and Pleasure," a paper found on the US National Library of Medicine of the National Institutes of Health's Web site, researchers described the neurobiological state of happiness as "a state of pleasure without disruptive desires, a state of contentment." The secret to happiness lies in being so mentally engaged in what we do that there is no room for anything else but an overriding sense of purpose. When researchers Jordan Muraskin and Chris Berka were looking at their charts and graphs, the fMRI images of a thinking brain in action that they saw were images of brains so engaged with the present that they were experiencing a state of contentment that a Zen Buddhist would probably describe as "being in the moment."

Completing the circle between the old and the modern, the internal and the external, the anecdotal and the scientific, the theoretical and the practical, the military and the business environment is Takuan Sōhō, the man credited with influencing Zen Buddhism to fifteenth-century Japan. A hugely influential, eccentric figure who befriended and played a part in the development of some of Japan's most notable warriors and leaders, Sōhō used words that describe a state of mind not unlike that of neuroscientists describing a state of happiness and fulfillment or charting the neurobiological signature of a state of flow:

When the swordsman stands against his opponent, he is not to think of the opponent, nor of himself, nor of his enemy's sword movements. He just stands there with his sword which, forgetful of all technique, is ready only to follow the dictates of the subconscious. The man has effaced himself as the wielder of the sword. When he strikes, it is not the man but the sword in the hand of the man's subconscious that strikes.

His words bridge the gap of more than four hundred years to add context to Mike Durant's own account of how Gary Gordon and Randy Shughart conducted themselves in the face of mortal danger: "professional and deliberate to the point that they looked like they were planning a parking lot. They didn't seem alarmed by the situation that we were in. It was just focused on the task . . ."

FINDING YOUR CENTER

So, how do you get to be like that? How do you attain that coveted sense of serenity without packing up your job and joining the army to train as a sniper or giving up all worldly delights to train as a Buddhist monk?

If there are internal similarities in the brains of baseball players taking a swing and top snipers taking a shot, what are they? What are the connecting threads which then lead all the way to a CEO making a critical decision? A team leader choosing how to best motivate his team? A husband contemplating whether to take a job in another city, or a boyfriend deciding whether his relationship with his girlfriend can be saved? You and I trying to decide the best city to live in? Or the next step that will define the trajectory of a good chunk of our lives?

How can we learn to activate these threads so that our thinking is clearer?

One method is to practice the basic four-step process every major decision is filtered through:

- Make it personal
- Make it real
- Make it credible
- Make it actual

Each step has a list of activities attached to it which depend upon the situation and its participants. They allow for complete customization, fitting into the details of the event, the experience of those involved and the degree to which they are engaged in it. Translated into a real decision-making context the approach can become very granular, very quickly:

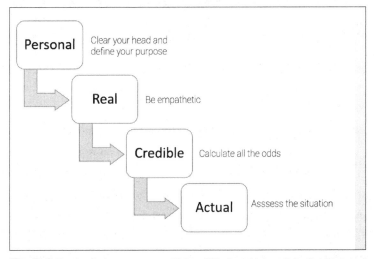

Fig 3.6 Each of these steps will be different for each individual and different for the same individual facing different circumstances.

Personal—Abstractions create oversimplifications. Personalize each decision. Understand what it is that drives you and what affects the decision you're about to make and how you and those around you will be affected by it, in return. Make decisions consistent with your character and principles.

Real—Be empathetic. Empathy is a literal game changer. It rewires the brain, fostering upon it a role-play that transforms a perceived "them" into "us." Its role then is to break down barriers, destroy compartmentalized silos, and open up the mind. This impacts immediately on everyone around you.

Credible—Weigh everything up. Mindless action without a real understanding of the ramifications is only likely to result in serious miscalculations or a colossal waste of time. Avoid both by using your judgment, filtered through both knowledge and experience. Use common sense and logic as a counterbalance to emotion.

Actual—Every situation is different. No two decisions are alike. Use your prior knowledge but also utilize your skill and carefully weigh every single variable. This is where everything you know and everything you are learning come into play.

If you employ these four steps you are well on your way toward creating the kind of inner presence required to have a solidly anchored sense of identity and, with it, a sense of purpose.

Is this enough? No, which is why there is more.

Snipers are highly empathetic. Empathy acts as their moral compass, allowing them to have a sense of faith in the righteousness of their decisions. It was empathy that enabled Gary Gordon and Randy Shughart to volunteer to sacrifice their lives in order to save those of their fellow soldiers. Once the decision is made however, it is the analytical part of the mind that kicks in.

Empathy is no longer in the picture. Once on the ground Gordon and Shughart became cold, analytical, and calm. The job at hand and their competence at performing it was absorbing all of their neural resources.

If you want to have a moral compass you can trust, you can develop empathy through an eight-step program often prescribed by occupational psychologists to help people develop empathy at work:

1. Focus your attention on the welfare, interests, and needs of others—genuinely care. Don't pretend. People have a story that matters. Pay attention and understand it.

2. Key into shared human values—empathy thus involves the ability to key into shared human values across diverse interpersonal contexts and cultures. Understand what these values are and how they affect people and also gauge their impact on yourself and the reasons for it.

3. Don't judge—by suspending your judgmental nature you give yourself permission to connect with another individual regardless of who they are.

4. Walk in their shoes—unless you are willing to view things from the perspective of another person you are unable to truly understand the underlying logic of their argument and their motivation.

5. Use self-reflection a lot—Think about your motivation. What is deeply important to you; what isn't. Discover the things you will not compromise about. In other words, find out who you are and hold on to that. If it's important to you, it is not affected by others. It is immutable to the pressures around you. It is your core. In other words, the real you.

6. Learn to listen truly—Don't just stay at the surface value of the words. Listen for context and underlying meaning.

7. Be transparent—Self-disclosure, where appropriate, can be disarming and can help overcome many perceptual barriers. It creates a very human point of contact that can help you build relationships with others.

8. Be fair—Use objectivity to assess other people's points of views and perspectives. Even when you disagree with them be willing to treat them with respect.

While empathy helps you be human, maintaining your composure and achieving the kind of focus that allows you to operate in a mental state of flow requires a process.

The acknowledged seven steps that get you there are:

- Knowing what to do
- Knowing how to do it
- Knowing how well you are doing
- Knowing where to go (if navigation is involved)
- High perceived challenges
- High perceived skills
- Freedom from distractions

The best advice I could find on how to put these into practice came from an unexpected source. Under the heading "Environment and the Mental Game," the respondent told me:

Making good decisions, quickly, especially in the heat of battle, is not easy. As mentioned, your environment and mental state are two of the biggest contributors. The best decision-

making is done without really thinking about it—you process the visual and aural information you have in the moment, and make a decision weighted toward success. This makes it somewhat subconscious—you're not necessarily going through a decision tree in real time in your head, because chances are by the time you run through the plays, the enemy has collapsed on you.

Are you half eyeballing your phone? Are you thinking about a stressful day at work? Seriously, do you have to pee? Are you hungry? Thirsty? Sleepy? All of these contribute to slower cognitive processing—your head is trying to prioritize multiple things while you're playing, instead of prioritizing only elements of the game.

So how do you get around this? First, you may want to listen to Sports Psychologist Steve on Crucible Radio. He has great advice for the mental game. But two of the most relevant pieces of advice are:

a. Deep breathing. Do it between battles and more at the start. Big bellyfuls of air, into your diaphragm, hold a second or two, and out.

b. Grounding yourself. What I do is, I focus on something else in my room, and either out loud or focused in my head, I recite: three things I can see (window, pillow, water bottle), three things I can hear (fire engine, PC fan, footsteps outside), and three things I can feel (thermal socks, my couch, my glasses).

These practices both calm your nerves and get you refocused. Highly recommended.

This is sound advice and it was widely publicized in a Reddit thread discussing the tactics that most benefit Guardians, the primary characters in *Destiny*, the online-only, first-person-shooter video game that was developed by Bungie and published by Activision. With over five million players worldwide the game and its strategy and tactics have attracted considerable conversation and attention. There are many online forums discussing its philosophy and studying tactics that work.

What is interesting is that from a cognitive point of view a simulation is the same as the real thing. The brain engages equally in the pixel world as it does in the analog one. The information that needs to be processed is just as complex, the responses from a physiological and neurobiological point of view are exactly the same.

Destiny players may not have to dodge real bullets in their living rooms but their minds and bodies, in a somewhat eerie echo of the plot of Orson Scott Card's *Ender's Game*, go daily into battle nevertheless. Empathy was also a central, game-changing emotion in *Ender's Game*. It transformed not just the outcome but also its key character.

Finally, extrapolating from snipers' actions in battle we can extract the sequence of practical steps that allow the analytical part of the brain to kick in and the practical, analytical decision tree process to coolly take over:

- **Relaxation**—This is key because performance anxiety creates mental confusion and inhibits peak performance. Both anxiety and physiological arousal must be regulated before peak performance and flow can occur; breathing and even the heart rate need to be brought under control. Exercise is a basic treatment for all types of anxiety. Fitness routines and meditation lower the resting heart rate and increase brain plasticity.

- **Imagery**—The use of imagery can engage the power of the senses, especially visualization, to mentally depict what peak performance should look and feel like. Snipers tell themselves just how capable they are and how special their training has made them. Mental rehearsal is effective because mirror neurons activate various muscle groups via the peripheral nervous system in the same way as with physical practice. It's that simulation thing again. Snipers think about possible scenarios, run imaginary missions in their heads, and use their direct experience to create new scenarios with fresh parameters.

- **Goals**—Setting targets and meeting them is a motivational tool used to direct efforts toward optimal performance. Goal setting allows the practice of very specific routines which help maintain skills. By setting goals you also begin to get into the habit of breaking them down into actionable steps.

- **Self-talk**—Giving yourself a pep talk is key to the psychological relationship between the person and the performer. This in turn helps maintain a positive outlook and mental toughness when under stress. Research shows that positive thoughts and feelings promote creative thinking whereas negative emotions stimulate critical thinking that can lead to self-consciousness and undermine confidence.

- **Concentration**—No challenge can ever be met if you cannot concentrate on it. Attention, skills, mental discipline, and creative thinking are only possible if you can concentrate your efforts without feeling distracted either externally or internally. Concentration allows you to immerse yourself fully in the moment and engage with the task. Think back to the battle of Mogadishu example and the incredible performance of the two Delta Force snipers. It was concentration that allowed them to behave on the battlefield, against all those odds, with the equanimity of two guys going through a drill at the shooting range.

• **Pre-performance routines**—To get into a state of flow you really need to frame your mind. The key tools to finding that optimal performance mind-set are breathing and centering activities. Breathing deeply helps calm the mind and oxygenate the body. Having a routine to go through creates a deep sense of assurance that transforms any jitters into focused energy.

There is one final step you need to take to bring all of this together: Believe in who you are and what you do. We've already seen from the studies cited how believing in something deeply totally affects the outcome. Colorado College researchers went one step further and actually used placebo effect experiments to study the way the brain responds if it thinks that something positive has happened and it is better off than it should be. As expected, their evidence showed that human subjects who, for instance, thought they had slept better than they actually had, performed cognitive tasks as if they had actually slept better. Even more amazingly, they found that the brains of dogs, cats, and hamsters involved in the experiment also performed better if the animals had been conditioned to believe that a pill they took allowed them to feel calmer.

Obviously humans tend to be more aware of medicine and overthink a study involving a placebo, but animals know nothing about medicine and the placebo effect. The fact that they also responded reveals the common denominator between animal and human minds: conditioning. It also reveals exactly why a routine is necessary to prepare the mind to perform at an optimal rate. Conditioning allows the brain to be transformed, just like the body, into a weapon that can be called upon at any time to perform in a way that provides a true edge, under pressure.

THE SNIPER SKILL ACQUISITION LIST

In this chapter you learned:

- Empathy provides a psychological advantage. Empathy can be developed through a series of activities and approaches.
- Performing optimally and remaining calm under pressure requires us to achieve a state of flow.
- The right tools for the job are part mental and part physical. We need to practice using both.
- Clarity of thought leads to clarity of action. Both demand frequent practice.
- Clearly defined boundaries create certitude which leads to confidence.
- Confidence provides a strong sense of identity.

The final weapon is the brain, all else is supplemental.
—JOHN STEINBECK, *THE ACTS OF KING ARTHUR AND HIS NOBLE KNIGHTS*

4

Smarts: The Brain Is Your Ultimate Weapon

IN THE 2003 INVASION OF Iraq, Welsh Royal Marine sniper Corporal Matt Hughes was participating in an operation with the marines' Brigade Patrol Troop when they came under enemy sniper fire. It was heavy enough to effectively halt the troop's advance and pin them all down in a compromising position. Sniper fire, beyond its incredible accuracy has a deep psychological effect. It makes every man feel vulnerable. In their minds they can picture a sniper trying to get a bead on them.

Working on the principle that it takes one to catch one, Matt Hughes was called upon to deal with the threat. A sniper firing at incoming enemy is one thing. A sniper trying to find and eliminate another sniper is something else entirely. The hit movie *Enemy at the Gates* showed just how important a sniper's role can be in bolstering troop morale and it highlighted the mental chess game that's involved when one sniper hunts another. Both consummate professionals working with a mutual knowledge of the rules of the game and possessing roughly equal abilities, makes it an even match. Winning here becomes a mental game more than a physical one. One sniper has to somehow outwit the other in order to gain the advantage.

When Matt Hughes was tasked with the job, he was facing some steep challenges. One was the wind which was blowing tremendously. In the movies sniping appears easy. You look at a target through the crosshairs of a scope, take careful aim, and squeeze the trigger. But that's not how it is in real life. The position of the target you're looking at through a scope is not the same with the position of the target when the bullet finds its mark. In the intervening time between aiming and firing the Earth has shifted, gravity has kicked in, and the wind has blown. Hitting a target, for a sniper, is a game of sheer prediction. It requires the ability to presciently see the future, and for that you need to draw heavily upon the past.

Snipers record every shot. They remember previous engagements where the distance or the wind or the temperature or the elevation played a key role. They are the living embodiment of Takuan Sōhō's admonition of oneness. A sniper becomes his gun.

Matt Hughes's sniping spotter, Colonel Sam Hughes, who shared the same last name but was not related to him, had found the enemy sniper. He was hiding at a fortified, elevated position a little over half a mile away, which placed it over the 800-meter mark. With just his head and chest showing and a gale force wind blowing across his sights, the enemy marksman could see just how challenging the conditions for long range were and must have felt safe enough from any counterattack.

The rifle Matt Hughes was firing was the L96A1, the sniper rifle of choice for the British Army. The L96 originally competed successfully against the Parker-Hale Model 85 rifle in the mid-1980s to become the standard British Army sniper rifle, replacing the aged Lee-Enfield L42A1 series. The engineering process incorporated light alloys, plastic, and metal into the design. The system itself is designed to allow the single user the ability to carry out all but the most major repairs by himself in the field with the necessary tools being three Allen wrenches and a screwdriver. The drawback of the rifle is that its "first shot accuracy" is only 2,000 feet (600 meters) and it is designed for "harassing fire" on a range up to 3,600 feet (1,100 meters).

To put it mildly Matt Hughes was looking to make a first shot count at a target who himself knew all the tricks of the trade, so was out of effective range and hiding in a fortified position that covered 85 percent of his body, and he needed to do it against a strong crosswind that made the trajectory of the bullet almost impossible to guess.

If the gusts of wind had somehow remained steady and everything else was equal, to hit his mark Hughes would have to

Fig 4.1 British sniper training with his L96A1 sniper rifle.

curve his shot, firing the bullet 56 feet (17 meters) away from the target he was aiming at, using the wind velocity and angle of firing to make up for the effective range deficiency. It was a trick that used physics to extend the range and power of his gun, much like we might use a small incline in a road we're cycling on, to accelerate faster than our pedaling of a bike allows us to so we can make it farther up the other side of the incline.

When you add all the variables together, consider all the parameters, and take into account the margin for error, it all rapidly adds up to "impossible." This is the point where mere mortals say it cannot be done and cite the technical evidence of their equipment (Hughes's target was beyond the effective first-shot range of his weapon by at least 700 feet, or 200 meters), the difficulty of the conditions, and the impossibility of it all. Hughes, of course, was not a mere mortal. As a marine sniper he had received some of the toughest, most expensive, focused training in the world. Both mentally and physically he was more than just up to the job.

In a newspaper interview months later, Hughes would recount how:

> *My training then took over and I got myself quickly but calmly into the perfect sniping position.*
>
> *We follow a set pattern, placing parts of our bodies in the optimum position in strict order starting with the left hand followed by the elbow, legs, right hand and cheek.*
>
> *Finally we're trained to relax and to start to control our breathing focusing solely on the target.*

His words make taking the impossible shot sound easy. To prove the power of high-quality training to overcome impossible odds, his spotter and sniping partner, Colonel Sam Hughes, next to him, also successfully took an identical kill shot, against similar odds, seconds later.

One "impossible" shot being taken like that could be ascribed to fluke. Freak circumstances coming together or Matt Hughes being, perhaps, an exceptionally gifted sniper. A rarity. Two separate ones, happening so close together, by two separate snipers is something else. It's about the kind of training that shapes the minds of men and makes them able to perform at an incredibly high level.

Just how critical is the role played by the mind-set becomes obvious with an example given to me by Thomas M., a serving marine sniper.

Let's play a game. You are in a building alone. You have with you the weapon of your choice. Whatever you think will give you the greatest advantage. Inside that building are two men. They have orders to kill you, but they both must stay alive. You need kill just one for the threat to be over. You can choose which one to tackle.

Opponent No. 1 will be armed with the .40 or .45 semi-auto pistol of his choosing, fully customized to fit him (regardless of cost, he will get the best that money can buy). It will have night sights, a rail mounted flashlight and a laser sight. Plus, it will be loaded with the nastiest, flesh-shredding, man-stopper hollow points known to man, and Opponent No. 1 will be equipped with as many spare magazines as he wishes to carry. He will also have a state-of-the-art switchblade knife and the backup handgun of his choosing.

Opponent No. 2 will have a 1970s-vintage, two-inch, .38

caliber, five-shot revolver. However, it will be loaded with only three rounds, of .38+P+ hollow point ammunition. He will have no additional ammo or other weapons.

Which one would you pick to face?

The no-brainer, knee-jerk answer here is to pick Opponent No. 2, but experienced snipers, he explained to me, always ask, Who's behind the gun?

You see, Opponent No. 1 is a weekend shooter. He has the flashy guns and the ammunition. He has all the kit you can imagine. But he shoots maybe once a week, busting off one hundred rounds. Opponent No. 2 is a combat vet. He has with him his weapon of choice. Now who would you choose to face?

The point of his story was that it's not the weapon that makes the man. It's the mind-set he has that makes the weapon. And that mind-set is always the result of mental preparation and training.

THE SCIENCE: The brain is like a muscle. In order for it to function well it has to be primed or warmed up. Priming preloads mental heuristics that allow the brain to recognize potential threats and opportunities and respond faster. The principle applies equally across all situations that generate a heavy cognitive load.

CREATING THE MIND-SET

John Dean Cooper was born into a well-to-do family in California in 1920 and enjoyed a family and education background that made him probably the least likely person to be associated with the creation of a code employed in life-and-death struggles.

He earned a political science degree from Stanford University in 1941 and, later that same year, he also earned an honor graduate commission in the US Marine Corps a few months prior to the Japanese attack on Pearl Harbor. Called "Jeff" by his friends, Cooper went on to fight in the bloody Pacific theater during World War II. There he saw close-quarter armed combat involving small firearms which allowed him to formulate some of his theories. He later went on to also serve in Korea, eventually rising to the rank of lieutenant colonel. A passionate advocate for effective handgun training, after the war Jeff devoted a large part of his energy to formalizing and refining the rules for handling and using handguns that are today enshrined in the US Marines' training and the code of practice of most law enforcement agencies.

As a matter of fact, by the time of his death in 2006, Jeff Cooper was widely acknowledged as being the father of modern pistol shooting. By then he'd founded a shooting academy and revolutionized the way handguns were held and shot throughout the world, not just through his own efforts, talks, and writings, but by influencing everyone else who also talked about handguns. Cooper was instrumental in developing and popularizing the modern handgun grip (and stance) that make shooting pistols more accurate. He helped develop and formalize the five-step draw method that makes it easy, safe, and quick to draw a holstered weapon and fire it. He also advocated and popularized the four basic rules of firearm safety, rules that are still taught by the military and law enforcement across the United States.

For a man who had such an impact on process and standards, through the technical practicalities of handguns, rifles, and shooting, Cooper put a lot of store on man's ultimate weapon: the brain. In his book *Principles of Personal Defense*, Cooper specifically described how the mind-set one carries is the key to survival in a hostile situation. And, ever the man to codify and formalize a step-by-step response principle, he created a four-color code known as Cooper's Color Code to help ensure survival by cultivating the best state of mind for the situation.

In 2005 he simplified it further, making it even more accessible:

*In **White** you are unprepared and unready to take lethal action. If you are attacked in White you will probably die unless your adversary is totally inept.*

*In **Yellow** you bring yourself to the understanding that your life may be in danger and that you may have to do something about it.*

*In **Orange** you have determined upon a specific adversary and are prepared to take action which may result in his death, but you are not in a lethal mode.*

*In **Red** you are in a lethal mode and will shoot if circumstances warrant.*

Cooper was to admit in his comments later in life that his color code, successful as it was in military and law enforcement debriefings throughout the world, was not as easy as he had thought, to apply. His approach was too cerebral, his focus on the mind, the invisible things that happen inside a person's head that make all the difference to the eventual outcome, was too difficult even for the US government to understand. It had adopted a version of Cooper's Color Code, however, finding it extremely useful but failing to understand the divide between function and form (which means that in typical bureaucratic fashion it had also missed the connection between the two), the government was using it to assign a level of threat to a particular situation when the level of threat may be present even though it was not evident enough to be measured.

"We cannot say that the government's ideas about colors are wrong, but that they are different from what we have long taught here," Cooper said. Ever loyal to the army, he was being charitable. The problem is this: your combat mind-set is not dictated by the amount of danger to which you are exposed at the time. Your combat mind-set is properly dictated by the state of mind you think appropriate to the situation.

Cooper was training the mind long before anyone else thought it was important to do so. Using his hard-earned experience as a real combat vet, he was making connections between the level of alertness a person has inside his head and his chances of coming out alive from a life-threatening situation. Ever the pioneer, he would say, "You may be in deadly danger at all times, regardless of what the Defense Department tells you. The color code which influences you does depend upon the willingness you have to jump a psychological barrier against taking irrevocable action."

There are a number of subtleties here that are truly worth unpacking. The obvious one is that it's thought that moves things from the cerebral or imaginary plane to the real through the binary requirements of available tools and mind-set. What is inside our heads can never be made real if our mind-set is inadequate for its articulation or if we do not possess the tools necessary to make it a reality.

You can apply this to countless situations: Nikola Tesla invented electricity but it was Thomas Edison who gave us the lightbulb. Digital Equipment Corporation pioneered interactive computing but it was IBM that won the battle and market share. DEC's mind-set in particular can be traced down to Ken Olsen, its founder and chairman, who in 1977 gave us this infamous line: "There is no reason anyone would need a computer in their home."

Thoughts are the result of information. Even when we are not fully aware of it our brain processes data. But though we use computer-related terms for what the brain does—*data, processing, input channels*—this is not how the brain works. We are not reactive machines that come to life the moment data enters a consciously defined channel. The picture of the real world we have inside our heads is built up of data and neural sensations that start long before we become conscious of it all. When he formulated his four-color code, John Dean Cooper knew nothing about the unconscious part of the brain that David Eagleman would make a central character in *Incognito* but he had sufficient experience to allow him to see patterns of behavior.

Drawing both from himself and others he could see why a man with a gun survived in a situation that another man with a gun did not. And it was not the gun that made the difference. Something happened in the brain that allowed one person to enjoy a tactical advantage over another, and it was that something that Cooper was trying to understand and codify.

Cooper was unable to use anything other than his own talents, his observations, his instincts, and plenty of common sense.

He drilled and thought and drilled again using a scientist's approach in standardization and an artist's passion for elegance until he thought he had something that not only would work for him but would work for anyone, anytime, anywhere.

What he lacked, of course, was data-backed evidence. The kind that would require time travel to get. Nearly three quarters of a century into Cooper's future, Jordan Muraskin and his lab partner, Jason Sherwin, would find themselves looking at the data that Cooper would have gladly given his right arm for back in the 1940s, the journey that had taken them there as weird itself as two people's chance meeting in a Columbia University bioengineering department. Muraskin was researching Alzheimer's and aging, and had been analyzing the efficiency of magnetic resonance imaging (MRI). Sherwin was studying the neural composition of cellists. It took just one lunchtime chat to convince both that each held part of the picture and brain analytics held the answers they were looking for.

That's how they found themselves looking at the brain of a baseball player as he was about to take a swing at an oncoming pitch. Michael Lewis, the author of *Moneyball*, understood the critical role the mind plays in the game. Assessing what batters did he would write in his best-selling book: "Only a psychological freak could approach a 100-mph fastball aimed not far from his head with total confidence." *Freak* is a term reserved for anything so outside our experience that we cannot even fathom the path that would get one there.

Muraskin and Sherwin began a series of experiments that showed them how to trace the path that so-called freaks could see. In retrospect it is remarkably simple. Wearing what looked like a luminescent swim cap with wires leading off it, baseball players were asked to look at a blank white screen. As Muraskin explained it to each player: "In a few seconds, a countdown will appear. It will indicate which type of pitch to expect: fastball, slider, or curveball. The pitch is just a green dot that darts straight or swerves, depending on the pitch. If the pitch is what you were told to expect, you press the button, *J*, to swing. Simple."

The simulation may seem crude to someone who doesn't understand the dynamics involved. A player after all doesn't sit still on home plate staring at a screen to press a button. He moves around, his legs are twitching, he flexes his arms, gets in position, takes deep breaths. But all that is a dressing. It is not unlike the gun that Cooper saw so many people hold. It's very much like the mental game Thomas M. asked me to play. What is important is what we can't see. The mind that's holding the bat. The mind that's holding the gun. The mind that guides the person who does whatever action is required of them. The way that mind sees the world and reacts, the state it is in and the processes that actually get it there, these are the real game-changers. From the perspective of that mind the simulation was as good as the real thing. If anything, one would assume that lacking any other distractions the mind would be able to perform better, not worse, in the simulation much like a fighter pilot or a video-game player, knowing that they cannot really die, can afford to take chances that in the real world they simply wouldn't take.

Except the brain doesn't work like that. A simulation activates the same command and control centers that govern the decision-making process as the real thing. What Muraskin and Sherwin saw as they looked at seven different data categories with names like Neural Decoding Performance, Decision Position Metrics, and Neural Discrimination Strength, was the brain working before action was physically taken at a conscious level. The brain deciding which parts of it to activate based upon its prior knowledge and its assessment of skills, efficiencies, and the situation. Described like this the baseball decision tree sounds eerily similar to what a sniper faces as he looks down his scope. Decisions have to be made extremely fast based upon an assessment of the situation and a recognition of the facts.

Good eyesight is important because visual information provides a clear, immediate data stream for the brain's decision-making apparatus. The sharper the vision the better the quality of the information supplied to the brain, and the faster. Visual cues that would be noticeable at a later stage, then become apparent earlier. When Phoenix Cardinals team ophthalmologist Louis J. Rosenbaum arrived in 1992 at the spring training facility for the Los Angeles Dodgers in Vero Beach, Florida, to run some player acuity tests for a theory he was formulating, he ran into some problems straightaway. Rosenbaum was testing the players for traditional visual acuity, dynamic visual acuity (the ability to see detail in moving objects), stereoacuity (the ability to detect fine differences in the depth of objects), and contrast sensitivity (the ability to differentiate fine gradations of light and dark). For the visual acuity test he used commercially available Landolt ring charts.

Also known as the Japanese vision test, the Landolt ring chart uses circles with a gap in one section of each that the viewer needs to pick out as the circles get progressively smaller the farther down the chart we go. In Russia this is used widely in conjunction with the Cyrillic alphabet in what is known as the Golovin-Sivtsev table. The problem with the Landolt rings is that commercial models only test down to 20/15. That means that what the viewer sees at 20 feet most people with 20/20 vision can only see at 15 feet. The players on the Dodgers were killing it; their tests were off the chart completely.

Undeterred, Rosenbaum broadened his test population to include Little League as well as professional baseball players, collected his data, completed all the other acuity tests, and came back the next year with a new, custom-made chart that went down to 20/8, the theoretical limit of human visual acuity. What he discovered blew him away. All the LA Dodger players had visual acuity that was 20/10. Major league players had better vision than minor league players and minor league players had better vision than collegiate basketball athletes (whom he also tested, for reference), and collegiate basketball athletes had better vision than everyone who was a nonathlete. More than that, there was such good correlation between athletic performance and strong eye test results—for visual acuity, depth perception, contrast vision, and the ability to see detail in moving objects—that he was able to predict which minor league candidates would be good major league players based just on their eye tests.

To understand how exceptional the eye test results were consider that in the two largest population acuity studies to date, one from China and one from India, out of 13,849 eyes tested, only one had 20/10 vision. Just twenty-two were found to be 20/17 or better and yet here we had the LA Dodgers with 2 percent of their players dipping below the 20/9 mark, hovering at the theoretical limits of human physiology.

Pro baseball players it would appear, could make great fighter pilots, seeing their prey long before anyone else. In the Baseball Hall of Fame, few names rise above the rest. After all, every name there is a star in the baseball firmament. Even so, Ted Williams is a brighter star than most. Joining in 1939, he played his entire

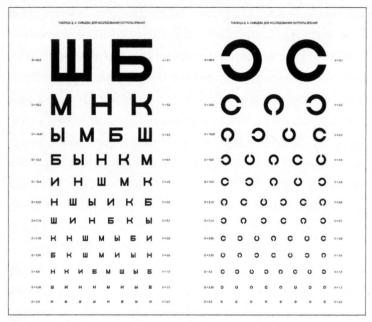

Fig 4.2 The Golovin–Sivtsev table is a standardized table for testing visual acuity, which was developed in 1923 by Soviet ophthalmologists Sergei Golovin and D. A. Sivtsev. In the USSR, it was the most common table of its kind. The right side of it consists of Landolt circles.

nineteen-year major league baseball career as a left fielder for the Boston Red Sox. His lifetime batting average of .344 is currently the highest of any MLB player with 302 or more home runs and he is still the last player to finish a season with more than a .400 batting average (he batted .406 in 1941). Williams was a seventeen-time All-Star, a two-time recipient of the American League Most Valuable Player Award, a six-time American League batting champion, and a two-time Triple Crown winner.

Visual acuity tests undertaken when Ted Williams applied to be a fighter pilot during WWII, unsurprisingly, showed that he too had a visual acuity that was 20/10. This is the moment to lose hope. If great eyesight is a requirement of excellence, much like a great telescope such as the Great Canary Telescope (GTC) whose size makes it the biggest optical telescope in the world, then it comes down to construction, which means genetics. The GTC has an effective aperture of 409 inches (approximately 10.4 meters), which makes it two and a half times bigger and six times more sensitive than the Discovery Channel Telescope at the Lowell Observatory in Arizona.

The average human eye has about 4.6 million cones which act as its primary photoreceptors. Some people have as many as six million cones, which make their eyes more photosensitive than others and the sharpness of their vision is better as a result. Visual acuity is determined by the number of cones in the macula, an egg-shaped spot in the retina of the eye. There is a direct correlation between the cone density, expressed as the number of cones per square millimeter of macular surface area and the quality of the vision one enjoys.

If visual acuity is determined purely by genetics to the degree that Rosenbaum suggested when, bereft of all other data, he used the results of baseball players' visual acuity tests to help him pick likely winners in new recruits, then we all just have to wait until cybernetic vision improvements come along and we all start to enjoy the kind of vision that gives us a competitive edge in sports, combat zones, and, arguably, everyday life since it conditions us to be more alert and trains our brains to process a greater stream of data.

There are, however, two parts to great vision: one is indeed predetermined by genetics. There is nothing we can do about that

Fig 4.3 The Gran Telescopio, or Great Canary Telescope, at Roque de los Muchachos Observatory, in La Palma, Canary Islands. Its 409-inch/10.4-meter wide aperture makes it the finest optical instrument of our times pointed at the sky. It initially used twelve segments of its primary mirror, made of Zerodur glass-ceramic by the German company Schott AG. Later the number of segments was increased to a total of thirty-six hexagonal segments fully controlled by an active optics control system, working together as a reflective unit.

without having to go back in time and choose a different set of parents whose DNA we have screened to help us get better eyes. The other part is mental. The way the brain processes data is critical to the picture it forms of the world. To put it a little more bluntly, the GTC telescope, despite its size, is only as good as the scientists it has who interpret the data it captures. A better quality of scientists may actually "see" more with the exact same data.

It's the same with us. Unlike our eyes, we have brains that are subject to neuroplasticity. Provided they are given the right kind of stimulus they can be remade at any age, redesigned to do new things. Way more so than the rest of our bodies, our brains are the

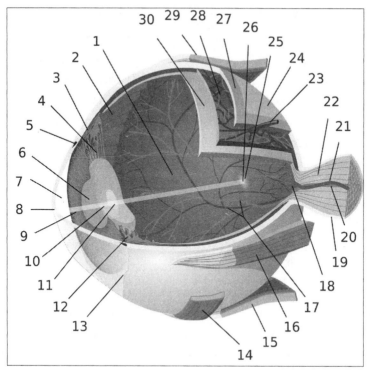

Fig 4.4 The human eye structure: 1: posterior segment of eyeball; 2: ora serrata; 3: ciliary muscle; 4: ciliary zonules; 5: canal of Schlemm; 6: pupil; 7: anterior chamber; 8: cornea; 9: iris; 10: lens cortex; 11: lens nucleus; 12: ciliary process; 13: conjunctiva; 14: inferior oblique muscle; 15: inferior rectus muscle; 16: medial rectus muscle; 17: retinal arteries and veins; 18: optic disc; 19: dura mater; 20: central retinal artery; 21: central retinal vein; 22: optic nerve; 23: vorticose vein; 24: bulbar sheath; 25: macula; 26: fovea; 27: sclera; 28: choroid; 29: superior rectus muscle; 30: retina.

ultimate adaptive machines. This means we have the power to change how our brains process visual data as well as information of any kind. We can make them faster in their responses and more accurate in their assessments. We can teach them to preload responses long before we become aware of them because they can learn to understand the context of what they see and can prepare to act upon the information long before we have a conscious need for it.

John Dean Cooper drew from his own direct experience and understood this. Snipers and pro baseball players, Special Forces soldiers and fighter pilots, intuitively get it. There is a fine line deep within the mind that makes self-belief and confidence, the defining elements between success and failure in any circumstance. How we learn to activate them without running the risk of lying to ourselves is the key that unlocks the superhuman lying dormant within us.

YOU HAVE TO WANT TO BELIEVE

X-Files fans are probably familiar with the popular 1990s television show's recurring motto, handily displayed in a poster over Fox Mulder's basement office wall that blithely said, "I want to believe." With the picture of a UFO hovering above the words, the poster and the statement perfectly capture the emotional ambivalence embedded in the sentiment.

Somehow, wanting to believe smacks of self-delusion. There is a sometimes very hard to see defining line between fervent belief of the kind that can move mountains and blind hope of the sort we charitably nod our heads to. Luckily science has some hard data on how the former, rather than the latter, can move the needle of our performance past our perceived limits.

Ellen Langer is the first woman to gain tenure in the psychology department at Harvard University, but that's not what makes her remarkable. In a series of studies that have provided proof that belief has a direct, measurable, physiological effect, Langer has carried out experiments which show that aging and decision-making can be positively affected by preparing the brain properly and that our sense of control of a given situation can often be proved to be just an illusion.

Ellen Langer calls mindfulness "the psychology of possibility," and her experiments show, among other things, how the mind-set we have affects the way our bodies perform. Langer has frequently said, "Many of the things that we think we can't do are a function of our mind-set rather than our abilities to do them." There is no better way to show this than by testing whether what we think affects something as seemingly immutable and genetics driven as our eyesight.

In an experiment which took advantage of the belief that pilots have good eyesight, Langer and her researchers brought college students who were in the Reserve Officer's Training Corp (ROTC), a college-based officer training program for training commissioned officers of the United States Armed Forces, into a flight simulator. The students were given green army fatigues to wear to enhance the role-playing and were told to fly the simulator. They used the throttle, compass, and other trappings of an actual cockpit to execute flight maneuvers.

They then did an eyesight test by reading markings on the wings of planes ahead, which in fact were lines from an eye chart. A control group of ROTC students was put in the same conditions, but they were told the simulator was broken, and that they should just pretend to fly the plane. The people who had performed like pilots, as opposed to those who just pretended, saw 40 percent better.

Langer reran this experiment, in one case telling the controls they could motivate themselves to have better vision and in another actually giving them eye exercises. But the pilots to whom no mention of vision was ever made at any point still outperformed them. In other words, simply believing that pilots have good vision was enough to sharpen the volunteer-pilots' eyesight.

When psychology trumps biology, it becomes obvious why the army invests in so much ritualized training designed to place recruits under intense stress and then remold them into new people who understand that their limitations can be overcome through focus, determination, and teamwork.

There is data from several different disciplines that is beginning to come together and point at the same thing. Cooper was convinced his color code, simple as it was, saved lives by increasing reaction speed and shortening the decision-making process. Rosenbaum swore by the ability of his eyesight tests to predict the success of untested baseball players. Muraskin and Sherwin, looking at their elaborate charts and graphs, could see that successful baseball players and top-level snipers seemed to respond mentally long before their bodies moved and they took the swing or the shot. Langer was now bringing in research findings that tied peak performance to belief.

Ted Williams, the superstar baseball player famously said, "Hitting is 50 percent above the shoulders." The brain plays the key role here and the brain has to be trained and primed (or warmed up). Cooper's Color Codes clearly prepared the brain to take specific action by alerting it to the situation and allowing it to preload stored responses. Being mindful sounds like an energy-intensive state of mental and psychological alertness, but stored responses that kick in the moment a trigger is identified make being mindful an energy-efficient way to respond to a particular situation. In psychology and cognitive science, stored responses are called a schema which describes an organized pattern of thought or behavior that further organizes categories of information and the relationships among them.

A schema then is a complex conditioned response, a cognitive shortcut. It is a mental heuristic that allows us to operate fluidly when dealing with a load of data by assigning it values drawn from our predetermined worldview. It's a miracle of energy optimization in mental information processing. Unfortunately it is also a trap. The most common reaction to information that does not fit a schema is to ignore or forget it. Or simply not see it. Snipers rely on this failing to become invisible in their camouflage.

Without training (or priming), no amount of alertness is going to actually help you improve. One classic example of this is the famous case of Jennie Finch. In 2004 Jennie was the Team USA softball pitcher. At the Pepsi All-Star Softball Game, an exhibition featuring Major League Baseball All-Stars such as Albert Pujols and Mike Piazza, Jennie, standing just forty-three feet away from home plate and pitching underarm, pitched out one All-Star player after another.

Speed here was not the issue. At the distance she was pitching from, her balls were equal to a fastball pitched at 95 miles an hour. Fast, but nothing these players could not handle. Rather, it was the underhand angle from which Finch released the pitch that these top hitters found discomforting. It was like nothing they had faced before. Their database of knowledge from years of practiced learning was useless. They had no special ability to determine where her underhanded pitches would travel.

This personal database of knowledge plays an important part. While, as Langer showed, you can sharpen your physical responses and overcome limitations through self-belief, without prior training or knowledge of some kind you are still at a disadvantage. Snipers record every shot they make in a sniper's log book. It's a practice first pioneered by British Major Hesketh Hesketh-Prichard in 1916 in France, and it has since become the basis of every sniper's skill.

The reliance on this "database" is not restricted to snipers. Ted Williams, in his book on baseball published in 1971, *The Science of Hitting*, wrote that he could recall everything about his first three hundred home runs, the pitcher, the count, the pitch itself, and where the ball landed. At the plate, he was a "guess" hitter, surmising what pitch would be thrown where depending on the count and the situation on the field, which he could deduce because of his knowledge of pitchers' tendencies.

Science, in bits and pieces, from many different quarters is giving us the components that build a fearsome brain:

- Visual acuity, both physical and mental, that allows good collection of information
- Mental alertness, the result of situational awareness and assessment, which prepares us for action (Cooper's Color Codes is pivotal here)
- Self-belief in one's training and capabilities, necessary to silence the mental dissonance of doubt
- Prior knowledge or experience of the situation and a set of possible responses that can be employed quickly (training)
- A personal database of past events with a similar context that can be used to make quick decisions

From all these we can see the means through which a sniper's skills, both conceptual and practical, can be transferred to a business setting.

THE BUSINESS CASE

Here's how a business organization could take the five components of a sniper's mind-set and create a business culture that is focused, united, knowledgeable, nimble, and predictive.

- **Visual acuity**—A business is not just the eyes of its people, it is also their minds. A business organization that has everyone within it looking at the marketplace, looking at the competition and considering the information that they see, collectively, has a far greater sight than any of its competitors. It can recognize opportunities and threats faster and position itself quicker to take advantage of them.

- **Mental alertness**—Business organizations that accurately assess the environment they operate in are better positioned to recognize the direction it is heading. Periods of fast growth, stagnation, or recession require specific sets of actions which need to be taken sooner rather than later. Businesses that are alert are not caught up in the reactive cycle that their nonalert competitors will find themselves in.

- **Self-belief**—An organization that does not believe in its mission statement, its reason for being in business, and in its ability to meet all challenges will struggle to find the necessary energy to deal with unexpected adversity or to even successfully deal with expected challenges as they arise. The same applies to individuals within it. A sense of mission and the knowledge that each belongs to something greater than themselves is required if they are to deliver the sort of peak performance modern business challenges require.

- **Prior knowledge or experience**—Organizations that fail to learn from the past are doomed to repeat their mistakes until they fail. Knowledge (and experience) means that the organization has worked out a way to retain it even after the people that were directly involved in an event or activity or crisis have moved on. Successful organizations, like successful individuals, invest in their own cognitive development. They have internal knowledge bases, some have colleges which they staff and use to augment their own, immediate cognitive skills. They run scenarios, play "games" which challenge their notions of what they do, and why. They run activities that challenge their identity and their understanding of where they are in the marketplace. Similarly, entrepreneurs and executives invest their time and effort in acquiring the kind of knowledge and experience of the past that allows them to better understand the present.

- **A personal knowledge base**—Smart organizations invest in archives and archivists. Their corporate history, the company successes and failures, moments of triumph and moments of crisis are recorded there. These then should be kept fresh, pored over and analyzed for insights on how they made survival possible and how they may do so again. Business executives who are switched on use their knowledge of past events as a springboard. Each time they face a new problem they can draw on their keen awareness and detailed knowledge of what made success possible in the past, what were the exact variables, which of these have remained the same, and which ones have now changed.

THINK LIKE A SNIPER

As a business executive, company CEO, entrepreneur, or start-up owner, what are the direct lessons that snipers have taught us so far? From the battlefield, through the science that is backing the sniper mind with direct evidence, there are five lessons we can draw that will change any businessperson and any business that applies them into a force to be reckoned with.

- **Snipers stop only when they are done.** The goal defines the parameters of their operation, not how tired they are or how they feel. If we constantly think about the softer alternatives available to us we subconsciously yearn for sleep, entertainment, a night out, a holiday, respite from the pressure of work. By setting a goal and itemizing each step required to get us there we simply go from one to the next. Our focus is on each step, not on the enormity of the task or the number of steps still left to us. We know that, like snipers, we also will stop only when our goal has been achieved and there are no more tasks left on our list. This is why it is important to have clear missions with detailed, clarified objectives and a path that will achieve them that is feasible and logical.
- **It's not the tools you have that make the difference, it's what you do with them.** Snipers have powerful rifles and great scopes but ultimately it is their mind that makes them so effective. A business has to rely on expertise rather than equipment to gain a competitive advantage. A sniper on a mission is not just a person with a rifle. He is cognitively active, calculating odds, figuring out angles,

factoring in variables, and carefully picking targets. There is nothing on autopilot where he is concerned. A business that relies on technology is easily cloned or surpassed. Even a business that has significant knowledge is not safe, in the sense that knowledge is only good when it is applied. It is only when a business makes full use of its cognitive surplus that it begins to become a force to be reckoned with in the marketplace.

- **Snipers pick their shots for maximum effectiveness.** They are patient and they are precise. That makes them efficient. A business that uses the battlefield equivalent of "spray and pray" is wasting resources to little effect. Create internal processes and marketing strategies that make full use of resources in an intelligent, precise manner. Learn to identify your "targets," assess the benefits versus the effort involved, and then act in a focused, intelligently directed manner. Classic examples of wasteful efforts include e-mail campaigns that go out using databases that have not been cleaned in years, advertising and marketing campaigns that are carried out in a haphazard manner because, obviously, something needs to be advertised and we really have to market something, and résumés or (for journalists) article pitches that are sent indiscriminately to all and sundry without any consideration of target audience or the suitability of the person who is receiving it.

- **Snipers get the best shot they can get. Not the perfect shot they want.** Things are always difficult. There are always variables you cannot control. Waiting until the conditions are perfect frequently means that great opportunities are missed. Provided you bring all your skills, patience, accuracy, analysis, and determination to bear, waiting too long before taking action will only cause the kind of relaxation that happens within organizations that have worked hard to prepare and have yet failed to act. Morale plummets. Doubts set in. The entire organizational edifice wobbles and all sorts of problems begin to surface. When it comes to executing a plan, at some point analysis simply has to stop and action has to take over.

- **Snipers can change the course of battle with just a few shots.** Snipers are force multipliers. They have clarity of purpose and a focused mind. They work to do what they have been trained to do. Businesses that are focused and driven, with a clear sense of purpose and a defined idea of their place in the world, are truly unstoppable. Their every action has a far greater effect than masses of wasteful marketing activity from their competitors.

What happens when these lessons have not been applied? Organizations and individuals become vulnerable to a crisis and frequently falter. The department of political science of the University of Stockholm spent over two years examining critical decision-making during the acute phase of the Chernobyl nuclear fallout crisis of 1986. It defined a crisis as a moment that presents three distinct variables:

- A threat to basic values
- Urgency
- Uncertainty

In a business setting, a threat to basic values threatens the very core of the organization. Urgency is presented because the situation is fluid and things are moving fast and there is uncertainty in terms of the magnitude of the threat and the outcome of any attempted action.

When there is a cultivated approach that reflects a sniper's mind, the crisis is just another challenge that needs to be met. When, however, there is no such cultivation then a crisis becomes a dangerously destabilizing event which threatens the very existence of the business organization, the individual, or (as in the case of the Chernobyl crisis) the state.

How do you make sure that you are always ready? After all, in a business environment it's not like work can stop and everyone can go off to boot camp for twelve weeks. From a personal perspective, everyone already has their plate full. It's not like they can find a lot of extra time each day to absorb and then practice new techniques.

There is a solution, of course. In behavioral psychology shaping is "a conditioning paradigm used primarily in the experimental analysis of behavior. The method used is differential reinforcement of successive approximations." Unsurprisingly it was pioneered by B. F. Skinner, who also gave us operant conditioning with its binary reward/punishment structure.

The principle of shaping is that instead of setting a desired outcome as a task like "become more alert," it is always easier to break it down into stages, identify how to get immediate feedback so those stages can be assessed, and increase it incrementally.

An organization then does not go from being an inward-looking one that is totally oblivious to what is going on around it, to one that has a business intelligence unit, two analysts, and a team of futurists working for it, overnight. Instead smaller tasks are set and assessed, like mapping how many competitors it has and what they do. First, understand each competitor's unique selling point and verify it. Then identify each competitor's marketing strategy and verify it. Then identify each competitor's strengths and weaknesses and verify them. Each of these steps may take months, but by the end of the approach the organization ends up with a detailed, fully functional knowledge of the marketplace, itself, and everyone else around it.

In sniper parlance all this is broken down into a simple guideline that goes: *Do it! Practice it! Live it!*

There is zero value in putting a lot of effort into developing and acquiring a skill set which then is never used. Everything that you put in place as an organization has to become fully integrated into the functioning of your business.

Even that is not enough. There are more practical steps that can be applied, one taken down directly from the birthplace of professional sniper training: the World War I trenches in France. It was there that Major Hesketh Vernon Hesketh-Prichard pioneered the use of scopes on rifles, taught riflemen how to operate them, trained snipers to work in pairs, and introduced *Kim's Game*, a game derived from Rudyard Kipling's 1901 novel *Kim*, to help train observational skills.

Kim's Game is truly effective in this regard, not to mention fun, and it is detailed in full in appendix I at the back of this book. It can be used in any kind of business training setting to help improve cognitive recall and analysis and help its participants develop their observational abilities.

In addition, online computer games like *The Last of Us*, developed by Naughty Dog and now published by Sony, are helpful. The game itself requires a strong team dynamic and helps develop critical, tactical thinking as well as situational analysis.

Its online nature makes it perfect for a corporate team that can be put together during off hours, and a follow-up analysis of what went wrong and what worked (and why) can become part of the discussions at work.

All of these help in the development of skills and a mind-set that gives a business a distinct, competitive advantage.

In a slightly more formal way, consciousness is linked to awareness. A fully conscious brain that is aware cares not just about what it knows but how it knows it and what this then reveals about itself and the world it lives in. So consciousness is a phenomenon that requires awareness to complete it. Who we are, who we become, is the brain's theory of its own existence. Become fully conscious and reap the benefits.

THE SNIPER SKILL ACQUISITION LIST

In this chapter you learned:

- The brain is the most powerful weapon in your armory. The mind-set you begin with can truly make a difference. Flow can only be achieved in a fully aware, mindful brain.
- You can prime your brain to work beyond its normal limits by preparing it for what lies ahead.
- Observational skills are key. Attention to detail provides data and memories provide even more data. Both sets allow you to understand what is happening faster and react quicker and more appropriately.
- Self-belief plays a pivotal role in success. Acquiring skills and becoming good at using them provides the level of self-confidence necessary to perform at peak level.

Don't fight forces, use them.
—R. BUCKMINSTER FULLER

5

Science: Use Fight Science Knowledge to Work Smarter, Not Harder

Every day during training you wake up at 4:00 a.m. Your head is not quite clear at that time but you need to try and keep your shit together. Within thirty minutes we are all out, running maybe six, seven miles, the whole platoon carrying this forty-pound weight we keep passing around so we can rest up on the go. It becomes everyone's responsibility to keep it going, and to fall not too far behind the instructors and, at the same time, it makes each of us responsible for everyone else. When we get to base there is an obstacle course we have to get through, followed by a 500-meter swim.

We then have maybe thirty minutes to clean up and get to class where we work on navigation, tactics, strategy, and mathematics. Basic physics and geometry. Then in the afternoon we go and shoot. We are in pairs, just like in the battlefield, only now we have to make an 8. We need an 80 percent accuracy score or we flunk out. And it's not like it's a turkey shoot. The instructors mess with our heads. They put us under pressure. Shots we make are labeled a "miss" and we cannot argue against them. Targets are not quite right in the way they have been set up. The range they give us might be off by a hundred yards or more. Each bullet we have is counted and we have very little time to learn and recover.

Sometimes the instructors will wake us up in the middle of the night so we can carry logs or go on a midnight run with rucksacks weighing anywhere from sixty to seventy-five pounds strapped to our backs. We still have to be up at 4:00 a.m., ready for physical drilling. Each day, the pressure only goes up. The difficulty rises as they try to push us until we crack. We say to each other: the easiest day was yesterday. You are tired, your body aches, you feel like shit. You can't get the time to eat enough. Yet you have to concentrate, perform, deliver each shot with perfect accuracy in conditions that are never perfect.

It doesn't matter what is happening, what has happened, how you feel. They are making you into a fighting machine. On the battlefield there will be no breaks. If you can't take it they want you to fail, tap out, become one of the 80 percent of the guys who can't take it anymore. What you have to do to survive is clear: Adapt. Overcome.

A SERVING SNIPER WHOM I shall call Harrison gave me this account of training to be a part of the marine scout snipers, a very specialized army unit whose members frequently find themselves operating alone in very isolated positions, usually far from any immediate help and with the enemy near. He made it through, joining the 20 percent of army personnel who then go on to train at sniper school to learn techniques such as camouflage, stalking, observation, and "bubble compartmentalization"—the ability to block everything out except specific visual and observation skills. The training is designed to toughen you up to the point that the

Fig 5.1 Marine Corps Base Camp Pendleton, California. Marines with Force Company, 1st Reconnaissance Battalion, 1st Marine Division hike with 50-pound packs and carry a 60-pound container full of sand during a physical training exercise, November 7, 2014. The physical training exercise also incorporated activities to improve proficiency in marksmanship and memorization.

rigor of the battlefield is not something that can easily break you and it has a specific name: stress inoculation.

The training Harrison was subjected to mirrors that of a Special Forces operative whose account of his training broadens the perspective even more: "Your hands are tied securely behind your back. Your feet are tightly bound together. The strap of a dive mask is placed between your teeth. You are then thrown into a pool. At that point you know that you're not going to get much breathing done. You have seconds to figure out how to make the most of it, work out a way to survive." The account, given to me by one of my respondents whom I shall call Ben Sherman, is of an until-now secret training program carried out at Fort Bragg in southeastern North Carolina.

The program is tough: the recruits who enroll in it are destined to fill the ranks of the army's elite Airborne and Special

Forces units. The drop-out rate is 80 percent, sometimes even higher. As you sink to the bottom of the pool, unable to swim, your body's natural response to the lack of oxygen and the water all around is to struggle. Your mind wants to scream in fear. There are changes taking place inside you when all this happens.

Some of those changes are purely physical. Your heart rate goes up insanely, using up more oxygen than you have to spare in your bloodstream. The oxygen content in your blood begins to go down as a result. The concentration of cortisol, the stress hormone, begins to rise. More neurochemical changes begin to kick in. Some recruits exhibit specific behaviors as levels of a neuropeptide simply called Y begin to rise. NPY is an abundant amino acid in our bodies and we shall learn more about it and how to control it in the next chapter. Here it helps to know that it aids in the regulation of our blood pressure, appetite, learning, and memory. It also works as a natural tranquilizer, controlling anxiety and buffering the effects of stress hormones like norepinephrine, one of the chemicals that most of us simply call adrenaline.

All of these diverse changes, however, can be measured and, as science has begun to show, they can be controlled. The training facility at Fort Bragg, high drop-out rate notwithstanding, is actually designed to help recruits become mentally and psychologically tougher, which is where its "stress inoculation" name comes from.

All the carefully controlled chaos, mock captivity, simulated torture, and physical deprivation that those who sign up for the process have to endure are designed to do a relatively simple thing: enable the recruits to develop personal resistance strategies so that they can stay level headed and clear thinking even when they find themselves under the most extreme physical and psychological pressure.

The problem with the approach is that it is Darwinian. The selection process has a basic premise: put up impossibly difficult conditions that will push the mind and body of anyone placed there (physical training, psychological pressure, sleeplessness, you name it), get a bunch of raw recruits together, screen them to find likely candidates, throw those who pass the screening in the mix, and let nature take its course.

Despite its primitive premise, historically there is a good reason for it, which is best explained by Brandon Webb, one of America's seasoned warriors, a Navy SEAL sniper instructor who had to go through it all himself.

There is a tremendous amount of science involved in making all these observations, but the art of it is bringing them all together into an extremely precise picture of the overall scenario. What is the weather doing at your position as the shooter? Looking down the range halfway to your target, what's happening at that position? Is that valley funneling the wind a certain way? And what's happening 800 yards away, all the way down to where the target is sitting? Is the wind calm there, or moving, and if so, in what direction, and how strongly? Calculating all those factors, then assembling them all together to arrive at an estimation of exactly what you think is happening and precisely how it all applies to your weapon, and then making the perfect shot . . . it's incredibly complicated—and there is zero margin for error.

In a battlefield the sniper will have to make life and death calls, juggling all of the variables Webb wrote about, in less than optimum conditions, while under pressure and never having enough time to reflect.

Webb wrote a book about it all called *The Red Circle* where he mentioned, repeatedly, the mental and psychological pressures that are applied during sniper training, to push recruits to their limits and then to see how far beyond them they are willing to go.

Those who survive this brutal process are usually the ones who find the means to forge the inner pathways inside their own heads that unlock the special kind of fortitude they need to get through it all. It works but it's a slow, messy process and it churns up people. It has other drawbacks too: it is not infallible. Talented people may slip through the cracks because of unfortunate circumstances, clashing personalities, or the luck of the draw on a particular day. It is also almost impossible to replicate outside a military setting. The rigor required to forge the type of highly skilled warrior Special Forces requires is not the kind of thing you can self-impose at home, on the weekend. On your own, you simply cannot apply sufficient pressure to fully plumb the depth of the resources you can draw upon when you have no other choice.

"Reality is what we take to be true," David Bohm, the pioneering physicist who helped us advance some of our thinking on quantum mechanics, said in a lecture (which can be found in the 2001 book *The Quantum and the Lotus*). "What we take to be true is what we believe. What we believe is based upon our perceptions. What we perceive depends on what we look for. What we look for depends on what we think. What we think depends on what we perceive. What we perceive determines what we believe. What we believe determines what we take to be true. What we take to be true is our reality."

Sniper training changes the sniper's perception of reality through the gateway of the mind. By recruiting higher thought under duress and training the mind to function in flow, Harrison's "bubble compartmentalization" reality becomes less distorted. More real. More prone to control. More subject to self-determination. Details acquire greater value. Connections are made between almost imperceptible things. The mind functions, without thinking about it, joining up dots like a semantic search engine. Everything in its field of vision is connected through a web of tangled, interrelated interactions. Is air flowing faster over a building? Is the wind ruffling blades of grass by a roadside differently? Is the light glinting off somewhere it shouldn't? Is the length of a shadow longer than it should be? Sniper training opens up the world of the real into many more layers, each one rich in the information it can provide. A mind looking at the world through sniper-trained eyes sees a richer tapestry than any nonsniper can imagine.

These are mental skills that are too good to be restricted only to the few. Science has always been about working smarter not just harder and in the case of a sniper's mind it looks to do what science has always done: find the mechanisms in operation, replicate them at will, short-circuit natural selection, and produce results to a standardized formula almost anyone can apply. We call this "fight science."

THE SCIENCE: Critical decision-making under pressure operates on a bounded rationality principle where time, resources, and information are limited. The quality of the decisions can be significantly improved by applying a satisficing algorithmic approach in tandem with the utility model of decision-making to prescreen some choices and arrive at much better decisions.

THE DECIDING MACHINE

We all make bad decisions, all the time. There is another way to look at this sentence: *We all fail to make good decisions, all the time*. There is a subtle but vitally important difference between the two which is at the very heart of current neuroscientific research. The first implies a conscious direction toward bad decision-making which is predicated on choice (as in, having to choose between decision A and decision B, we just choose one and hope for the best) and the second, more accurately, suggests that our decision-making process needs improving.

When we are on a night out with friends or alone shopping in the supermarket our brains are using two distinct systems to help us reach a decision. One is a valuation reward system whose task is to examine every choice we have available to us in terms of how it will benefit us. From having those extra four shots in the pub or not before walking home alone to whether to buy that extra-large pack of donuts instead of the lettuce and walnut salad, everything gets filtered through a "what's in it for me?" lens.

But the brain also has a cognitive network involved in the decision-making. That cognitive network brings a broader perspective to bear which then changes the weight ascribed to our choices by the brain's internal valuation of those choices. Four extra shots on a night out might be a great way to join in the fun and shed the week's load of stress, but they are also likely to make us drunk. A walk home, alone, on a Friday night, inebriated, may raise red flags regarding personal safety which would then dictate against the four shots, no matter how tempting. Similarly, the donuts may taste great and they may be cheap to buy, but their impact on our waistline, in relation to our lifestyle, broader set of aspirations, and even our social status, may be such that the lettuce and walnut salad becomes the one we go for in the end.

This helps explain why children, for instance, given the same admonition we may give ourselves, will still go for the cookie over the carrot when presented with it. Their brains are good enough to understand our words and their importance but the cognitive network that presides over the valuations of their choices is not yet populated with a sufficient number of connections for it to be as effective as ours. They have fewer filters and fewer restraints, as a result.

In a balanced mind every value-based decision we make is filtered through the brain's cognitive network that associates the binary good/bad outcome of our selfish choices with a broader web of complexities. Each decision then is a choice between selfishness and broader social responsibility. When snipers submit themselves to training they know that they will experience pain, discomfort, and a sense of loss of self as their instructors bear down upon them and start the process of stress inoculation.

Those who survive that training are mentally and psychologically tougher. That toughness is actually expressed by the complexity of their cognitive network. It all sounds simple enough. There is a little more to it than that. Decision-making under pressure doesn't have the luxury of time that would allow us to create a complex decision tree that takes into account all the available information and weigh everything carefully to find the best possible outcome, before reaching a decision.

A sniper aiming at a child running toward the soldiers he's protecting has only a split second to decide whether the youngster is a threat or not before he shoots (a situation encountered by *American Sniper* Chris Kyle in his first deployment in Iraq). A CEO guiding his company toward the future cannot afford to endlessly wait for the business intelligence unit to do its work and come up with a one-hundred-page report that will most likely be obsolete by the time it's written. It may not always be possible to make a decision about your career or your personal life with a sheet of paper in front of you neatly divided in two so you can list all the pros and cons of all your likely choices.

So what do you do, then? How do you make sure you make the best decision possible? To answer this question, we need to understand why perfectly sane individuals choose to stay and put themselves through the incredible rigor of stress inoculation training instead of making the seemingly more rational decision that would say: "Well, I have an easier job in my current army unit. I really do not need to go through all this sleeplessness, physical pain, and mental anguish." And in order to understand this seeming illogicality we need to first accept that without training most of us are very bad at making good decisions.

Evolution is to blame. If the decisions we are hardwired to make were indeed so bad that they always worked out against us, we could argue that over the course of history so few of us would now be around to read this that there wouldn't be much of a point in writing this book. But that's not the case. We have survived and thrived because of the way we are hardwired to respond to threats and make decisions on the go.

The brain, which takes up as much as a fifth of the body's total available resources, is incredibly complex and yet far from completely mapped. As a matter of fact, a consortium of brain researchers used recent data from a five-year, multimillion-dollar study, called the Human Connectome Project to discover almost one hundred new regions in the brain whose purposes are undefined. Despite its complexity and ever unraveling mysteries, as a whole it is easy enough to segregate into three distinct areas: forebrain, midbrain, and hindbrain, each of which performs distinct functions.

These three areas correspond to the neocortex or neomammalian brain, limbic or paleomammalian brain, and the reptilian brain. Tempting as it would be to assume that these three areas are completely isolated from each other and working in sequence as we rise from primitive beings banging on hide shields with sharpened sticks to higher beings capable of appreciating music and poetry and the refined tastes of ethnic cuisine, this is not quite how it works.

The primary processing area for some very specific activities may be a particular area of the brain, like the midbrain or the hindbrain but to carry out its work successfully, each area recruits regions from all over the brain. The integration model suggests that the brain works in a holistic, cooperative way that makes our basest desire or most abject fear as expressive of who we are as abstract thinking of the highest order. That means that we are all equal part snakes, monkeys, and spacemen.

The inference here is that higher brain functions in the neocortex, the part of the brain where we do most of our rational thinking, have the ability to affect the other parts of the brain which control emotions (like fear) and involuntary responses (like heart rate and breathing).

When a person finds himself in a combat zone, under attack, having to fight back, in fear of getting hurt or killed, and capable of hurting or killing others, this is what happens to his brain: capillaries and secondary veins in the body experience a significant slowing down of blood flow. Doctors call this vasoconstriction:

the muscular wall of the vessels contracts, narrowing the blood vessels, raising the blood pressure, and restricting the flow of blood to capillaries. It also allows the main arteries and the core of the body to hold twice the amount of blood coursing through them than before. Vasoconstriction prepares the body to take damage to the extremities and bleed minimally. It also restricts blood flow to the forebrain. When that happens complex rational thought pretty much shuts down. The midbrain takes over and conditioning and training kick in. Brandon Webb highlighted this in his book where he spoke about his training: "It was as if I were standing inside a minuscule red circle, hurling the bullet to its destination by an act of sheer mental concentration. In those moments on the range everything else disappeared and my world shrank, like the near-infinite compression of matter in a black hole, into that red circle." Similarly, if we think back to the actions of the two Delta Force snipers in the *Black Hawk Down* incident in the battle of Mogadishu, their flawlessly calm performance in the face of what amounted to certain death is a classic example of how a trained brain operates when under stress, so that it is not overwhelmed by the stress and fear.

In Frank Herbert's award-winning sci-fi novel *Dune*, there's a passage that reads, "The mind can go either direction under stress—toward positive or toward negative: on or off. Think of it as a spectrum whose extremes are unconsciousness at the negative end and hyperconsciousness at the positive end. The way the mind will lean under stress is strongly influenced by training."

Hyperconsciousness is what soldiers whose brains have been trained experience under the extreme conditions of combat. But in order to get there they have to be made to experience that kind of stress in their training environment. You cannot throw raw recruits into combat simulators or even combatlike environments and hope they will somehow learn to switch on their thinking in a way that allows them to survive by making supremely rational decisions in the blink of an eye. No. They have to systematically be shown how to think for survival, through a progressive load of work that they have to do in order to get through their training and a progressive increase in the difficulty of the conditions they have to do it under. That's where the traditionally raw load of physical training snipers undergo reveals itself to be a form of fight science, refined by experience, over time.

How does the valuation-reward system of our critical decision-making kick in during the time Special Forces soldiers and snipers are trained? To understand this we need to discuss the concept of bounded rationality, a valuation we use to make everyday decisions when the data we have at our fingertips is insufficient or overwhelming. Although we would like to think that we are all completely rational all of the time, the truth is that we are only partially rational, part of the time. There are practical, realistic constraints on our time, energy, resources, and on the information we have available to us.

So to make a decision our brains take into account all the constraints to form a snap judgment. This becomes even more obvious when the additional constraint of time is introduced. On our way to the checkout do we go for the lettuce salad or the donuts? Faced with a child running toward troops we are protecting do we shoot now or not? The brain here looks for mental shortcuts. Bounded rationality lets us see speed-dating in a different light, which helps explain why finding lasting love this way is harder than usual. Bounded rationality relies on mental shortcuts, called heuristics, to help us speed up the decision-making process.

Fast-talking salesmen and some e-commerce Web sites have realized the value of activating bounded rationality and the heuristics it operates with by introducing a very obvious time factor in their sales pitch: a special offer, a single-day sale, a limited-offer sale, a today-only discount. Amazon used the exact same principle to pull off its biggest single sales day in twenty years of doing business, with Prime Day in 2016—an otherwise ordinary day in July during which Amazon Prime subscribers could take advantage of special offers and discounts not available to anyone else.

Bounded rationality scenarios create an imperative to action in our brains that makes it harder to step back and examine the valuation-reward choices available through the more rational cognitive decision-making based on longer-term goals.

Bounded rationality however is not a trap without an escape door. It adds a handy, on-the-spot cognitive assessment layer through the use of a mental heuristic (or algorithm) that is called satisficing, whose purpose is to help us reach a reasonable outcome in the decision-making process. Satisficing gets its name from a fusion of satisfy and suffice, which is a direct clue of how it works. Given great constraints on time and additional layers of pressure we face two options: make a decision that we think is optimum in a simplified setting or make a decision that we think is satisfactory given all the constraints we are operating under.

Do you shoot the child running toward the troops you are protecting or not? When Chris Kyle famously took that exact shot he had limited information. He was the only one who'd thought he'd seen a pipe bomb carried by the child. He was told to make

Fig 5.2 The auction countdown timer on eBay creates a time imperative as it counts down seconds that activates our bounded rationality decision-making process. When we fail to understand this we end up buying items we do not want based upon criteria that are narrow and have been circumscribed by circumstances.

the decision and he made it based on the information he had at hand. An optimum scenario in such a situation might run along the lines of shoot to wound. But that works in a simplified world where snipers' bullets are hyperaccurate, targets framed in sniper scopes move in entirely predictable ways, and there are no variables at play which will affect the bullet trajectory between a gun barrel and a target. When Chris Kyle made his decision he opted for a satisfactory solution to a real-world situation. The child looked likely to be a threat; the lives of troops he was protecting were on the line. It was his job to stop threats and it was his career and reputation he was risking if he got it wrong. He made a decision based upon what his instinct told him was happening and what he was willing to risk (if he was wrong) in order to meet the stakes he was facing.

It sounds reckless. Yet his training had been complete. Sniper recruits have to force their brains to make rational decisions under incredibly pressured conditions. To help them speed up the process they do extensive internal modeling and role-play. They run scenarios in their heads. They go over the shots they have recorded that did well and try to understand why. They look at the missions that failed, see how they could have improved them, and apply everything they know to everything they see so that they are learning all the time. Over time this helps them build the handy mental shortcuts that greatly speed up their decision-making process.

This is where the brain's cognitive network is activated and the second major decision-making system kicks in. Scientists call this utility-based decision-making. It requires the person making the decision to assess all likelihoods, evaluating every option and assigning a value to it in regard to a likely outcome. Utility-based decision-making is the most rational way to make a decision, but it requires effort and time. It is also subjective. The person making the decision is key to ascribing the value to the variables he is weighing. Sniper recruits who employ it to justify the hardships of training do not drop out of the course because they have dug deep within themselves and can rationalize their willingness to suffer sleep deprivation, fatigue, pain, and psychological torture in order to graduate as trained snipers. They have already decided they are ready to pay the price in order to achieve their long-term goal and are willing to withstand the discomfort training requires. They have a firm grasp of what we call the bigger picture. As a result their bubble compartmentalization techniques have started to evolve.

This is not an entirely foreign concept. Deferred gratification, resisting the temptation for an immediate reward and waiting for a later reward, is familiar to every little boy and girl who could not go out to play with friends until their room had been cleaned or could not have a cookie until homework was finished. We all have that mechanism, but without a complete awareness of it and some real reasons to consciously employ it, it runs a little like a latent system: it kicks in haphazardly with us because we don't always know we are employing it.

Snipers are not like that. Because the training is so physically hard, the recruits who remain and become snipers like Chris Kyle understand how their brains make decisions. It's drilled into their training day in, day out. They are forced to confront it every time they are pushed to their physical limits and beyond and then asked to think analytically.

By the time he took the shot at the boy running toward the troops, Kyle had worked out his mental shortcuts. He had his set of sniper mind–trained heuristics in place. He was at the hyper-conscious, positive end of the spectrum of Frank Herbert's notion of a trained mind. As a result he understood what was at stake and he had confidence in his ability to assess the situation within a limited frame of time and limited available information.

The approach helps many different people operate successfully when under pressure. Jack Nicklaus, the legendary championship golfer, used to say that when you're making a difficult shot, 50 percent of it is the mental picture you create, 40 percent is how you set it up, and 10 percent is the swing itself. In that respect, sniping is a lot like golf: 90 percent of it is how you see the picture, compose it successfully, and make your decision and just 10 percent of it is how you get your shot lined up.

Some call this "gut instinct." The moment when all the

information comes flying at you from everywhere and the pressure ratchets up to intolerable settings and you can still find the direction your decisions should be taking because you, somehow, just know.

GOING WITH YOUR GUT

The way to a man's heart may, famously, be through his stomach but despite the popularity of the phrase the stomach is not linked directly to the heart or the brain. That, however, does not mean it cannot feel or think, which means there is a traceable connection between the gut and the central nervous system. Connected components form a network. The network is influenced by the number of connections between its components and the strength of the connections.

Our brains are full of the heuristic shortcuts we use for decision-making. For example, a child looking at a "Fire Sale" sign is using a brain as complex and sophisticated as an adult's to work out the implications. That young brain, however, is devoid of real-world knowledge and experience. Lacking the mental shortcuts of its elders it takes a long time to arrive at its conclusions. To understand the power of these mental heuristics to change the meaning of what we observe, consider the different impact the "Fire Sale" sign has if it's written in a comic font as opposed to a more standard font. To the child's mind the words would convey the same message, but to an adult mind the meaning and context would subtly shift.

With some 500 million neurons the enteric nervous system (ENS), which is also known as the intrinsic nervous system, has come to be recognized as a "second brain" communicating with the central nervous system (CNS) through both the sympathetic and parasympathetic nervous systems. Producing upward of thirty neurotransmitters, many of which are identical to the ones found in the central nervous system, the work of the ENS has found its way into everyday vernacular through such expressions as "gut reaction," "gut instinct," "gut feeling," "sick to my stomach," and "butterflies in my stomach." Studies have shown that relationships commonly reported between gut feelings and intuitive hunches may share a common, poorly understood, perceptive origin.

While intuitive hunches can be attributed to factors such as expertise now lying dormant in the brain, unconscious somatic

Fig 5.3 These two signs say the exact same thing, but only one may actually be serious about it and the other may be just a promotional sales event.

influences, and the reading of cues that are too subtle to be anything other than subliminal, there are still instances of intuition and gut feelings being right that cannot be accounted for in this fashion.

The gut, responding to environmental and perceptual data not yet visible to the conscious brain, produces neurochemical signals and enzymes which prepare the body for a "fight or flight" response. This, in turn, uses both the sympathetic and parasympathetic nervous systems to communicate with the CNS. The heartbeat begins to elevate. The pupils of the eyes dilate and the breathing begins to change. Capillaries close to the skin begin to shut down and blood supply is diverted to the main organs, deep within the body. Long before they become noticeable, all of these changes can be seen initiating deep within the brain using fMRI techniques, priming it for action.

Intuition, itself a mental heuristic, is triggered when the brain knows it needs to decide something fast on relatively little information and needs some guidance to ascertain its threat level. Mental heuristics keep us safe when they tell us not to get in *that* car and not to take that shortcut via a back alley, or when we enter a place and can "feel" the tension in the air.

Studies have shown that the signaling is bidirectional. When the gut talks to the brain, the brain kicks into high gear, carries out its own subliminal assessment, and talks back. The enteric nervous system is an ancient evolutionary holdover we share with insects, snails, and marine polyps and its role is to allow the rapid assessment of a situation in the most energy-efficient way possible, so it's not even uniquely human. The cross-signaling that takes place with the brain, however, is.

The moment it is activated by a gut reaction, the trained brain brings its considerable resources of knowledge, experience, and training to bear and achieves seemingly impossible feats. Consider the case of the now legendary "miracle on the Hudson." On January 15, 2009, barely two minutes into its takeoff from New York City's LaGuardia Airport on a domestic flight, US Airways Flight 1549 experienced catastrophic twin engine failure because of a bird strike. The incident rendered the aircraft completely powerless at 3,000 feet.

Within just 208 seconds, veteran pilot Captain Chesley B. "Sully" Sullenberger and First Officer Jeffrey Skiles had made aviation history. In that brief space of time they had assessed a complex situation for which it was impossible to practice. They had then gone through every option possible while also working to calm the passengers, communicating with the control tower on the ground, continuing to attempt to cold start the two dead engines, and all the while gliding the completely powerless A320 Airbus, turning it around until they could coolly land it on the Hudson River. Ditching the plane, the fast thinking of the pilots saved everyone on board. This feat has been described in a book and a major movie, and a recording of it has become one of the most popular YouTube videos, with millions of views.

Despite the fact that the cockpit of an A320 that has just lost all power is far removed from the ground on Mogadishu and the rough, open terrain of Musa Qala, the moment shares more than just a few overt characteristics with the feats recorded in those instances. Again, there are two professionals battling with complex, shifting variables, a life and death situation that is impossible to practice, a ticking clock rapidly winding down, and options they have to quickly choose from. There are other similarities too, which are more than mere coincidence: The participants all share good eyesight and memory, experience, and training. They have brains trained to use heuristics, to listen to their gut instinct that says "do this, do not do that" and then allow the more analytical part of the brain to double down and go to work. Even the fact that they work in pairs, trusting each other implicitly to pick things up in sync so that their efforts are coordinated, is not coincidental. Every sniper has his spotter and the effectiveness of the pairing is such that at the Marine Corps Base Camp Lejeune, in North Carolina, one of four such facilities across the United States where snipers are trained they have a saying: "Two is one. One is none." Similarly, a plane like the A320 requires two pilots to fly it. Each acts as the extra brain, eyes, and ears of the other. Together they form a complementary presence, two brains in sync.

The cockpit recording from the Flight 1549 incident, available to listen to on YouTube, sounds eerily calm, the voices of the pilots measured like it's a training video. Their controlled diction as Captain Sullenberger talks to his first officer and the control tower are reminiscent of the account of the banter between the two brave snipers in the *Black Hawk Down* incident. The cool, methodical manner in which they prioritize options, pick one, and then take action is virtually identical in approach to Craig Harrison's when he was desperately fighting to save the men he was watching over in Musa Qala, while battling with the limitations of his equipment and the variables that were stacking the odds against him in his location.

A months-long investigation carried out by the Federal Aviation Administration afterward during which various expert pilots flew the same flight in simulators concluded that given the shifting variables and time available to them, Captain Chesley B.

"Sully" Sullenberger and First Officer Jeffrey Skiles had made the only decision that could have saved the lives of everyone on board. The results of the simulated flights that FAA investigators asked for were quite eye-opening.

The filed reports indicate that as part of the investigation nearly two dozen emergency simulations were flown by experienced pilots, including an Airbus test pilot, at the manufacturer's headquarters in Toulouse, France. Four out of four attempts to return to the closest La Guardia runway were successful. There were nine additional simulated attempts to land at La Guardia, either at different runways or under a scenario in which the plane was more severely disabled. Of those only three were successful.

But the simulator pilots had an obvious advantage: They knew exactly the kind of emergency they were facing. From the perspective of Cooper's Color Codes they were starting out on Red, their brains already warmed up, primed, and looking for ways out, already functioning at peak. The simulator pilots who immediately decided to turn back toward LaGuardia after the simulated engine problems had used up every second of time allotted to them to act, their decision tree already preconfigured. The investigating board's document acknowledged that fact, concluding that such a scenario failed to "reflect or account for real-world considerations such as the time delay" in recognizing the bird strike and the extent of the damage and then being able to "decide on a course of action."

Verdict: the US Airways Flight 1549 pilots were heroes with cognitive abilities just like a sniper's. Faced with a novel situation they had never encountered before they coolly relied on their experience and knowledge to trim down the available options and choose the best course of action. They then executed it in a by-the-book preternaturally calm way, prioritizing every step along the way in a manner that saved everyone's lives, including their own. And, once on the water, they continued to exhibit the same high level of performance in their professionalism.

With the plane taking water, Sullenberger and Skiles calmly oversaw the evacuation of the passengers and then, at the very end, with Skiles also gone, Sullenberger walked through the cabin twice to make sure it was empty. Only then did he board the last slide raft, and before long climbed onto a rescue boat. He was the last to leave.

Summarized down to a single line the sniper mind, or the pilot mind for that matter is reduced to: *Before you can act you must choose. Before you can choose you must know. Before you can know you must feel. And before you can feel you must be trained.* It seems bizarre to have to be trained to do what surely ought to be natural, but the fact is that training allows us to both better understand what it is our gut is telling us and know exactly when to trust it so we can make better decisions.

If business decisions were consistently made to the same high level of operational quality we would be seeing a lot fewer mistakes, a lot better leadership, and much bigger calm. Like snipers, business executives often face decisions that have to be made on a ticking clock, with high stakes, insufficient information, volatile variables, and uncertain outcomes. The pressure is immense. The difference is that their brains have not undergone the same kind of training as a sniper's has. Unaware of the decision-making systems they employ they frequently err the ways amateurs would. Sometimes, spectacularly so.

THE BUSINESS CASE

Filmmaker and director George Lucas hardly needs an introduction. He has a reputation as a shrewd dealmaker who understands how to extract value from everything he does. That reputation was not known to 20th Century Fox execs in 1977. Their focus therefore when negotiating with him on buying back the sequel rights to *Star Wars* (which he owned) was the money they'd make from another film, so when they were offered distribution rights theatrically and video around the world for seven years while George Lucas retained everything else and got back the merchandising rights (which Fox owned at the time), Bill Immerman, who was the head of Fox's business affairs, readily agreed.

Disney's purchase of Lucasfilm for more than $4 billion plus all the billions of dollars *Star Wars* merchandising has made over the years since 1977, in retrospect, shows the sagacity of George Lucas's decision. Yet, at the time, from their perspective 20th Century Fox was getting the better deal. Faced with a situation where they simply did not have sufficient information (as they had no way of predicting just how big the *Star Wars* franchise would eventually become) and with the clock ticking on negotiations with George Lucas (via Tom Pollock, his lawyer at the time, who would go on to become chairman of Universal Pictures), Fox used bounded rationality and satisficing as its reasoning mechanism to reach an acceptable outcome, instead of the best possible one for them.

How could it have been different? This point is now pure conjecture, but seeing all that we know about how large businesses operate today it is not impossible to imagine the pressure Immerman must have been under to deliver the best possible deal in terms. His focus would have been on what he could deliver immediately to demonstrate a tangible gain to those he answered to. It is highly likely that had Immerman been trained on how to make decisions under pressure he would have operated differently. He would, in all probability, have gathered way more data on film trends and merchandise income potential and the changing habits of the audience. He would, most likely, already have been intimately familiar with the way hundreds of films had performed and would have known what made each one work (much like snipers keep logs of their shots and know what makes each one work).

He would probably have weighed all that against the potential of making a few hundred million dollars extra over seven years and, I imagine, he would have said no and he would have bargained differently. It would have been a gamble tinged with uncertainty but in a business as huge as Fox was at the time, the gamble would have been worth taking. However the very visible, very direct temptation of immediate gains was apparently too much to resist.

In a different scenario, the Eastman Kodak Company was 131 years old by the time it went bankrupt in January 2012. Once the dominant force in photography the company actually invented digital photography in 1975 when engineers Steve Sasson, along with some colleagues, demonstrated to company executives the world's first attempt at "film-less photography." The clumsy, toaster-sized device they were using could capture images, save them digitally, transfer them onto tape, and then view them on TV by attaching the camera to it.

Had company executives known then what we know now about digital photography, they would have leaped at the chance to dominate the globe once more, leveraging the household brand name that was Kodak. But the data sets they were working with were circumscribed. While they knew all about film and what it brought to the company and understood how to create value for their customers with their current products, they did not at all see the potential of digital photography or the demographic shift in the public that it would precipitate.

Bounded rationality demanded that they go for the most profitable solution that was still working, which was analog cameras and film, and satisficing led them to decide that the best path available to them was the one which they were already on. Sasson was ordered to file his invention away. Such was the narrow focus on what the company was doing with film that eighteen years later, Kodak vice president Don Strickland would leave the company, unable to persuade it to manufacture and market a digital camera. He would say in a later interview with Britain's *The Independent* newspaper, "We developed the world's first consumer digital camera but we could not get approval to launch or sell it because of fear of the effects on the film market."

Just how do you stop your company from becoming another Fox or Kodak? How do you learn to make decisions like a trained sniper, taking in everything the moment gives you, operating under its constraints, and still achieving a deeper, more mature perspective that will enable you to make better choices in your decision-making and have better outcomes as a result? In essence this is what fight science promises to deliver and it does so through some very prescribed processes we can all learn to use.

THE FOUR-STEP PROCESS TO BETTER DECISION-MAKING

Stress destroys our ability to make smart choices. There are two distinct strategies to help us cope with stress and still make good decisions and each activates a slightly different pathway in the brain. Both take practice to perfect.

This account by Tommy N., a sniper, showcases how snipers bring their training to bear in everyday life:

> *In stressful situations, it can be hard to calm down when the mind isn't focused. By exercising breath control and learning that even my breathing affects my movements, I've come to the realization that it is important to calm myself first by clearing my mind. This can be done simply by breathing exercises and focusing on my breath while being aware of my surroundings.*
>
> *I got into a really big fight with my spouse and knew my blood pressure was going well beyond what I am used to. I'm talking about seeing red. I punched the wall a few times and that didn't help. It just made matters worse. Once I realized what I had done, I started to do breathing exercises and focused on my breathing. My mind began to clear. Once things finally calmed down, my wife and I were able to resolve the issue.*

Another sniper, let's call him Ronnie, gave a more business-related account:

> *I deal with sales teams. We have monthly targets and quarterly targets to hit. A few things happened at once. Our share price plunged (it was a combination of factors, none of them*

of our own making) so we lost money virtually overnight. The reports I was getting showed we would miss the quarterly target. That's really bad news. It had the potential to send our stock off a cliff. Jobs would be lost, mine probably among them. It was incredibly stressful and all this was happening while we were rolling two new products out the door. I took an hour to walk around the block. No phone calls. It cleared my mind as I started to put the pieces together in my head, decide on the plan of action. Who to call. What to say, when. I got back to the office, called for a meeting with all sales reps the next day. I spent the next six weeks on hot coals, helping each sales team get the details just right. Making sure their morale was up, they chased every lead, went after every call. We made target. Just. It was such a close thing that had I just let a week or so go by while I wallowed in panic, we wouldn't have pulled it off.

Different as these two accounts may be they are united by the exact same process: Training > Feeling > Choice > Action.

It seems perverse that we need training in order to do what must surely be the most natural thing in the world, but the truth is that unless training has, indeed, been undertaken our feelings are too diffuse to totally make sense of it all and our actions become muddled and ill-considered. However, with training we accumulate knowledge that, when appropriately filtered, becomes experience which then transforms the four stages of the sniper mind's process into four action-oriented steps:

- **Frame**—Decide the scope of the problem you are facing and then accurately detail the resources you have in relation to the resources you need in order to deal with the challenge you are facing.

- **Find**—Decide on the kind of decision you need to make quickly. Is it a major decision or a routine one? Major decisions often are very specific, one-time events involving high personal commitment and a considerable investment of resources. Routine decisions are not quite as energy intensive and their impact on your "mission" is also likely to be minimal. The thing is it is not always easy to distinguish one from the other and often there is an overlap between them. Hiring an assistant for the CEO of a business, for instance, sounds routine but if the assistant is going to be organizing all the meetings and scheduling other business-critical stuff, hiring the right person can be a major decision with far-reaching consequences which could affect the smooth operation of a business. It is important to set your criteria correctly here so that decisions can become easier to make with a higher degree of certainty about whether you should listen or not to that all-important gut instinct.

- **Evaluate**—Weigh all the options available to you. Consider cost, time, commitment level required, and desired outcome. Be thorough. Use experience to find valuable shortcuts. Look for the best applicable decision that will help you achieve the outcome you want. Be as quick as you can but do not let the need for speed blind you. If the two previous steps are true then your gut instinct can be relied upon to guide you.

- **Apply**—Detail each of the actions required to deliver the outcome that is needed. Be thorough in laying them out and also describe what each one entails. Whether you do this in a written format (as an exercise) or in your head as a mental exercise is irrelevant, as long as you do it and stick to it. Patience, perseverance, and attention to detail are sniper mind traits. They form the bedrock of discipline which turns a "can't do" mind-set to a "can do" one.

While this may sound simple when detailed out like this the part where most people stumble is persistence. Not everyone has the ability to simply go through each situation in such a methodical manner until it reveals itself to the analytical gaze.

These are the same steps applied by the top management of consumer industry giants like Unilever. The company is trying to teach its management talent how to make better decisions under pressure by running a company-wide, internal course called Decision Making Under Uncertainty, or DMUU for short. In typical high-end company-speak the literature Unilever uses to internally promote the course to its management staff explains that "DMUU is a disciplined, methodical/structured approach to decision-making, with probabilistic analysis at the heart of its logical reasoning."

Unilever expects those who have been trained to apply their training; the discipline they learned during DMMU to make strategic decisions (which they call "choosing the right path") and proactively manage risks and opportunities (which they call "running the path").

One Unilever case study cited:

In 1999, DMUU was used to move pro.activ through the Novel Foods regulatory process in Europe. Prior to the analysis, key decision makers were in disagreement and considering several alternative options (including cancelling the project outright)—whereas, the application of DMUU won senior management commitment to a single course of action that drove the pro.activ product on the market. This analysis resulted in major product launches in all major European countries within nine months, with global sales in excess of €160 million per annum.

THE SNIPER SKILL ACQUISITION LIST

In this chapter you learned:

- A trained mind is a controlled mind. Training and experience become the foundation for exceptional analytical performance under pressure.
- A good memory and a willingness to carry out mental games or scenarios is part of the response strategy that a trained sniper mind employs.
- Better decisions and better responses happen when the brain is primed. A primed brain is a brain that is both knowledgeable and experienced.
- Knowledge is as essential as experience when it comes to making a good decision. You need to cultivate both.
- There is a four-step process through which you can control your decision-making mechanisms and make better choices.

Once your mind-set changes, everything on the outside
will change along with it.
—STEVE MARABOLI, *LIFE, THE TRUTH, AND BEING FREE*

6

Mind: Special Qualities. Develop the Special Ops Mind-set for Success in a Fluid Situation.

You're on enemy ground. You are aware that even tiny mistakes can kill you so you judge everything around you on the help or hindrance it will give you. That's everything, the ground, people, objects, equipment. Everything has a value to you that can be positive or negative. Positioning is key here. First, if you have made the wrong choice to begin with you will have limited options or greater danger to deal with. Then, you need to be able to reposition yourself without being seen. Positioning gives you a clear advantage. Your thinking is key. You know the mandate of your mission. If you have clear targets you also have a clear plan of action. You know what you have to do. The mission is not the place where you will learn if you are prepared to do it or not. This thinking is done long before. When you are on a mission you know exactly where you will draw the line and do not hesitate as a result. Hesitation can get you killed. An unclear mind will get you killed. Anything

that distracts you from the task ahead will get you killed. Your
job is to get your task done and not get killed.

THE ACCOUNT IS BY TONY M., a serving US Ranger sniper. The only way you can function effectively in this manner is with the bubble compartmentalization snipers can switch on that allows them to focus on what they have to do to the exclusion of everything else. Someone who performed at this high level and got the job done was Carlos Hathcock, a marine who became a legend during the Vietnam War. In the dramatized account of just one of his stalking exploits, shown on the History Channel, Hathcock talks about being dropped behind enemy lines on a solo mission, tasked with hitting a North Vietnamese Army general at his headquarters, deep in the jungle. The high odds against success had made the mission "volunteer only," but that did not deter Hathcock. From the landing zone he had to trek through dense jungle and then 1,500 yards of open field crisscrossed by enemy patrols and watched over by machine gun nests. It was a journey that took four days and three nights without sleep, crawling inches at a time, camouflaged with sticks and vegetation, blending in with the landscape. We get the measure of the man from his own words:

At one point I came across a bamboo viper defending its ter-
ritory. I had to freeze and wait for it to move away before I
could resume my crawling. As I was nearing my firing point I
was almost stepped on by one of the enemy patrols scouring the
area. Had I been discovered it would have been instant
death. Luckily the enemy soldiers were feeling secure so deep
in their territory and didn't spot me. I reached my firing posi-
tion some 700 yards from the General's HQ and waited. He

didn't take too long to come out. I knew I had just one shot so I had to make it count. I went for a shot to the chest. Aimed, slowed down my breathing, and when I had everything timed so I could shoot between heartbeats, I took the shot. He went down. The enemy came to life like an angry beehive but I was already moving, getting back by the escape route I had prepared, hidden by a ravine. Once I made it back to the tree line I knew I was safe. I hot legged it then to the evac point.

Hathcock himself attributed his ability to survive in such a hostile environment to his ability to "get in the bubble," to put himself into a state of "utter, complete, absolute concentration," first with his equipment, then his environment, in which every breeze and every leaf meant something, and finally his quarry.

> THE SCIENCE: There are specific steps which can condition a brain to activate neurochemical changes that help trigger bubble compartmentalization, which increases focus. This helps it weather stress, fear, worry, and uncertainty, better than an untrained brain.

THE QUEST FOR CONTROL OF THE BRAIN

The inventor and polymath Nikola Tesla used to say about his brain: "My brain is only a receiver, in the universe there is a core from which we obtain knowledge, strength, and inspiration. I have not penetrated into the secrets of this core, but I know that it exists." His words, seeking to frame the mind and the seemingly magical place from which its experience, knowledge, and insights arise, is part of an ancient quest that seems to date as far back as Ancient Greece.

In 387 BC, Plato is known to have suggested that the brain was the seat of all mental processes. In 1637, René Descartes posited that humans are born with innate ideas, and forwarded the idea of mind-body dualism, which would come to be known as substance dualism (essentially the idea that the mind and the body are two separate substances). From that time on, major debates ensued through the nineteenth century regarding whether human thought was solely experiential (empiricism) or included innate knowledge (nativism). Some of those involved in this debate included George Berkeley and John Locke on the side of empiricism, and Immanuel Kant on the side of nativism.

Conceptually, the question of which of these ideas was true about the mind, an intangible, invisible construct of the brain, could well have gone on for several hundred more years, but in the twentieth century something happened that created strong imperatives for practical applications of all these nice theories: war broke out.

Conflict on a major scale and in quick succession marked modern times. World War I got the ball rolling, but it was with the development of new warfare technology during World War II that the need for a greater understanding of human performance came to prominence. Problems such as how to best train soldiers to use new technology and how to deal with matters of attention while under duress became pressing for military personnel. Behaviorism provided little if any insight into these matters, and it was the work of Donald Broadbent that integrated concepts from human performance research and the recently developed information theory that forged the way in this area.

Developments in computer science would lead to parallels being drawn between human thought and the computational functionality of computers, opening entirely new areas of psychological thought. The cognitive revolution was about to begin and the way the brain creates the mind became an area of intense study.

One of those who paid close attention to the mind, its behavior, and the modes of operation it can go into was Edward E. Smith. Born during World War II, he was to hold the William B. Ransford Professor of Psychology chair at Columbia University. His work in cognitive psychology, a field of research that did not become properly recognized until the 1960s, would bring together distinct areas such as learning, cognitive control, working memory, semantic memory, and perception in one common thread.

In his book *Cognitive Psychology: Mind and Brain*, Smith would write, "Mental activity, also known as cognition, is the internal interpretation or transformation of stored information." It's a simple sentence that launches a thousand thoughts. Everything is information. The things we see and the thoughts we remember. The skills we have learned and the strategies we have been trained to implement. All of it is stored inside our memories. Memories are stored in specific areas of the brain and they become the fuel for the furnace of the mind, the moment we start to think.

There are ten distinct areas that are directly affected by our mental processes:

- **Perception**—This is the processing of information from the senses. What we hear, see, smell, and feel. The telltale signs that let us assess how we are doing.

- **Emotion**—This includes such as the anxiety surrounding the task at hand. Emotion can arise when we perceive something and interpret it in view of the results we want to achieve.

- **Representation**—In long-term memory, our actual memories of previous relevant experiences as well as the memories of our training and the memories of our skills are stored in a representative format that can be retrieved.

- **Encoding**—This is what happens when we enter new information into memory or pull up information from long-term memory (critical if we are going to use previous experience).

- **Working memory**—This is what allows us to hold information in awareness. It's sharpened by playing mental games like Kim's Game and it is used when we carry out a situational analysis. It is particularly important if we try to scope out any themes or patterns that are emerging from the situation we're facing.

- **Attention**—This allows us to focus on specific information, including words and nonverbal signals, which then allows us to filter out irrelevant information (such as external sounds).

- **Executive processes**—These manage our other mental events, allowing us to pause before we speak and to inhibit ourselves from saying the wrong thing. They enable us to act on our decisions.

- **Decision-making**—This is problem solving and reasoning which allow us to figure out what tasks we need to perform and how to best apply them in order to reach the outcome we want.

- **Motor cognition and mental stimulation**—These involve setting up responses, mentally rehearsing them, and anticipating the consequences of our behavior (useful for anticipating likely responses to unexpected changes in scenarios).
- **Language**—This is what we use to communicate with both ourselves and others.

These ten areas form part of a modular approach to cognition control that snipers and, really, all Special Operations people are taught to employ. Knowledge, in its most inclusive sense, is information about the world stored in memory that is likely to either be true or to be something we have justification for believing. That means, however, that we also know what's untrue and what should not be believed.

Inside a sniper's trained mind, details which may seem inconsequential to an ordinary person acquire special significance and greater meaning.

To understand how we can achieve a trained sniper mind without having to necessarily undergo the grueling physical training that snipers do, we need to look at another area of body/mind research and its effects: mindfulness meditation.

The textbook definition of mindfulness meditation is given by Jon Kabat-Zinn, professor of medicine emeritus and creator of the Stress Reduction Clinic and the Center for Mindfulness in Medicine, Health Care, and Society at the University of Massachusetts Medical School. It is one that every sniper will instantly recognize: "Mindfulness is awareness that arises through paying attention, on purpose, in the present moment, nonjudgmentally. It's about knowing what is on your mind."

Like sniper training, mindfulness meditation changes the internal pathways of the brain. It changes the way we think, which means that our perceptions also change and we experience the world around us differently. How exactly?

A recent study with the title of "Alterations in Resting-State Functional Connectivity Link Mindfulness Meditation With Reduced Interleukin-6: A Randomized Controlled Trial" describes research carried out by J. David Creswell, associate professor of psychology and the director of the Health and Human Performance Laboratory at Carnegie Mellon University, among others. It reveals exactly what happens when we meditate: "mindfulness meditation training functionally couples the DMN with a region known to be important in top-down executive control at rest (left dlPFC), which, in turn, is associated with improvements in a marker of inflammatory disease risk."

Broken down into plain English, the research suggests that a mind that has been taught to meditate has access to neural pathways that are not available to a mind that hasn't. Creswell's research focuses broadly on understanding what makes people resilient under stress and these neural pathways allow the brain to handle stress way better than usual by changing the way information is processed. More specifically meditation changes:

- The posterior cingulate, which is involved in mind wandering and self-relevance.
- The left hippocampus, which assists in learning, cognition, memory, and emotional regulation.
- The temporo parietal junction, or TPJ, which is associated with perspective taking, empathy, and compassion.

- An area of the brain stem called the pons, where a lot of regulatory neurotransmitters are produced.

The amygdala, the fight or flight part of the brain which is important for anxiety, fear, and stress in general, gets smaller in size. The change in the amygdala is also correlated to a reduction in stress levels.

At mindfulnet.org, a Web site that has become a repository of content from mindfulness practitioners, both academic and self-taught, the meditation experience is described as a process that begins with the clearing of thoughts out of the mind. Devoid of direct thoughts the brain's attention association area begins to quieten. The frontal cortex that is normally active with immediate attention tasks becomes inactive and any sensory information that is not important is filtered out as the results of a study cited by the Web site illustrates:

> *Attention is drawn to the present-now experience, which triggers a shift to right-brained activity, as attention is predominantly a right-brained function. This shift from "intellectualized" left-brain thinking is a further explanation of why the experience cannot be described or analyzed: the right brain does not have the ability to categorize and analyze the experience; it intuitively "feels" it.*
>
> *At the same time, the meditator also becomes less aware of sensory information stemming from his external environment, and therefore less aware of his orientation in space and time. This dissolving of the self/nonself boundary is reflected in a decrease of activity in the right parietal lobe. Not only does it have an impact on activity in the right orientation association*

area (leading to a loss of sense of space and/or time), but it also has an impact on activity in the right verbal-conceptual area, leading to an inability to convey the experience efficiently through language.

How do you learn what an experience feels like when experiencing it seems to negate the very language you need to describe it? You bypass speech and go straight to the brain itself, that's how. And fMRI scanners that have been so instrumental in looking at mental states are, again, key here.

Sara Lazar, a neuroscientist at Massachusetts General Hospital and Harvard Medical School, was one of the first scientists to use fMRI to test anecdotal claims about the mental and psychological benefits of meditation and mindfulness.

Here's what she found: Those who practiced mindfulness meditation for a long time versus the control group who did not had an increased amount of gray matter in the insula and sensory regions of the brain which control the auditory and sensory cortex. When you're mindful your senses are enhanced. You're aware

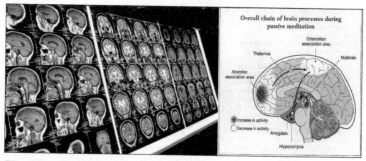

Fig 6.1 MRI scans during mindfulness meditation have shown, repeatedly, the shift in activity of the brain from the centers which process analytical thought to areas which work more holistically, "feeling" a moment or a concept.

of your breathing and the sounds around you. You're squarely in the present and analytical cognition is shut down. The brain scans also showed that those who meditated had more gray matter in the frontal cortex, which is associated with working memory and executive decision-making. Their brains were wired not just to be more aware but to also make better decisions.

Rationality creeps into our decision-making when the over-reaction initiated by the fear response is kept in check. That means that instead of reacting to every environmental stimulus and sensation as a potential threat we can assess each piece of information our brains collect more impassively, with greater empathy. This greatly reduces the stress we experience and introduces a center of calmness in our decision-making that the Japanese call *mushin*. Its closest English translation is "no mind," and it basically is a mental state into which very highly trained martial artists are said to enter during combat whereby emotions like fear dissipate and decisions become supremely rational. In martial arts (where the concept of *mushin* is predominantly encountered), it is talked about in terms familiar to any practitioner of flow. The self-centered, hypercritical "Me" area of the mind is silenced as the highly empathic holistic "We" kicks in.

Despite the "silencing" that takes place there is no segregated shutting down of brain centers. As we saw in chapter 5 each region of the brain contributes to the others through the associated neural networks that develop as a response to training. This is no exception. Mindfulness meditation increases and strengthens the connections between specific parts of each area of the brain and weakens others. This careful mental pruning and augmenting that takes place is what transforms the mind into a potent, rational, analytical weapon.

Kirk Warren Brown, associate professor at the department of psychology at Virginia Commonwealth University and a colleague of David Creswell's, has written that *mushin* or flow is "a quality of consciousness manifest in, but not isomorphic with, the activities through which it is enhanced." In other words, it takes a lot less effort to elicit a flow state of mind than previously thought and the benefits far outweigh the effort involved.

There are other physiological changes that take place which are symptomatic of the changes in the rewiring of the brain. At the elite Navy Diving and Salvage Training Center in Panama City, Florida, researchers ran blood tests on recruits undergoing intensive physical training and they discovered their bodies exhibited levels of the adrenaline-moderating neuropeptide Y (NPY, again) that were almost double that of a control group who were not undertaking the same elite training.

If adrenaline is the clarion call that sounds when we sense danger and our bodies prepare to spring into action, then NPY is one of the buttons the brain pushes to silence that alarm, dampen fear responses, and keep the frontal lobe parts of our brain working longer under extreme stress.

A three-year study commissioned by Defence Research and Development Canada, the research arm of the Canadian Department of National Defence, to examine post-traumatic stress disorder (PTSD) and the long-term effects of combat stress on Canadian troops who had served in Afghanistan during the tension-escalating period of 2002 to 2008, showed that snipers report being less traumatized by the war. Although they exhibited escalated levels of psychological stress after taking a test known as the Kessler Psychological Distress Scale, their stress levels were actually lower than the average scores of their fellow soldiers. So, not only does NPY allow us to make better executive decisions under extreme stress but it also helps our brains recover faster, afterward.

All of this is good news as we look at just how to change our daily decision-making habits to create the triggers we need in order to experience a state of flow. We shall also see what activities we can engage in that will harden our brains to shock and allow us to make better decisions, sniper mind–quality decisions, under pressure.

Appendix II at the end of this book has a detailed guide to mindfulness meditation that may prove helpful.

THE BUSINESS CASE

Johnson & Johnson, the New Jersey–based global giant knows its business executives are key to the company's success. With four distinct divisions that stretch across consumer healthcare, medical devices, and pharmaceuticals, and a presence in 260 countries, the company knows its leadership needs to be at peak performance all the time.

This is the reason they ran a two-and-a-half-day-long executive training course which, according to company literature, "begins by emphasizing the connection between personal purpose and daily behaviors to help ensure alignment. Aligning energy investments with one's deepest values and beliefs represents a critical component to skillful energy management."

Through its Human Performance Institute, Johnson & Johnson has been a pioneer in linking the mind with the body and ascertaining that quality in executive decision-making is directly linked to good physical and mental health. Just like a top sniper or a Special Ops member must be fit and in tune with his body, a person making high-quality decisions in key business positions requires the commitment and awareness of a trained sniper.

Johnson & Johnson advertises the course to its executives as one "designed to strategically help participants become more productive and effective under pressure by managing their energy more effectively." And it goes on to detail that "participants work side-by-side with highly skilled Institute experts who have received specialized training in performance psychology, nutrition and exercise physiology."

Like a corporate version of sniper school training, the Johnson & Johnson Human Performance Institute's ultimate training objective is to "help strengthen individuals to become more resilient and able to thrive in even the most demanding and stressful working conditions." The similarities between the mind-set needed to address the mental stress experienced in corporate positions and the trained warrior's mind-set do not stop there either. A study by Kelly See, Elizabeth Wolfe Morrison, Naomi Rothman, and Jack Soll, published in *Organizational Behavior and Human Decision Processes*, concluded one characteristic of powerful and successful leaders is high levels of self-confidence.

All of this can be manufactured with the right kind of mental training and the development of suitable mental triggers, as a first step.

MENTAL TRIGGERS AND HOW TO CREATE THEM

Mental triggers are external events or circumstances that produce specific mental states. Mental triggers are necessary because they prime the brain to behave in specific ways and form new habits. New habits rewire the mind and enable it to be able to function at peak even when under pressure. Flow or *mushin*, for instance, can be activated with the right kind of mental trigger.

Cooper's Color Codes is, in a manner of speaking, a trigger that prepares the brain to perform at a high level by registering the threat level of the environment around it. In clinical psychology a trigger is simply an event or action that will kick off an automatic reaction. Without mental training most of us already have some kind of response to triggers that takes over and guide us. Unfortunately, these tend to be negative for the most part: the need for a stiff drink when a big project looms and the pressure ratchets up. A desire to smoke when feeling stressed. Overeating in order to compensate for a sudden increase in pressure in our decision-making. These are all handy examples most of us intuitively agree with. The fictional detective Sherlock Holmes would reach for his stash of heroin every time his famous deductive reasoning was blocked and he felt he was losing his edge.

Triggers are stressors: financial worries, increased anxiety, work-related problems, relationship worries. In most cases all these are examples of triggers we feel we do not control. I am not going to debate this here. What is important to us is the powerful sense of action that follows a trigger which, indeed, makes us feel impotent, being swept alone by an invisible tide that is now guiding our actions.

Now imagine creating, quite deliberately, mental triggers that are positive. Here's how snipers train themselves to form positive mental triggers:

- A trigger can be an event or an action. It is a cue that allows something else to happen, automatically.
- A trigger needs to be energy efficient. If we have to do a lot of work in order to activate a habit then it becomes harder and harder to justify the effort.
- A trigger should be automatic. There have to be clearly defined parameters in which a trigger is activated.
- A trigger should be familiar. Because we will be linking a trigger with a new habit, the trigger can't be so alien to us that it distracts us each time, nor can it be so removed from the new habit we are trying to form that it is a struggle to associate the two.

Once we have created the trigger (or are about to) linking it to a new habit requires just three things:

- Identify what the new habit will be.
- Make definitive time for this new habit.
- Identify the trigger associated with it.

In order for something to become a habit it requires repetition, so practice, and lots of it will be in your future. Repetition requires priority. A habit that is struggling for time to take place in, is unlikely to ever really be a habit.

A serving marine sniper I interviewed—let's call him Carl—told me his secret for getting into the calm frame of mind that we know as flow:

I can see everything piling up. Decisions to make, things to consider. Changes to the schedule. Commands that are asking you to use initiative and decide on something. It gets crazy with a lot of variables and a totally fluid situation on the ground. There is always a slight sense of panic that starts off at the back of my mind. You know, that voice that asks, "What if I can't do it? What if this is the time I choke?" Then you feel fear. Real fear because failure in your mission means that lives will be lost, yours probably included. I feel all that. Then I tell myself I am a killing machine. I know how that sounds and it's how I do it. In my mind I have this picture. The perfect machine. No flaws. No fear. No mistakes. It's like I am a Cylon Centurion. And my brain goes into high gear. Everything happens more slowly, at a distance. I can see things clearer then. What to prioritize. What to do next, what to do last or leave off completely. And I feel calm. In control. I become the killing machine of my mind, all gleaming chrome and steel. That's how I get in the zone.

Carl's account highlights the personal nature of the mental trigger. The apparent illogicality of it which, however, works. For him, the idea of a chrome-clad Cylon, impervious to fear and incapable of making mistakes, is all that's required to send his brain into a higher orbit. With the many snipers I interviewed who were willing to talk about this, the intense personalized nature of it always came through. None mentioned duty, patriotism, valor, a sense of being a hero. To them it is always about something small and intensely personal. It's about feeling empathy for those around them. Never wanting to let them down. It is about something that conceptually transforms them into something else. What I found fascinating is that being snipers, they all used the same trigger phrase to activate the mental imagery they needed: "Adapt. Overcome."

This is testament to the quality and stickiness of their training and, I suspect, to the tried and tested formula they use to function at peak efficiency. Like a mantra, the words unleash exactly the kind of sense of confidence, capability, and skill in a person that a sniper needs to complete his mission. None of this should come as a surprise to anyone who's tried positive psychology. Starting the day with a positive mantra like, "I know I can do it," "I can overcome any obstacle," "I am reaching my success goals every day," leads to the same kind of confidence and mental focus snipers attain that actually makes things happen.

DEVELOP MENTAL ALERTNESS STRATEGIES

We can all make mental focus a habit by drilling our brain to work in very specific ways. The condition of going through the day in an unfocused manner that allows thoughts to surface at the wrong moment and become distractions is what impairs our performance.

Thinking about work or relationship issues while driving, for instance, is a classic example of unfocused, distracted behavior. When the traffic around us is flowing normally and there are no problems we can get from A to B without compromising our own or anybody else's safety. But driving in that distracted manner can become a potentially serious problem the moment things around us change and we fail to perceive it because we have not been paying attention properly.

The example with driving also occurs in many other aspects

of our day-to-day lives. We may find ourselves thinking about holidays when at work, thinking about work when we are with our family and friends and thinking about everything when we are struggling to fall asleep. All of these are instances of a lack of focus that hurts more than it helps us.

Snipers are masters at using their training in their everyday lives. In psychology this is called "transfer," and it is the application of skills developed and knowledge acquired in a specific, bounded area of performance, like a video simulation or a battlefield, to another, like everyday life.

"Britain in 2009 was not a happy place." The former British sniper I was talking to, let's call him Scott Green, had just been released from the Royal Marines after two tours of duty in Afghanistan. "Jobs were vanishing, the economy was shrinking. My computer engineer degree earned in the army was out of date for civvy street." Britain was feeling the same fiscal pressures as all the other Western economies reeling from the collapse of Lehman Brothers. Members of Parliament were embroiled in the expenses scandal that involved politicians from every party. Public confidence was low, consumer spending was down, and no one was hiring.

"I'd come out of the army with savings but they were clearly not going to last long. I needed a job and I needed it fast," Scott said. Although he'd gone back to living at home Scott was engaged and planned to marry a woman named Susan. "It was ridiculous," he recalled. "It was like being back at school and dating. My relationship with Sue was suffering because we weren't even sure if we could get a mortgage at that stage, let alone pay for a wedding."

Scott spent the first nine months after coming out of the army doing the usual. "I went to the local job center, I sent out CVs and covering letters. I went for interviews." The story was the same everywhere. Army personnel were not regarded as highly skilled. In a stalled economy no one wanted to risk hires.

"I knew I had skills. As a sniper you are trained to operate on your own for long periods of time. You are meticulous in your approach to every situation. You learn to assess, think, plan, extrapolate, project, analyze, and then reassess. I thought it was perverse because these were skills business most need during a recession yet no one was willing to give me a chance."

Scott decided to take matters directly into his own hands. "I knew of a medium-sized engineering company in the Midlands, near my parents' old home. Engineering is a tough environment. A lot of the production processes and quality control are highly standardized, yet there are fluid situations where you need to be able to make critical decisions fast. I was certain I would be able to add value to them as part of their quality control and systems' production overseeing process, but I needed to get their attention."

Instead of following the usual route of sending an email with a covering letter and a CV to human resources, Scott decided to go down and check out the factory. He made a note of times trucks came and went, the lunchtime patterns of lunch being delivered to the premises by those who ordered it from outside. He checked what he could publicly find about production schedules and output goals. He then went one step further and looked at the truck cargo drop-off points and local traffic and railway conditions.

"The cost of transportation is important," Scott said. An extra couple of hours spent in traffic increases fuel costs and wear and tear on trucks. "The company was using its own delivery vehicles to transport machinery parts. Some of the heavier items going across country would be taken to the railway depot to be delivered by rail and picked up and delivered by a third party at the other end. As a sniper I know timing is everything."

He wasn't wrong. What he found was that truck drivers out on deliveries would consistently time it so they arrived back to the depot in time for lunch and then picked up and dropped off the next load. It created an invisible bottleneck. Because their trucks were being loaded while they were having lunch, no one noticed the pattern.

"I used the Internet to check motorway traffic loads from the Midlands to major cities. I mapped out delays due to rain, congestion, and traffic accidents in hourly intervals. Lunchtime traffic on the M6 was at its lightest consistently. But that was the time when the truck drivers were having lunch. After lunch hour, traffic congestion went up. That's when you also experienced the greatest delays due to weather conditions or accidents."

To Scott, the action required was clear. But first he had to make sure. "I checked the cost of wear and tear per hour in traffic on the kind of trucks they used," he said. "I factored in fuel. Then I looked at the driving conditions they'd meet at the other end when they came off the motorway."

He found similar bottlenecks in the train delivery timetable. Delivery dates were being missed because loads delivered to the train depot would miss the window for delivery and pickup at the other end.

"It was a question of synchronization. I realized it was affecting the perception of reliability for the company from the customer's point of view, yet their reputation for what they made was solid."

He spent a month methodically putting together a monetary value to all that. "I created a mission file, the way I'd been taught. Marked out everything in terms of operational procedures and objectives. I don't think anyone at the firm had ever done anything like this before."

When Scott was sure of his findings and figures he sent in a single e-mail. The subject line was "Hire me and save £40,000 [$50,000] a year." In the cover letter, he explained a little of his background and that he was looking for a job. He mentioned that he was confident he could help the company save that amount of money at least in missed deadlines, vehicle fleet repair, and productivity gains. All he wanted was a chance to explain.

"They called me back three days later," Scott said. "Asked me to go in the next day, gave me thirty minutes."

The meeting was with the company's service manager, the man in charge of production schedules and deliveries. "I had my file with me. I began laying out the picture. Ten minutes in I saw that he was flabbergasted. He wasn't sure what to say. No one had thought of looking at the problem in quite this way. Delivery timetables outside what time a load was ready to go, they felt, was something they could do nothing about.

"He went over the figures I gave him," Scott continued. "I explained how I had done it. What point of view I had employed, what assumptions I had made. He made notes as I explained my methodology. At the end of the meeting he asked me if he could keep the file and said he would call me. I suppose you always think that he could have taken all this and claimed it for himself but by then we had overshot our allotted thirty minutes by almost an hour. I liked the man."

Scott left, leaving the file behind. He heard nothing for almost a week. He was beginning to think his judgment had been wrong, that he had made a mistake trusting the service manager, when he received a call.

"I am still working with them now," he said. "They did not have a position for me so they actually created one. I am roaming projects manager. My task is to see what current challenges the company is facing, communicated by management, and then see if I can find a solution that will solve them or make them easier to work with.

"If I had not decided to put what I knew to good use, if I had relied on the traditional approach to employment, I may still be out there today, hoping to get a job, making it harder to get one the more time I spent as unemployed. It was my sniper's mind that created this opportunity for me."

Another way to look at it is to think that the opportunity was always there. Scott's sniper-trained mind simply took advantage of it.

There are three very basic things we can do to help our minds think like Scott's:

- **Pay attention**—Being aware of where we are, what we are doing, how we are perceived, who else is sharing the space with us teaches our brains to process information without getting overloaded. Paying attention is expressed in many other practical ways too: listen to others, not just what they are saying but how they are saying it. Everything is information if we know how to look for it. But for the brain to process it properly it needs to be primed for context, beforehand. Information without context is unfiltered noise. It overwhelms, distracts, confuses, and exhausts us. Context allows the signal to emerge from what appears to be random noise.

- **Look at details**—When you are in context look at every detail. Do not assume that everything is perfect and gloss over details as unimportant. Everything truly matters. From the tone of voice someone is using to the kind of car they drive. In a restaurant the flow of the waiters, the people coming and going, the positioning of the tables and the chairs, and the intensity of the lights all play a key role. Learn to appreciate the details of where you are and what you do. Expectations build up suppositions in the mind that make us overlook changes in the environment we are in. Get into the habit of building your own mental picture of the world you operate in.

- **Show initiative**—In the example cited earlier, this is exactly what Scott did. He did not wait for things to happen according to some kind of perceived rule. He realized he could not rely on the system to help him find work quickly so he took matters into his own hands with a very direct approach. Exercising initiative is not just about taking control. It is also about making sure the information you are receiving is correct, verifying data sources, making sure that the mental picture you are putting together in your head is always as correct as possible.

TRAIN YOUR MIND

Edgar Morin, the French philosopher and sociologist expresses the need for a trained mind that is constantly being put through its paces in a very elegant way: "If knowing is always performed by somebody, then that somebody can be viewed as an instrument, an instrument that has to be tuned, studied, practiced. Limitations and blind spots have to be assessed and brought into consciousness."

By "knowing" he does not mean just knowledge but also awareness. The Know Thyself of the Ancient Greeks and the temple of Apollo at Delphi. This kind of awareness is always hard to practice alone. All too frequently, old habits creep in before the new ones have the time necessary to become the norm. We can get overwhelmed by circumstances. Snipers may at times operate solo but they are always part of a larger group which forms their default support network. This helps them maintain the standards they have been trained to. The same goes for athletes, martial artists, soldiers, and first responders.

In a business environment this is not always the case. This is why it is important to have a personal eight-step methodology that helps us become able to perform at peak, at will.

The eight steps that follow are used by everyone who has the attitude of a trained warrior:

- **Use your mind**—Snipers never rest on their laurels. They run imaginary scenarios in their heads. They think, "If this happens, what happens next?" They look at past scenarios where they know the variables and they play with them, imagining what different outcomes would be like. Again, this is a case of "transfer." The internal modeling that goes on during these mental exercises allows our brains to perform at peak when encountering a scenario we cannot train for, like when Captain Sullenberger landed US Airways Flight 1549 safely on the Hudson.

- **Use vision**—Use your eyes to gather information about the world around you. Understand the dynamic principles that govern your environment. Use your mental vision to see yourself in that environment the way you want yourself to be. Understand how perception works, what you have to do in order to be who you want to be or get the outcome you want.

- **State your goals**—Write them down. Articulate them in a way that allows you to focus so that you can be persistent. Trained snipers know how to keep their goals central in their mind.

- **Create positive habits**—Habits allow you to repeat and practice your skills and reinforce your goals. Repetition creates the kind of mental heuristics that make reaction to specific events feel completely instinctual and automatic.

- **Be ambitious**—When setting goals for yourself, be realistic but also get a little outside your comfort zone. Things that do not challenge you are unlikely to help you develop.

- **Use mental triggers**—At some point we all get tired and weak and feel helpless and falter. What gets us through this rough patch are the emotional triggers we have created to help maintain our drive. For some it is about duty to their family and friends. For others it is about identity and who they want to feel they are. This requires a little introspection and a lot of self-honesty. When you have your trigger, however, it is the one that will help you go when your body and your mind are telling you to stop. This is also how you begin to activate the focus necessary for bubble compartmentalization to happen for you.

- **Believe in yourself**—If you cannot believe in what you can do it is unlikely anyone else will either. Develop the attitude of feeling capable that snipers and elite Special Ops soldiers learn to develop. This is different from arrogance. Confidence in yourself comes from the inner understanding that you can do what you set out to do and nothing will stop you.

- **Change your mind**—The plasticity of the brain means that we can teach ourselves new habits, new skills, new abilities even. We can use the inner power of our minds to improve our memory and even our eyesight. All changes we want to see in the outside world and our environment start from within. We are the ones that need to change first.

THE SNIPER SKILL ACQUISITION LIST

In this chapter you learned:

- Mindfulness meditation changes the mind as well as the body. The changes it produces make handling intense pressure and prioritizing easier.
- Bubble compartmentalization can become a learned response provided the right mental triggers have been set up beforehand.
- Positive habits are crucial to success. There is a transfer of skills and knowledge from visualized scenarios to real-life situations.
- Training the brain as well as the body results in better, overall coping strategies for stress.

- Awareness of the environment and awareness of ourselves are requirements for creating the sniper mind capable of quickly assessing a situation and finding the best solution to a given problem.

I developed a mechanism so that whatever mistakes I made, I would bounce straight back. Whatever was happening off the pitch, I could put it to one side and maintain my form. Call it mental resilience or a strong mind, but that is what we mean when we talk about experience in a football team.

—GARY NEVILLE, *DAILY MAIL* INTERVIEW

7

Fortitude: Build Bulwarks Against Mental Fatigue, Uncertainty, and Fear with the Navy SEALs Method

It was cold. There was snow and ice everywhere and I'd spent the last eight hours going through the forest, trying to be as quiet as possible which was not easy as I was wearing specially issued snowshoes. I knew there was enemy all around, looking for me, but their position was unspecified. I was trying to stay low, hoping to get eyes on them first. My first night in the forest was a disaster. I was trying to use what I know, keep myself warm by burrowing deep into the snow, carving a small igloo for myself. But I had obviously done a poor job of hiding my tracks or hiding my sleeping place. I woke up to yelling voices and the sound of guns being cocked. I tried to come out with my hands up, my brain trying to get a sense of what was happening, when someone slapped me hard on the back, sent me sprawling to the ground. My hands were quickly zip-tied behind my back and a hood was forced over my head. For good measure I also got a punch to the solar plexus.

I knew I was caught.

I was pushed onto the back of a truck and driven for a long time. Mentally, I was trying to count the left turns we took so I could have a bearing on the place they were taking me, but one of my captors must have sensed what I was doing. He used the butt of his gun against my ribs. It was not a serious blow but it hurt like hell and for a while my head was just full of pain. My sense of direction completely lost.

When the truck stopped, they unloaded me by kicking me off the back of the truck. Someone took the hood off and that's when I saw the other members of my squad. We'd all been captured. They too were squinting against the sudden light and they all looked roughed up.

We were all led to individual cells, blindfolded. I was made to sit on a box about a foot or so high. My hands were placed along my legs, palms up. "Move and you will get shot." A few hours into this uncomfortable position and the pain was beginning to make itself felt. My captor came back in, removed my blindfold, and he pointed to a tin can lined with a plastic bag in the corner and explained that it was for my toilet needs, but I had to ask permission. I noticed he had a thick accent, which I could only half-guess as Syrian. "You are war criminal number Two-Two-One," he said. From now on that was how I would refer to myself. And the position I was in had to be kept at all times.

The moment he was out of the cell I allowed myself to relax a little. It was a mistake. He came back in seconds later.

Slapped me. Made me assume the position at gunpoint. "You do again and no toilet," he said. I hated him.

I assumed I was being watched at all times, so I started working out just how I could move my body, relaxing each muscle a tiny bit at a time without it being noticed. I really felt I was getting somewhere when I had managed to ease the pain on my body and no one had rushed in to slap me when the psyops stuff kicked in. A loudspeaker started blaring Rudyard Kipling reciting his poem "Boots" again and again and again until I thought I would go insane. When "Boots" was not being recited there was a real cacophony of music, drums, cymbals, saxophones, that felt like an assault on the ears. It made it hard to think.

The only break was the heavily accented voice again yelling in English, coming over the speakers: "War criminals wishing to use the toilet must ask permission using their war criminal number and yelling at the top of their voice." Despite the fact that I knew what all this was, part of me was really thinking that this was it. This was a place from which I may not make it out alive.

THIS IS AN account given anonymously. All Survival, Evasion, Resistance, and Escape (SERE) recruits have to sign a nondisclosure agreement and take an oath of secrecy regarding the exact nature of the training program. Harrowing as the account may be, narrated by a former marine sniper whom we shall call Eric, it's nonetheless nothing more than a training exercise. SERE is a program offered to those members of the US Armed Forces that are likely to find themselves behind enemy lines, facing the probability of capture and having to rely on their wits to survive until extraction becomes possible.

Before SERE became what it is today it was the brainchild of World War II airmen who used the experiences of the British and American pilots who managed to escape from and then evade the Germans and return to friendly lines. They formed private clubs to first learn and then teach the skills required to help them survive, escape, and then evade capture. It was formalized in 1948. It was championed by General Curtis LeMay who realized the value of the training program to the survival of airmen and special operatives stranded behind enemy lines. The program was not officially named SERE until the 1990s. It has, however, become the lifeline of every sniper and Special Ops personnel, with many acknowledging that it has given them skills that would have been impossible to develop under different circumstances.

The exact nature of the training is a closely guarded secret. Snippets, however, like the account provided by Eric here, have surfaced across the Web. Sometimes they appear in military forums where specific aspects of the training are discussed, like the fact that SERE used enhanced interrogation techniques during the captivity part of the program, a few of which have now been discontinued due to the degree of stress they impose on the subjects, and at other times on question-and-answer sites like Quora, where former snipers and marines openly discuss some aspects of SERE.

Piecing together their stories, a picture emerges of what goes on there. Soldiers from many different parts of the armed forces (navy, air force, army) are taught how to carry out specific tasks that include surviving off the land, keeping themselves safe from the elements, learning to navigate using the stars, and learning how to avoid and evade enemy patrols looking for them. The training offers expert guidance beforehand by personnel who are at the very top of their field.

When the more academic part of the program is over, the recruits must complete a loosely scripted mission which, however, goes wrong and they get "captured." What they face next is something which they have never quite expected and they have to use everything they have been taught to get through it.

The official US Army Web site says that "regardless of a soldier's background, the SERE-C training approach exploits his or her weakness in order to induce the most amount of stress safely and effectively." And SERE training is all about exploiting weaknesses and creating both physical and psychological stress. Lasting between five and six days the program aims to introduce recruits to a combination of physical, environmental, and psychological stressors in as realistic a way as possible.

Fatigue, sleeplessness, extreme heat and cold, as well as hunger and thirst are carefully introduced to push SERE trainees to their breaking point. Interrogation techniques are employed with physical discomfort being a constant.

The aim is to peel back the onion layers of each person's defences and force them to create coping strategies that will enable them to develop physical, psychological, and mental resilience. The military calls this "hardening."

The reason all of this is relevant to us who (thankfully) will not undergo SERE training and will not experience the very real sensations of fear, exhaustion, and psychological stress, is that it proves there is no separating the body from the mind. Every physical response, every psychological change, and every mental transformation starts with the mind.

Snipers who have undergone SERE training testify to having access to a well of psychological and mental resources they can call up when necessary to help them cope with unexpected adversity so that their decision-making process is not affected.

Every time we make a high-level decision we are struggling against the "elements." Work will tire us out, stress will deplete our natural resources, uncertainty will make us question our judgment, and fear will cause us to hesitate. We will find ourselves mentally alone, in a dark place. The army has always known about this "dark place," and it has devised the highly effective mental training techniques that it teaches the SERE recruits to deal with it. The French Foreign Legion codified it in what it called its "barrel set" and its soldiers used it to get safely across the Sahara, simply going from one barrel buried in the sand to the next, following a rope, joining them together.

Snipers and Special Ops operatives from Rangers and Navy SEALs to the British Special Air Service (SAS) call it "stress testing." Each time the scenario is different, depending on the particular nature of each Special Ops team. What unites them all, however, is the effect stress testing has on the human psyche. Its destructive, identity-stripping work affects the decision-making part of the brain.

What modern warriors benefit from so can corporate warriors. How the body/mind connection works to affect such deep changes in such a short training course, so that performance at peak becomes possible at a much later date is the subject of much scientific analysis. What we are learning is of direct use to corporate warriors facing their own version of environmental stressors.

THE SCIENCE: Extreme physical, mental, and psychological stress forces the body and mind to adapt through physiological and neurochemical changes. By studying the architecture of these changes we can learn to emulate the effects.

"ADAPT. OVERCOME."

Evolution has geared the human stress response to last about thirty seconds. It's enough time to facilitate fight or flight. Evolution has not adapted our brains or bodies to handle weeks or months of prolonged stress—the kind that can feature in the two-month Ranger school or yearlong combat tours.

In a stressful situation, the brain's amygdala activates the body's hypothalamic-pituitary-adrenal axis and the sympathetic nervous system, which produce the physiological and metabolic changes to the body. The amygdala is itself regulated by two other parts of the brain: the hippocampus which helps place the stress in context, and the prefrontal cortex, connected to executive function and working memory, which helps abate fear.

The prefrontal cortex helps a soldier to feel in control of a battlefield stressor and make sound decisions under fire. When a trained sniper applies his "Adapt. Overcome." principle, he is basically using his prefrontal cortex to own his fear and get past it so that his emotional stability is not affected.

To understand what makes a better soldier, the army examined the stress levels of soldiers who have gone through the SERE training course. In one study, the levels of cortisol, a hormone that prepares the body for stress, were measured. Researchers found that students taking the SERE course experienced significant changes in hormone levels, which the military described as some of the greatest ever documented in humans.

More specifically, by analyzing saliva samples from a test group undergoing SERE training and comparing them to a control group of soldiers who though physically fit and mentally capable, had not gone through SERE training, the researchers were able to prove that there are specific hormonal, physical, and, by inference alone, psychological changes which marked those who had been stress inoculated by the training as different from the average soldier.

Although a relatively large number of hormones are affected by stress, the researchers focused on four specific ones:

Cortisol—This is one of the most frequently studied stress hormones. It prepares the body for stress. Cortisol increases a person's level of anxiety and alertness. By increasing the metabolism of carbohydrates, cortisol also increases the amount of blood sugar available to the body's cells.

Testosterone—This helps the body to maintain secondary sex characteristics and plays an important role in the body's ability to repair tissues. It helps the body's immune system to work properly, and it helps protect against the effects of stress.

Adrenaline—This is released quickly when a person is under stress. It enhances alertness, increases blood pressure, and aids in the formation of threat-related memories.

Neuropeptide-Y, or NPY—This is produced by the same glands that produce adrenaline. NPY enhances the body's production of adrenaline and works to counter the effects of stress:

it decreases anxiety and enhances the mental functions of attention and memory.

They also looked for instances of dissociation in the SERE participants. Dissociation occurs under stress when we see ourselves from the outside looking in. In psychological terms it is the separation of normally related mental processes, resulting in one group functioning independently from the rest. This allows those who experience it to function as if levels of discomfort that are being experienced happen to someone else and not them.

This last metric is a tricky one. Dissociation is a psychological defense mechanism. The brain activates it when faced with high stress levels so that it can cope better. Left unchecked, dissociation completely envelops the person, taking his mind away from the here and now (in a sort of mental safe harbor) while leaving his body to cope as best as it can. Dissociation at this level is clearly counterproductive when you are trying to juggle a dozen complex variables and deal with pressure and stress that simply keep ratcheting up. SERE graduates learn to use that defense mechanism to their advantage. They trigger dissociation sufficiently to help them cope with stress and pressure without losing touch of the here and now. The net result of this is an increase in the level of cognitive control they enjoy and a sense of calm that allows an increase in discomfort tolerance levels.

When faced with the enormous physical, mental, and psychological stress of SERE, the body and the mind do exactly what snipers are taught to do in order to accomplish their mission: Adapt. Overcome. Obviously, some of the physiological responses, like the rise in particular hormones, cannot be consciously controlled; however, they are frequently the result of a specific mental approach or attitude which in itself can become instrumental in

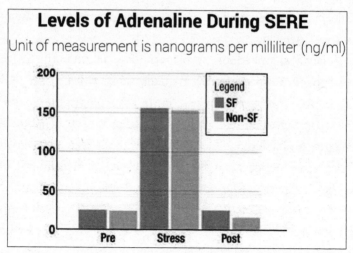

Fig 7.1 The chart shows average cortisol levels measured in SERE students compared to levels recorded in previous studies that looked at patients about to undergo major surgery, soldiers in Army Ranger training, pilots performing military flight operations, and novice skydivers making their first jump.

eliciting different physiological responses from the body and brain.

While none of them are likely to find themselves behind enemy lines and in danger of being captured or being taken as prisoners of war and interrogated, being physically and mentally resilient and psychologically adaptive is a great skill to have. At the very least it allows greater productivity even under prolonged pressure and it gives them the ability to develop personal survival strategies and adapt them on the fly.

THE BUSINESS CASE

In San Francisco's Silicon Valley, tech companies live or die by the energy, commitment, and focus of their employees. Twitter's human resources and wellness program manager, Amy Obana, knows that, which is why she looks to keep the company's one thousand employees fit, healthy, and committed with onsite yoga, Pilates, Wing Chun Kung Fu, and CrossFit classes.

Just the saving in productivity losses and absenteeism is enough to convince even the most hard-nosed corporate boss of the need for a comprehensive fitness program for employees. But helpful as these may be, no comprehensive fitness program will quite do the job that a sniper-trained mind and body will, or at least not without understanding the mechanics and doing a little work to emulate them.

In a landmark study of SERE participants called "Behavioral predictors of acute stress symptoms during intense military training" researchers showed that soldiers who adopted an active coping style fared better than those who took a passive or emotion-focused approach. This leads us back to the importance of the mind-set we examined in chapter 6. The study's implication is that a "fake it till you make it approach" works. For the same reasons a simulation can help develop skills, knowledge, and experience, which can be transferred to a real-world setting, so imitating the mind-set of hardened warriors can help us benefit from their mental and psychological resilience.

While pain and torture may never be factors in a corporate setting, sleep deprivation, stress, poor memory (as a result of these two), decreased concentration, decreased immune system resilience, and decreased drive are factors which occur frequently as a result of work-related stressors. From important meetings to presentations. From projects that need to be completed on very tight deadlines to unexpected crises that require extensive attention to set right. All of these are hard on the body and hard on the mind. Knowing how to cope with them and recover can be an incredibly useful skill.

DEALING WITH AN ALL-NIGHTER

In an ideal world all-nighters are the kind of thing we do when we're in college, because we must, and then for the rest of our lives we deal with things in an organized, determined, step-by-step manner. There is, of course, no ideal world, and the chances are that at some point in your working life you will have to do an all-nighter and still show up for work the next day and be expected to function at peak.

Studies have shown that a sleepless night elevates the dopamine levels in the brain leading to a heightened sense of euphoria. But at the same time, sleep deprivation shuts down the brain's key planning and decision-making regions (the prefrontal cortex) while activating more primal neural functions such as the fight or flight reflex in the amygdala region of the brain.

While this may sound like it is impossible to go through an all-nighter and still function adequately the next day, it clearly isn't. Carlos Hathcock did it in his legendary three-day crawl to complete his mission. Those who go through SERE have to learn how to manage it. The smart money is on having the forethought and planning time to not have to do anything like that, but should you have no choice there are four things you can do that will temporarily allow you to brush off the debilitating effects of sleep deprivation:

Stock up your sleep reserves—It may not always be possible to plan this in advance, but sleeping enough the nights that lead up to a sleepless night makes it easier to pull it off when you have to because your brain has that extra capacity to absorb the stress it undergoes.

Mark, serving with a marine sniper platoon, advised being smart. "If you don't have to, you should always try to avoid becoming sleep deprived. The one thing we all learn at SERE is that sleep deprivation unmans you. Your sense of orientation goes. Your sense of time disappears. Your memory becomes faulty. You can no longer trust your gut instinct. So always make sure you are operating with enough sleep hours in the tank, so you can pull it off at short notice."

In a pinch, as part of our personal survival strategy sleep experts suggest grabbing what they call a "prophylactic nap." At the Dayton VA Medical Center in Ohio, researchers associated with Wright State University have carried out studies to determine the best protocol for weathering a sleepless night without suffering ill effects in terms of performance. In a study titled "The use of prophylactic naps and caffeine to maintain performance during a continuous operation," they detailed how their group of twenty-four young adult males, being put through a sleepless twenty-four-hour period where their mental alertness and performance was monitored against baseline readings and a control group, managed to maintain near-optimum efficiency through a regimen of strategic napping and caffeine intake.

The "power nap" and a strong espresso strategy were found to be most effective when the nap was no more than ninety minutes long and the coffee intake was spaced out to help boost alertness when the effects of the nap were beginning to wane. Sara Mednick, an assistant professor at the University of California, Riverside, who's been studying the ability of naps to restore the brain to near-normal baseline performance cites how her studies show that napping produces the same sleep-stage-specific enhancements as an overnight sleep.

This ties in with anecdotal evidence from the accounts of serving soldiers who always try to get some sleep where and when they can. "I trained myself to switch off whenever I got the chance," wrote Mike, who's with the 15th Marine Expeditionary Unit. "Things happen fast when you're on the ground. You do not always know when you will be called up to leave base, and when you are, you can never be sure that you will get back on time. That's not the best time to find yourself short of sleep and with your head not in the game." His habit of catching naps any time things on base got slow allowed him to operate on the battlefield without exhausting his capacity to deal with stress and prolonged periods of concentration.

Have some stimulant ready—Wars may be won by bravery and they may require weaponry but they run on coffee. There is no nine-to-five in battle. And, just like when a crisis hits in a business environment, when things break on the battlefield, all hands are called to the task irrespective of the time of day or the kind of week they may have had. Snipers report having a strategic relationship with coffee. "If you need to stay up all night and are on lookout, you need to have coffee on hand. But that also means you can't go on drinking coffee all day, every day like water. Keep it in reserve. Come off it if you need a day before your all-nighter. Then it will work best for you."

Stay off the carbs—If you're preparing for an all-nighter and want your brain to function at peak then you should know that a large, carb-heavy meal will most probably lead to a crash as its "good mood" feeling kicks in. Snipers know that you need to fuel for combat operations so they need to pile in some calories to keep them going. "Since coming out of the army I have had a couple of occasions to pull all-nighters," says Tim, a former sniper who now works as a marketing manager for an international cargo transportation company. "I make sure that I have nothing to eat beforehand. The hunger keeps me alert and on form even at the end of a very long day. Plus I know I really earned my food afterward."

Stay active—Snipers on active duty have an active lifestyle as part of their everyday work. Although they constantly have to work on their fitness they do not have to specifically schedule in physical activity before they go on a mission. It's not quite the same for the rest of us who sit behind desks looking at screens all day, drive everywhere, and try to fit in exercise once or twice a week. Tim had this to say by way of advice: "Try to get some exercise in before an all-nighter. Nothing that would exhaust you so stay away from all the heavy stuff but a workout that makes you sweat a bit and lights up your brain makes you feel energized and ready for anything. Plus, when you are actually pulling an all-nighter try to be active. I do a few push-ups or stand up and walk about. All of this stimulates my body and keeps my mind alert."

RECOVERING ON THE FLY

When all's said and done, pulling off an all-nighter might be less challenging than having to stay alert throughout the next day and perform to a high standard. But even here there are three techniques to help the body recover faster and stay on track, and all they require is a little discipline and awareness of the kind trained snipers employ.

Rather than giving in to the sensation of fatigue, snipers make sure they take deep breaths to oxygenate their brains and look at the way they feel as part of the problem to be solved. This distancing, the dissociative element that snipers develop as part of their training allows them to apply fixes that are "good enough" to help them recover until they can rest properly again.

The approach is a product of the "you take the best shot, not a perfect shot" mentality that is drilled into every sniper during training. It reveals the decisive nature of the sniper mind intent on getting the job done and being capable, as a result, of temporarily disregarding every other distraction. The three most useful techniques trained operatives use to recover from a prolonged period of stress (apart from getting plenty of rest, that is) are:

Drink and nap—There is a sniper survival strategy that uses clever knowledge of the body's chemical processes and the brain's capabilities to reduce the adverse effects of extended periods of sleeplessness. Paradoxically, it requires some sleep. Snipers know that a fifteen- to twenty-minute nap grabbed opportunistically can take the edge off both fatigue and sleepiness. The danger with this tactic is that should the sleep last more than twenty minutes, a sniper risks getting deep into Rapid Eye Movement or REM sleep, which is a deep sleep stage. Waking up from that stage would make anyone feel like their brain has been run over as the brain's circuitry would require some time to fully come awake again. The sensation of sleep inertia we sometimes feel when we are woken up suddenly from a deep sleep is the sensation of mental and physical heaviness that result from an incomplete REM cycle. To avoid experiencing this sensation, some snipers drink a cup of coffee before they take their nap. Coffee clears the adenosine from the body. Adenosine is a nucleotide produced by the degradation of adenosine triphosphate (ATP), the molecule that serves as the "energy currency" for the body's various cellular functions. The amount of adenosine produced in the brain reflects the activity level of its neurons and glial cells. In other words the busier you are the more likely you are to hit the fatigue point past which you will want to sleep. Adenosine, as a result, is called a hypnogenic substance: its concentration in the brain is higher during waking periods than during sleep and increases during extended periods of wakefulness. Coffee takes a while to get through our system which means that we can drink a cup and go to sleep. By the time it fully kicks in, the fifteen- to twenty-minute nap will be over and we can wake up feeling refreshed, not just because we've napped without going into a deep REM sleep but also because coffee has dampened down the concentration of adenosine in our body.

Drink plenty of fluids—We don't always realize it, but stress has a strong dehydrating effect. Dehydration also helps increase the concentration of cortisol in the body. Cortisol is called the stress hormone because it is such a strong marker for it. Stress can cause dehydration, and dehydration can cause stress. Stress and dehydration exhibit many of the same symptoms such as increased heart rate, nausea, fatigue, and headaches, all of which affect our ability to function effectively. By remaining hydrated we send a clear signal to the body that there is little to worry about. It helps relieve the perception of stress and this eases cortisol levels in the bloodstream making it easier for us to control our body and mind.

Go toward the light—Those who like to work under low

light conditions will find it very difficult to stay mentally alert or physically awake for very long. Bright lights help the body fight off drowsiness and increase mental alertness, even when we are tired.

All of these help maintain the sharpness of the brain's executive actions, which means we make better decisions even when operating under extreme mental and physical fatigue.

DEVELOP AN ATTITUDE

These are practical steps, the kind of hands-on practices snipers employ to control their physical responses to fatigue and sleep deprivation. None of it is automatic. In order to be able to control our body's responses, we have to have the kind of focus and awareness that special operatives develop with time.

When it comes to performing at peak under difficult conditions most sniper trainers believe the 80/20 rule applies: 80 percent of the performance comes from attitude, 20 percent comes from skill and knowledge, divided equally between the two.

Attitude requires practice. In her 2010 book *Emotions in American History: An International Assessment*, Jessica C. Gienow-Hecht gave the psychological definition of attitude as "a relatively enduring organization of beliefs, feelings, and behavioral tendencies toward socially significant objects, groups, events, or symbols." This makes our attitudes the total synthesis of many of the mental components of our identities.

Snipers, like any other Special Forces operatives, are taught how to synthesize their belief in themselves, their understanding of their capabilities, and their trust in their training to create an attitude that helps them overcome the obstacles they encounter.

There are three specific components that create the sum total of the external behavior of a person we usually call attitude. Each of these represents an entire galaxy of psychological complexities that have to be gradually shaped to achieve the attitude we want to have. The components are:

Affective—As the name suggests this involves a person's feelings and emotions about a particular thing. For instance: "I can always adapt and overcome any obstacles placed in my path."

Behavioral—The attitude we have has a direct bearing on our physical behavior and actions. For example: "There is no obstacle I cannot analyze in a rational fashion and break down to its component parts so I can find a way to get around it."

Cognitive—This reflects the knowledge we have and the beliefs we fashion from it. For example: "Every obstacle is the direct result of constituent parts and circumstances. This means nothing is insurmountable."

Developing the kind of attitude that leads to success then requires personal awareness, self-control (discipline), and analytical thinking. These are exactly the type of skills corporate executives need in order to successfully lead their teams and respond to the pressures they face. Attitude truly emerges when the three components align so that there is consistency between behavior, beliefs, and feelings. Consistent behavior is desirable because it allows us to become dependable. Being dependable makes us trustworthy. Trust is the component that makes all of our endeavors, societal structures, business undertakings, and personal relationships work.

Consistency between our emotions, knowledge, beliefs, and behavior also allows us to trust ourselves, which makes it easier to respond to intuitive cognitive analysis (like our gut feeling).

When the cognitive and affective components of attitude do not match our behavior we sense the weakness in ourselves, the inconsistency. This leads to an attempt to rationalize the disconnect and compensate for it. The effort involved in such an approach is quite significant, which then leaves relatively fewer resources for getting anything else done.

The seemingly simplistic motto of trained snipers—"Adapt. Overcome."—is a mantra that expresses an attitude of capability and such deep consistency that it becomes a real strength. The psychologist Daniel Katz, who helped lay some of the foundations of organizational psychology, believed that attitude helps us define who we really are so it plays a role in forming our identity, it allows us to communicate better by mediating between our inner needs and the social structures we become part of and it helps add a sense of deeper meaning to our lives.

Until MBA courses come with a strong mental component designed to help in shaping a person's identity under pressure, developing the kind of attitude that stops us from giving up when we most want to, and rising above our limitations, training our minds to develop the right kind of attitude is a case of thoughtfulness, awareness, inward reflection, analytical thinking, and constant daily practice.

THE NAVY SEAL'S LIST OF MENTAL TRICKS

Of all the special force units, perhaps the Navy SEALs undergo some of the most physically and mentally grueling trials. During training they have to experience the sensation of drowning, fight sleep deprivation and hunger, deal with cold and fatigue, overcome injuries and fear and still stay mentally lucid, capable of recalling details of road signs they saw briefly in the dark, or the layout of rooms they caught only a glimpse of.

The SEALs are formidable in ways that few trained operatives are even in the exceptional world of Special Forces, and when SEALs are also trained as snipers they acquire an additional layer of skills and abilities that makes them even more exceptional.

All of this is achieved with a remarkably simple guide of just four steps:

Set goals—The setting of goals has been a constant throughout most sections of this book. Given the goal-oriented world of the military, it is to be somewhat expected. This is also what makes the military skill set so transferable to a business environment. Now Navy SEALs take goal setting to new levels. Not only do they set goals, but they break down their goals into micro goals, short-term goals, mid-term goals, and long-term goals. This almost obsessive way of deconstructing a task into its component tasks until everything becomes a series of small, manageable steps allows them to feel confident and stay focused.

Visualize the outcome—Just like Olympic sprinters who actually visualize themselves at the end of their races, crossing the finish line—even before the starter's gun has been fired—Navy SEALs train themselves to "see" the outcome they are aiming for. They prime their brains for success and this is then reflected in the attitude they approach each task with.

Cheer yourself on—Navy SEALs undergoing the aptly named Hell Week, give themselves pep talks telling themselves that many men before them have completed the course and so can they. They remind themselves that they should be able to pass no problem because they are more physically fit than their predecessors. They tell themselves to go on and not quit, no matter what. There is a small element of dissociation there where they see themselves as almost a third person, cheering themselves on. And it works. This relatively "cheap" mental trick frequently releases mental resources that allow a SEAL to not quit even though his body is screaming it has had enough.

Self-control—Control of arousal (such as anger or fear) is very difficult because the neural pathways through which these are expressed bypass the higher, analytic functions of the brain and make use of the more primitive parts of the brain. This makes such responses extremely fast, which means they are hard to resist. SEALs train themselves to resist and control them. By mastering the primitive parts of themselves SEALs become confident in their ability to "Adapt. Overcome."

Navy SEALs have no choice. Once they sign up for the course quitting is not really an option for them, so they learn to become the best version of themselves possible. The mental tricks they use to do what they do, however, are transferable to business and life. Resisting stress, developing a strong will and mental resilience, and maintaining fortitude against adversity are desirable characteristics for any person, not just a warrior.

THE SNIPER SKILL ACQUISITION LIST

In this chapter you learned:

- Decision-making does not have to be compromised when we are under pressure but we need to be prepared for the difficulties we face beforehand in order to resist them.

- How stress affects the body and what we can do to resist it.
- How to maintain mental and physical effectiveness when short of sleep and how to bounce back quickly afterward.
- The importance of attitude in shaping identity, resisting mental and physical pressure, and developing a winning approach to life.
- The secret mental tricks Navy SEALs use to survive their incredibly hard training and how to apply them to your life challenges.

The brain is a complex biological organ possessing immense computational capability: it constructs our sensory experience, regulates our thoughts and emotions, and controls our actions.

—ERIC KANDEL

8

Preparation: Create Mental Constructs, Use Situational Analysis Techniques, Set Up Your Environment, and Create Your Own Network to Maintain Your Edge

"GRENADE!" IS A CRY that freezes the blood of every soldier. It doesn't take a detailed knowledge of weapons to know that you don't mess with a grenade. It is essentially a small bomb and although the best are built to a specified standard, as ordnances go they are still pretty unpredictable which only adds to their ability to terrify. The sniper platoon with 2nd Battalion, 8th Marine Regiment, was used to difficult deployments in Afghanistan. Northern Marjah, in the heart of Helmand Province, was Taliban country.

For Lance Corporal Joshua L. Moore, Marine Scout Sniper, it was to become an unforgettable experience:

We were [attached] to Fox Company and left the morning of March 14 before the sun came up. We couldn't get to our main hiding spot so we went to our secondary [site]. We had all taken up positions and were waiting. You use your camouflage skills and then stay alert, watching for insurgents. In places where civilians happen along you need a little luck to be with you.

Two of our snipers were spotted hiding in the tall grass by a man wandering in the field. He almost stepped on them. He ran away from them and for our bad luck he ran right into a second team. He practically tripped over them too, I saw him fall on the ground clutching his chest. He must have been terrified, expecting certain death. A minute or two passed and then he was up and running like a rabbit. We were sure he'd go and warn the insurgents about us.

With their primary position compromised the marines fell back to their secondary one, an abandoned compound which they could use to set up defensive positions until they could melt away under cover of darkness. While waiting it out they were engaged by a small group of insurgents.

One of our guys was watching the north wall and said there were two guys running toward the wall carrying something in their hands. Those two guys threw grenades over the wall before we could intervene. One hit me in the back, rolled in between me and my buddy, and I picked it up and threw it back outside. It went off in midair. The second one didn't go off.

Let that sink in for a moment. With a firefight breaking out during which three marines were injured, Moore saw a grenade at his feet. He didn't freeze. He was, after all, a trained sniper. He knew fully well what a grenade can do to a man at close range. In a split-second decision then he ignored the natural instinct to seek cover away from the expected blast (snipers frequently run scenarios of how to survive a grenade in their vicinity), bent down, picked it up not knowing how much time he had before it exploded, and threw it over the wall where it would explode harmlessly in midair.

Call of Duty gamers will recognize Moore's maneuver as a "Press G to throw the grenade back" move, except this was real life in a fluid, hostile environment with sensory distractions and the obvious psychological and mental factors to contend with. To understand the true magnitude of Lance Corporal Moore's action that day consider that the question "What is the best thing to do when a grenade is thrown at you?" has come up on Quora.

Dan Rosenthal, former Foreign Service officer and a veteran of the Iraq War, with OIF I/II vet, Infantry/RSTA after his name, put things in perspective by explaining that the usual fragmentation radius of a frag grenade is 30 to 35 feet and you have as little as three seconds and a maximum of five seconds before it goes off. That means running is not an option; you'll never get beyond the blast radius in time. After the explosion most of the fragments fly upward so the best option for survival is to hit the ground and stay as low as possible.

Here's a war vet who has seen action explaining just how lethal a grenade is and how little time you have to do anything about it. Assuming you have just four seconds before the grenade goes off, two of which will be spent in flight time, you're left with just two seconds to "notice the grenade, react, reach down, pick it up, plant your feet, lift up, and throw it far enough that you're clear of the blast radius. Not going to happen except in the ultra-rarest of situations."

All the while there is incoming fire on your position because you're still in a combat situation. Of the two grenades that were thrown at them only the one he picked up was the lethal one. How did he make that decision? In a magazine interview long afterward, Joshua Moore would recall how he saw the rust on the second grenade and knew it might be a dud. Having saved his team from certain death Moore had no time to congratulate himself on his success. With three wounded marines outside the compound he left to help get them back. Enemy forces over 100 yards away fired at him, but Moore stood his ground and returned fire with his sniper rifle, forcing the enemy to retreat. He then stayed and provided security until a quick reaction force and another sniper section arrived and they could be safely extracted from the compound.

What Joshua Moore did that day went so far beyond what we accept as normal human reaction that upon his return from his tour he received the Navy Cross medal.

Was he just lucky with his grenade pick or did he intuitively know to maximize his chances of survival by picking up the newer looking grenade first? But an even more pressing question is, How did he manage to achieve zero hesitation time and a reaction speed that made it possible for him to survive what was, by most accounts, an unsurvivable situation?

The answer to that question is what makes snipers special and Special Ops soldiers different from everyone else. That answer also will help us maintain what we learn in this book so that it continues to benefit us long after the last word of the last chapter has been read. The secret, as described by Danielle Bassett, a systems neuroscientist and physicist and the youngest person to be awarded a 2014 MacArthur Fellowship, lies in networks.

There are networks that help us form habits and that determine our behavior forged inside our brains and there are networks of friends, family, and peers that we can use as an informal support group. The two happen to be connected so that whatever we do inside our heads has an uncanny way of being reflected in the physical setups we put in place in the outside world. Like so many things we are learning about how we can make better decisions under pressure and think like a trained sniper, this is not new. Tradition has left us countless instances where what we are about to discuss in this chapter has been codified. One of the four books of Confucian philosophy is called *The Doctrine of the Mean*. Unlike its three siblings, it is both a doctrine within Confucianism and a collection of sayings, teachings, and aphorisms that show how one can lead a better life, be a better person under adversity, and make better decisions under pressure.

One of the maxims contained in it reads, "What is within will be manifested without." Putting aside the tendency to dismiss this as either a fortune cookie saying or one of those aphorisms whose value is purely cultural and perhaps philosophical, it's worth deconstructing it a little. If the world within is reflected in the world without this is the mirroring effect Western magical tradition has summarized in "as above, so below." Its central tenet is the union of the microcosm with the macrocosm through human consciousness (usually via the efforts of the magician or witch).

Compare the Confucian idea of man and the world and the Western magical one with neuroscience's version where the internal modeling of the world inside our heads reflects our behavioral patterns in the world outside it. The assumption being that there is a constant dialogue going on between the outside world and what's deep inside our heads and we are barely aware of it most of the time.

If nothing happens without our being able to think of it, it stands to reason that the things we think of can and do happen and we are instrumental in their coming about. In many ways we imagine the world we live in, and our brains can remake not just our minds but also our bodies and can totally affect our everyday reality.

This cannot happen without some awareness of the things we want to change and some knowledge about how to go about changing it all. At Fort Bragg, North Carolina, home to the Green Berets, the Rangers, Delta Force, and the 82nd Airborne Division, this kind of training is called "Warrior Mind Training." Special instructors call it "mental push-ups" and teach the toughest guys in the US military how to beef up their minds so that their performance is enhanced, their attention is more focused and they make better decisions under circumstances of extreme stress. Sniper training is offered in all of these elite units. It involves awareness of physical, mental, and psychological processes, meditation, and learning how to reprogram the mind for emotional resilience.

All of this is attainable by anyone who can learn to apply certain techniques and has the discipline to stick with them until they become second nature.

THE SCIENCE: Neuroplasticity is the ability of the brain to reprogram itself through very specific, intentional mental and psychological exercises. It can learn to acquire new habits that become second nature and to learn to behave in ways that increase focus, change behavior, and directly affect peak performance. Key to this is the brain's ability to create new neural networks and the person's ability to create extensive social networks.

A WORLD WITHOUT DAY OR NIGHT

On a fine summer day in France in 1729, an astronomer by the name of Jean-Jacques d'Ortous de Mairan, whose obsession with the way sunlight could cause cold in winter and heat in summer would eventually lead his protégé to invent the photometer, noticed something peculiar. The leaves of the mimosa plant (scientifically called *Mimosa pudica*) opened and closed at the same time every day.

The mimosa is a heliotrope, belonging to a family of plants whose leaves or flowers move in response to the direction of the sun. Intrigued by the plant's timing, de Mairan isolated it in darkness and studied the times it opened its leaves. To his surprise, the plant stuck to the same times despite the fact that it was now housed away from any sunlight. This accidental observation laid down the framework upon which chronobiology, the branch of biology which studies natural physiological rhythms, was born.

Humans and plants have a lot in common in this area. In the

1950s the German biologist Jürgen Aschoff built an underground "bunker" to isolate human subjects from any external environmental cues and study their responses. His studies over twenty years confirmed two things: First, that humans lose body heat over a twenty-four-hour period and the heat loss depends upon the time of the day. Second, that we all have a built-in time clock (called an endogenous oscillator). That clock is somewhat personalized which means that each of us can be categorized into a particular chronotype. Our chronotypes are largely a function of when our bodies start and stop producing melatonin, the sleepiness hormone. Chronotypes are not set in stone. They can be affected by specific environmental triggers.

One of those environmental factors is artificial light. Another is stimulants like caffeine. Exercise may play a role as well as adrenaline. Chronotypes are at the heart of the jet lag we feel when we cross too many time zones. The fact that we can recover and adjust to a new sleep/wake cycle in a matter of days is what chronobiologists call entrainment, namely the ability of our internal clocks to adjust because of external factors.

The reason all of this is important lies in the fluidity of battlefield timetables. Combat is notoriously disrespectful of chronotypes and sleep/wake cycles. Sleep deprivation is associated with poor memory, poor attention, poor critical judgment, poor decision-making under pressure, and reduced operating efficiency. The modern battlefield is a world without day or night. Soldiers may find themselves in complicated situations where proper sleep may have to be foregone for extended periods of time, critical decisions may have to be made in a very short space of time, and complex scenarios that have not been encountered before will need to be effectively dealt with.

Under these circumstances to have sleep-deprived men running around carrying lethal ordnance and engaging in firefights sounds like a recipe for disaster. Yet the elite units whose tasks always involve some kind of mission-critical sensitivity are also the ones who are more likely to experience deployment where they will be least likely to get any normal kind of sleep. The brain is sharper when the body is rested and fully awake.

Reconciliation to this paradox requires a mixture of specialized army mind training and a hefty dose of natural processes. In recognition of the fact that its members have to be mentally tough and psychologically resilient the Department of Defense has started Warrior Mind Training courses at Fort Bragg and at the Naval Amphibious Base Coronado in California where Navy SEALs learn their craft. But it's not all an uphill battle. It turns out that the sleepless mind, properly managed, is actually more creative than usual.

Mareike Wieth, an associate professor of psychological science at Albion College, devised a study involving 428 subjects which tested for analytical thinking and creativity based on the chronotype of each person. What she discovered was that the sleepy brain has fewer inhibitions and is capable of delivering that overused cliché of "thinking outside the box." Fatigue apparently lowers what the scientists call "inhibitory attentional control," the filtering we do when fully alert in order to concentrate on solving a particular task, and this results in the brain activating a far deeper network thinking approach to its problem solving. In other words, being tired, the brain also becomes more creative.

In a world where the difference between day and night has been erased, soldiers have to be mentally alert enough to stop the debilitating effects of sleeplessness and disciplined enough to utilize the unfiltered state of their minds to creatively deal with the unexpected.

Compare this to what we usually do. We read self-help books that teach us how to use our memory better, perhaps, or be less distracted or become more productive and within weeks it is like we have not read them at all. We always revert back to who we were, our problems far from solved, our issues again appearing in multitude, our lives just as difficult.

It doesn't have to be this way. Yet, for most of us, there is no other reasonable way to be. We cannot learn something new and stick to it without a modular approach to application, positive reinforcement, and a real change of environment. Let me explain this a little further. Each of us is who he or she is because of the way we have set up our lives and the environment we happen to be in.

If we happen to work in the offices of a major publishing house, for example, we are aware of the cost of bringing a new book to the market, the latest books that did really well internationally, and the moneymakers for the publishers this year. We know who the up-and-coming authors are and who are on their way down. We know what subjects did well with the public and what didn't, and we understand why. Finally we know whether a proposed book will do well or not, because of our awareness of all this.

Now think what it would be like if instead of a major publishing house we worked for a small, local publisher whose biggest-selling title has been the local fishing guide. Our perception of the cost of bringing a book to the market will be different and we would have a different idea of expected returns. If we are aware of book titles that did well this year, it will be only circumstantial, not largely different from what the public picks up because of media interest.

Similarly, our ability to assess a proposed title may be way less honed. As a matter of fact, everything, including our salary, will be different. Yet we work in the publishing industry in both scenarios and we are largely the same person in each. So why do we then behave differently in almost every way? This is where the power of the networked mind becomes apparent.

THE NETWORK EFFECT

There are neural networks that help us form habits and that determine our behavior forged inside our brains and there are also external, real-world networks, such as the friends, family, and peers that we use to find out information, to mine their experience, and to act as an informal support group. The two happen to be connected so intimately that whatever goes on inside our heads has an uncanny way of being reflected in the physical setups we put in place in the outside world.

To understand the power of networking, consider the seemingly impossible feat of cheating death. At least for a while. The image conjures up money, lots of it. The money necessary to buy expensive gym memberships and to pay personal trainers, nutritionists, and dieticians. It takes a lot of money to reduce the stress of everyday life and to deliver a measure of security. It takes a lot of money to create the buffers we imagine are responsible for a carefree life and a carefree life is a high-quality one.

There are four or five places in the world which meet the scientific criteria necessary for longevity beyond average life expectancy even by Western standards and a quality of life that is high even in what we consider to be advanced old age. They are Okinawa in Japan, Sardinia, the Nicoya Peninsula in Costa Rica, Loma Linda in California, and Ikaria in Greece, just thirty miles off the Turkish coast. None of them has a rich or even fully employed population. Exercise (in the traditional sense) is nonexistent, and although the population in each place practices some form of healthy nutrition thanks to traditional diets, the vicinity of their countrymen and women provides a control group of sorts that excludes diet as the sole answer to living longer, fully active lives.

There are various factors that contribute to the long and healthy lives of the inhabitants in each of these places, and those factors include a diet rich in antioxidants, an active lifestyle, and a general abstinence from meat and processed food, but these factors, though undoubtedly contributory, are incidental. Within the target populations of each place, there are outliers who smoke twenty cigarettes a day and drink soft drinks and are still in good health.

In study after study, when all the relevant factors are analyzed in detail and normalized, these five places in the world, so-called Blue Zones, a moniker given to them by National Geographic Fellow Dan Buettner, whose research brought them to light, have one thing in common and just one thing: a tightly knit community spirit. People living in these places enter a social order where everyone is accepted, people pull together to celebrate or work, and everyone is everyone's friend to a degree that is simply nonexistent anywhere else.

In broad strokes and with a far enough removed perspective, this may all sound like some idyllic paradise where life is pressure-free and everyone gets along with everyone else, but the reality is quite different. Life in relatively poor economies (as all these places are) is complicated. Community spirit is a response to that complication, a tacit acknowledgment that the pooling of resources is a direct benefit to all and an identifiable strength of the local community. This "simple" life is actually quite complex and from an evolutionary point of view, we have evolved specifically for that.

Leading evolutionary psychologist professor Robin Dunbar from the University of Oxford has been part of a team looking at why we developed the disproportionately large brains that we have, when compared to other primates, and the indications are that we use the massive amount of computational power that is hidden inside our heads to "size each other up" in our social groups. Using computer modeling to unravel the complexities of decision-making strategies for simplified humans, human behavioral models that are based on specific preset assumptions regarding social interaction, Dunbar's group showed how, over time, "making relative judgments through helping others has been influential for human survival, and that the complexity of constantly assessing individuals has been a sufficiently difficult task to promote the expansion of the brain over many generations of human reproduction."

Actively engaged brains pack in more neurons per cubic milliliter than those that aren't which also may help explain how the aged populations studied in the Blue Zone areas display mental sharpness and alertness way past the age of eighty-five, which is the point at which many Americans begin to suffer from dementia.

We have seen that the popularized image of the "lone sniper" that movies and the media have pushed is not how snipers truly operate. They are embedded in units they support. Their decisions are often mission-critical. They have to be able to absorb a lot of information quickly and process it using mental heuristics that have been carefully built over time. In the complex pictures they create inside their heads, they factor in real-world knowledge of how people operate, how things work, what motivates humans, and how societies work. They are part of a larger support network made up of the army units they belong to and the regiments they are part of.

There is a deep and necessary element of empathy in their work. Empathy is a key ingredient in developing the emotional stability required to operate at a really high level without feeling isolated and, eventually, lost. There is a direct connecting thread, via the development of the mind, linking snipers operating under extreme conditions across the hot zones of the world with the mentally and sexually active nonagenarians living in the Blue Zone areas that researchers like Dan Buettner are studying.

What makes sniper minds different from everyone else's is the level of intuitive comprehension they can generate, the internal connections they are capable of making through the associative filtering of the things they know. This is the result of their very specific training. The aspects of their training that teach them how to control desire (in its broader sense) and have greater self-control have a clearly understood scientific basis that can be used to acquire positive habits and reprogram their minds to stop negative ones. As expected, the environment and the social network one is part of play a large role in this.

REWIRING THE MIND

Imagine if you could make every bad habit you have magically go away. Feeling tired? Bored? Unfocused? What if you could just rewire your mind and put in place mental triggers to help you overcome all that? Are you unable to control your desires? You eat too much? Drink too much? Exercise too little? What if you could reverse the way your brain perceives all this so that your lifestyle changes? What if there was a technique that would help you achieve the better version of yourself you know you are capable of being?

In a rational world none of the above questions would make any sense. We all know that exercise is good for us and drinking too much or eating too much are bad. We all want to be better versions of ourselves. The reason we fail lies in evolutionary programming that trips us up. But let's back up for a moment and say that everything that we do has its origin in the brain. It starts in subconscious processes that activate specific mental centers which predispose us to do certain things and which guide our actions, long before we decide to do them.

From an evolutionary point of view, this has been a good thing. Quenching thirst and satisfying hunger in the world of early human life necessitated activities that were not always safe. To overcome any fears about our safety or hesitations regarding danger that would have jeopardized our long-term survival, the brain resorted to a short-term craving and reward system to which we are still captive today. In an unexamined mind this system informs our daily decision-making, and in our modern lifestyle it is responsible for the creation of mental short-circuiting that can eventually break both the mind and the body, through the accumulation of bad lifestyle choices that can lead all the way to addiction.

This is how it works: The reward system in the brain identifies a target (food, drink, cigarettes, drugs, sex, and the like). Next it releases a neurotransmitter called dopamine. Dopamine helps control the brain's reward and pleasure centers. It also helps regulate movement and emotional responses, and it enables us not only to see rewards, but to take action to move toward them. Nearly all drugs of abuse directly or indirectly increase dopamine in the pleasure and motivation pathways and, in so doing, alter the normal communication between neurons in the brain.

Dopamine activates intense cravings and longing for short-term rewards because it makes us believe they will make us happy. That's not enough for us to act quickly, however. The body also releases stress hormones that make us feel discomfort or pain. The stress essentially tricks the body into believing the only way to feel better is to succumb to the craving so that not only will we experience happiness by giving in but we will also make all discomfort go away. The twin push-pull of wanting to be happier and seeking to feel less discomfort short-circuit the prefrontal cortex so that analytical thinking never takes place.

Run any addictive behavior you can think of through this mechanism and you can see how powerful it is and how difficult it is to resist. Resistance, of course, is possible, but resistance takes energy and effort and it can be depleted. A far better approach is to use the brain's own mechanism to rewire it so that behavior that may harm us changes to behavior that benefits us.

In experiments, cognitive psychologists have shown how this can be achieved:

- **Be mindful**—An awareness of the craving response allows us to examine how it affects us. Do we feel totally happy with it? Do we want to be controlled by a craving? How do we usually feel after we have given in to it? These are all questions that allow a broadening of perspective to take place. A broader perspective allows us to re-evaluate the motivation of the craving and establish a different one.

- **Create a different motivation**—You know that what gets you to your desired goals are your long-term goals. Weigh how they fit in with the instant rewards offered by satisfying your craving. Write down your long-term goals if necessary. Visualize them. This allows your brain to shift gears and see that there are better rewards that can stem from a different action. Stanford University psychologist, Kelly McGonigal, who's authored a book on willpower called *The Willpower Instinct: How Self-Control Works, Why it Matters, and What You Can Do to Get More of It*, calls this the "redirect moment." Cravings produce not just a want but a need, and the only way to redirect them is to replace that need with another, better, need.

- **Use triggers you can control**—A craving always has some emotional trigger. We've already seen in chapter 6 how the fictional detective Sherlock Holmes gives in to his craving for heroin when he is mentally blocked or feels defeated. It's a pretty good analogy of how a lot of cravings work. In that chapter we saw how we can create our own mental triggers. By using triggers we can control, we can supplant the negative craving with a different one that is positive.

- **Change your environment**—Where we are plays a key role in how we behave. Seek out, as much as possible, places where you can enjoy fewer challenges to your will-power or greater control. This is why the army manages to maintain discipline and a healthy work ethic in its soldiers. The environment they are in and the support network created by their fellow soldiers automatically creates a motivational push in the right direction. McGonigal calls this "dopamanizing your willpower challenges." Learn to feel good about the positive choices you make as opposed to the negative ones. Find ways to reduce the perceived threshold barriers to whatever you want to get done. If you need to answer e-mails in the morning, for instance, having no handy way to do so only makes the task harder and adds to the procrastination.

- **Change your rewards**—We can create tangible long-term rewards instead of abstract ones. Everyone wants to be "richer," "healthier," "safer," but doing something about it requires us to visualize the Ferrari we will buy, the six-pack we will sport, or the home full of loved ones we will have. All of these change the idea of a reward that is still in the future to a tangible object of desire that can replace what we currently have.

All of this begins with that first instance of self-awareness, the mindfulness that trained snipers possess that gives them their extraordinarily focused, controlled minds. As Jason D. discovered after he left the Rangers:

When I came out of the army I felt I was useless. None of my skills had any place in the real world. I felt out of touch with the concerns of all those who were in business who talked about social media and an online reputation. As I thought about it, it occurred to me that I was going about it the wrong way, looking at the limitations of what I had to work with. By approaching finding a job as a mission, I realized that I actually had skills that could be really useful. I am good at breaking problems down to first principles. I can see their moving parts. I am good at connecting with people when I have to. I can work on my own for long periods of time. I became a community manager for a national retailer. I got them to hire me at the interview stage. I was not that familiar with online communities. But that's just technical. You can learn this. Much harder is to be able to figure out what's important to the people in the community. Connect with them. Build up trust with them. Understand what motivates them. You need to be able to observe and understand. Listen. I just love what I do now. Love it!

THE BUSINESS CASE

In the fast-evolving marketplaces of tech, commerce, sports, and high finance, companies can no longer get by with contractually committed job descriptions for employees. The situations their staffs are likely to face are going to be fluid, unexpected, and probably something they cannot train for. Yet they will be expected to deal with them responsibly, intelligently, exercising their judgment, making critical decisions on the fly, and taking initiative.

Google, Zappos, Nike, and the Kodiak Capital Group are among the global companies that are emulating the US Army, looking at using power naps, networking, a tight-knit community feeling, and critical decision-making skills to enable their employees to deliver peak performance while they work long hours, under pressure, with irregular sleep patterns.

While decidedly different by setup and industry, the companies show remarkable overlap in their implementation strategy. They encourage on the job napping to recharge. They have people working in proximity to each other to foster natural networking, find support when needed, share ideas, spark off energy, and feel part of a larger community. They go to considerable lengths to create nonjudgmental, open atmospheres. They encourage the sharing of ideas and the sharing of solutions to difficult problems.

Even more important, informally but persistently, they encourage a methodology of working that utilizes three distinct steps:

- **Analyze**—Identify, grade, and list the obstacles that stop you from being the best you can possibly be.
- **Devise**—Have a set of routines that will help you overcome those obstacles or reduce their impact.
- **Execute**—Follow the routines you have devised in a way that reinforces your sense of self-worth and identity.

The similarities with the military do not end there, either. At the same time that each company tries hard to create the matrix within which its people work, it also encourages a strong culture of responsibility that's focused on the individual. In order to help cultivate the mental toughness that snipers have, these corporate giants use their internal culture to promote four "soft" concepts that are applicable in any setting.

- **Confidence**—To help build confidence the army makes snipers do tasks again and again and again until even complex tasks become second nature. Similarly, large corporations ensure that there is a routine structure to everyday work. Everyone knows what he or she is required to do and has the skills and tools to do it. This helps build confidence in a person's ability to cope with the workload. The same principle can be applied to an individual. Struggling with and overcoming smaller challenges is crucial to learning how to cope with larger ones. This is why hobbies like learning a language or learning to play a musical instrument are often found in the CVs of the best corporate performers. By extending themselves in those areas and stretching their skills, they open up parts of their minds they can use at work.

- **Duty**—Snipers know everyone has a job to do. They are drilled in the importance of doing their part so that others can do theirs. In a work setting we all have job descriptions. We also have "job descriptions" in our other roles like husbands and wives and friends and mentors. The only way we can succeed at each of them is if we have a very clear understanding of what each involves, all the steps required to do it correctly, and then we just do them. Snipers are methodical. Irrespective of how stressed or tired they may be feeling, they know they have to work their way through a mental checklist. By adopting the same example, we create a guided framework for our actions which enables us to act smoothly and without hesitation.

- **Team spirit**—Snipers, Special Forces operatives, even rank and file soldiers know that the moment bullets start flying and people start getting hurt notions of valor, country, religion, and higher belief systems evaporate. What keeps you sharp, focused, at your post, emotions firmly in check, and doing your job is your commitment to those around you which is fully reciprocated. If we cannot learn to function within our work teams and social groups with the confidence and reciprocal support that soldiers enjoy we are in the wrong job and with the wrong friends. We are truly social animals, at our best when our brains are engaged in a community or real-life social network.

- **Pride**—Snipers take pride in their ability to achieve extraordinary tasks. It is true that many of them receive commendations and medals but many of them also don't, and even those who do have tales to tell that are extraordinary and for which they will receive nothing. It is not the commendations or the medals that keep them performing at their peak. It is not the need for recognition that makes them constantly work to hone their craft and enhance their skills. They do it because they take pride in their work, in the abilities they have and the tasks they do. The satisfaction is for themselves. We always pour more of ourselves into what we do when doing it fills us with a sense of pride. Pride enables us to find ways to be creative when we are stuck with a problem. It becomes the gear that drives many of the soft activities beneath the surface of our actions.

By now we have seen the "secret" behind the success of snipers lies in a methodical, structured approach to the performance of tasks, constant learning, practice, visualization, and the use of mental triggers to reinforce positive attributes. Snipers develop a deep sense of who they are and what they can do and use psychological anchors to help them structure their belief systems.

Their biggest attribute, however, has to be adaptive thinking. When Bruce Lee gave his famous speech culminating in "Be water, my friend."[1] in an episode of the 1971 TV series *Longstreet*, he may as well have been thinking of snipers and their ability to flow with the problems they encounter and practice detachment in the face of adversity. Adaptive thinking can also be practiced.

HOW TO BE MORE ADAPTIVE IN YOUR THINKING

Just like snipers, who have a great support network when in barracks and are trained to an incredibly fine edge, corporate warriors are also required to be:

- Autonomous
- Responsible
- Self-motivated
- Driven
- Empathetic

The Special Forces field manual recognizes this skill set as part of the adaptive behavior that all Special Forces operatives, including snipers, must have. In their training they break this down into eight distinct components that are at the core of every job:

- Job task proficiency
- Nonsubject task proficiency

---

1. For a full explanation of how Bruce Lee arrived at that insight, plus the content of his speech, go to appendix IV.

- Written and oral communication
- Demonstrating effort
- Maintaining personal discipline
- Maintaining peer and team performance
- Supervisor/leadership
- Management/administration

There is transfer here in the sense that these components are part of all executive decision-making and adaptive thinking. The adaptive mind-set incorporates all the different skills and techniques we have learned to this point and, to define it further, adds a seven-point definition of what adaptability involves:

- Handling emergencies or crisis situations
- Handling work stress
- Solving problems creatively
- Dealing effectively with unpredictable or changing work situations
- Learning work tasks, technologies, and procedures
- Demonstrating interpersonal adaptability
- Demonstrating physically oriented adaptability

Forgetting for a moment that this is the field manual for Special Forces training to deal with the unexpected in situations where they are likely to engage with the enemy in a firefight, the eight components at the heart of every job and the seven points listed to clarify what the adaptive mind-set is could be today's average corporate candidate interview checklist.

Richard Cummings, a former Ranger who trained as a sniper

and saw active duty in Iraq and Afghanistan, gives his account of the adaptive mind-set:

Thanks to sniper training I learned a lot of patience. I was able to accept or tolerate delays, problems, or suffering without becoming annoyed or anxious. I would always tell myself: be patient, your time will come. You have to adapt and overcome. Some days I would have to crawl a mile to get into range, and then I might need to lay there for a couple of days for the target to come to where I was looking. You can't control everything that happens around you but if you are patient, you can hit your target.

Former snipers who are now in established careers give three tips on how to be best mentally prepared for anything that may come your way:

- **Visualize**—This is no "I see myself doing this perfectly and all's cool" kind of visualization. Go through a scenario in detail. Hear the sounds, smell the smells. See the problems that may come up. Think how you would overcome them. This is mental conditioning. In the service snipers call it "battle proofing."
- **Practice situational awareness**—Never be blind. Wherever you are try to guess what individuals around you are thinking. What's driving them. Notice how they behave and then look for anyone who doesn't fit in. Try to understand why. This helps you understand the flow of human behavior. Look at the place you are in, study its layout. Remember it. Be aware of yourself. All of this brings you

into the moment. It anchors you in a very real way that you will know the moment you start to practice it.

- **Have a purpose**—Don't just go through life. That's how your mind gets blunt. Think about beliefs. Think problems through. Break them down to their basic principles so you can see the dynamic that's driving them. Be empathetic. You will need this to understand people and yourself.

EMPATHY AND HOW TO PRACTICE IT

Of all the skills a sniper might need empathy seems a little odd, even a contradiction in terms. It stands at odds with the popularly perceived warrior nature of the sniper and the gruesome job he is often called upon to do. Transferring the sniper skill set to a more corporate, less lethal setting, it also seems to be a contradiction. High-level executives talk about developing "the killer instinct" and MBA classes often talk about the need to be "ruthless." How can empathy be made to fit in this mind-set? Why should it even?

This is where popular perception versus reality changes everything. With snipers each mission is personal. Each choice they make, however difficult, is going to have consequences. Make too many wrong choices and soon your confidence in your ability is undermined and you can no longer do your job.

Snipers get around this by displaying extreme empathy. They create a detailed weighing of their actions in their heads that enables them to have clarity of mind in what they do and why they do it. This is then reflected in the split-second timing of their decisions-making process where mission-critical decisions are made under pressure and for the right reasons.

Not everyone possesses empathy naturally. But we can all cultivate it. There is a five-step program that teaches the development of empathy in individuals. It is being successfully used in MBA classes to help high-flying executives who have focused too intensely in their careers to avoid burnout by being emotionally more stable.

The primary reservation when it comes to developing empathy is that it has a soft, touchy-feely kind of reputation (except, of course, when hardened Special Air Service types advise you to develop it because it will help you make better decisions). In a study of radiologists where they were shown a photo of the patient whose X-ray they were about to scan, they empathized more with the person, seeing that person as more of a human being as opposed to just an X-ray. As a result, they wrote longer reports, and they had significantly greater diagnostic accuracy.

The practice of empathy naturally leads to the next step. Duke University professor of psychology and behavioral economics, Dan Ariely explained in a *Time* magazine interview:

> *If I had to give advice across many aspects of life, I would ask people to take what's called "the outside perspective." And the outside perspective is easily thought about: What would you do if you made the recommendation for another person? And I find that often when we're recommending something to another person, we don't think about our current state and we don't think about our current emotions.*

At its core, empathy is the oil that keeps relationships running smoothly. The fact that empathy is an important component of effective relationships has been shown in studies by Antonio

Damasio. In his book *Descartes' Error: Emotion, Reason, and the Human Brain*, medical patients who had damage to the part of the brain associated with empathy showed significant deficits in relationship skills, even though their reasoning and learning abilities remained intact.

Empathy then is valued currency. It allows us to create bonds of trust, it gives us insights into what others may be feeling or thinking, it helps us understand how or why others are reacting to situations, it sharpens our "people acumen," and it informs our decisions.

A formal definition of empathy is the ability to identify and understand another's situation, feelings, and motives. It's our capacity to recognize the concerns other people have. Empathy means "putting yourself in the other person's shoes" or "seeing things through someone else's eyes."

The ability to keep a cool head and to be observant, analytical, yet empathic is sought after in every case peak performance is directly linked to mission-critical outcomes. Olympic athletes routinely need head coaches to help them get in the necessary frame of mind to succeed. Their routines mirror those taught by sniper training instructors at Fort Bragg. NASA trains its astronauts to operate in a similar way. Emotional decisions made 150 miles above the Earth can prove very bad, very quickly.

All practice a five-step routine to better decision-making:

- Use situation awareness to maintain a feeling of control.
- Prepare emotionally by visualizing how things could be worse.
- Monitor your breathing. Do not let your body descend into panic.

- Employ empathy. Understand feelings, points of view, and motivations even if you do not identify with them.
- Ask, "What advice would I give my best friend in this situation?"

It's a simple process. It can be life changing. At the very least it will immediately improve your decision-making under pressure. It has the potential to completely transform you. As one serving sniper who asked to not be identified said to me:

Sniper training changed my life. I learned to be patient. Controlled. Not upset by things I could not control. It taught me to clear my head and think things through and think of other people. It made me see just how little I know and how I cannot stop learning. Ever. I will not always be in the army. I have one more tour of duty left. I will be out then. But the learning will go on. Whatever lies ahead for me. The challenges. I am ready. My mind is ready.

THE SNIPER SKILL ACQUISITION LIST

In this chapter you learned:

- Hesitation is caused by confusion and lack of mental clarity. Controlling our instincts requires training and thinking.
- The brain can be rewired. We can be taught to overcome bad habits and replace them with good ones.
- Soft skills are as important as hard ones. Thinking about them and developing them is key to becoming a better version of yourself. Relationships are important to our mental

health, our ability to deal with stress and the decision-making processes we activate.

- Empathy is an important ingredient in the sniper mind psychological profile. Develop your empathetic capabilities and use them to better understand others and yourself.

- Practice the five steps to better decision-making that Olympic athletes, NAVY SEALs, and NASA astronauts make part of their everyday reality.

It's the repetition of affirmations that leads to belief. And once that belief becomes a deep conviction, things begin to happen.
—MUHAMMAD ALI, *MUHAMMAD ALI: IN PERSPECTIVE*

9

Response: Overcome Instincts and Use Intelligence to Turn Impossible Scenarios to Your Advantage.

The group of marines entered the Afghan village in a standard formation, as they'd been taught. Alert, guns at the ready, because this was hostile territory, they scanned rooftops and courtyards for signs of danger and kept a careful eye on the locals moving about the bustling market. Despite their vigilance the attack, when it came, managed to blindside them.

An improvised explosive device (IED) went off. Two of their number fell. The locals around the market and those milling in the streets yelled in fear and confusion, arms flailing as they scattered, clearing the streets. Plumes of smoke and dust wafted across the square where the empty market stalls stood. Two bodies clad in marine garb lay on the ground. One was still moving, the wounded man trying desperately to get his bearings and to understand what had just happened to him.

"Get the casualties to cover!" a marine ordered. A couple of them hugged the walls of the buildings on either side of the

square, eyes frantically scanning the rooftops overlooking it. The architecture of the village created a natural killing ground. The rest ran to where their two wounded friends lay and started to bring them back.

Boom! The second IED exploded in the town square itself. How it had been put there was something that would have to be explained later. One marine was caught squarely in the blast. Two other comrades were wounded.

"Contact!" came the frantic cry from the far right of the square, where a marine, hidden by the shadows created by the walls of the buildings, was now pointing at the rooftops around them which were crawling with shadowy figures outlined against a bleak blue sky. They were surrounded. And that's when insurgent sniper fire started to come in.

THANKFULLY, THIS IS ROLE-PLAYING. The village is real and so are its buildings, part of a training project in the foothills of Camp Pendleton, just north of San Diego. The IEDs and ammunition being fired are blanks—all noise and nothing else. The Afghan locals are experienced marines who've been drafted in to play that role and so are the ones looking down from the rooftops, all turbaned heads and Kalashnikovs.

The marines that have just found themselves in the thick of it, taking casualties and dodging imaginary bullets, are new recruits, learning the ropes. This is stress inoculation, and to them, the mock scenario seems pretty real. The IEDs make real noise and throw up smoke. The Kalashnikovs sound just like the real thing. There are scent machines that can pump out the stench of singed hair and rotting trash, and bomb victims gush fake blood. The village around them has authentic smells and sounds and the market is fully stocked with trinkets, fruit, and food, all carefully detailed and made out of plastic.

The idea behind such costly, detailed war theatrics is that the moment the things happen for real the marines will have built up the mental defenses necessary to keep their cool and think clearly. Just like when we get the flu shot that builds up the body's defenses against the flu virus by introducing weakened versions of itself that our bodies can beat, stress inoculation allows recruits to experience the fear, panic, and emotional uncertainty of an enemy attack without having to worry about really being killed.

It's an indication of just how far military thinking has shifted from the days when training consisted of daily runs, push-ups, menial duties, and rifle shooting. The understanding that wars are won in the minds before the warm bodies carrying the weapons are in a position to deliver victory is making the army prioritize building resilience and mental toughness on top of everything else. So instead of just going with the philosophy that if it trains its men harder the mental resilience will come, the military is using cutting-edge research to learn how to train its men smarter.

For those who will be asked to put themselves in harm's way and have to face a real enemy firing real weapons, it is the soft skills that can make the difference between coming back home with a tale to tell and not coming back at all. The military is trying to understand what's happening in soldiers' brains in moments of extreme duress, then train their minds to perform better. Taking the view that stress in unavoidable, the emphasis has shifted over the years from trying to find ways to avoid stress to undergoing training that makes stress under combat matter less. The difference is significant because the current training teaches each soldier's mind not just how to handle the enormous challenges that a battlefield scenario offers but also how to learn on the fly while doing so, and then use that knowledge to make better decisions at critical moments.

To understand the premium that the military now places on mental training, consider that in less than a generation soldiers have gone from feeling like disposable, albeit well-prepared, cogs in some mighty military machine to fully empowered warriors capable of becoming fulcrum points in a crisis. The marines deployed in the Iraq War had shot just as many rounds, spent as much time running, and done just as many push-ups as the marines that were flown into Afghanistan. But they had never been prepared for the effect of combat on their bodies and minds. By comparison, the average marine in Afghanistan is aware of his own body's physiological responses to stress and has been taught techniques to calm his mind and take back control of his body when things become critical.

Such is the importance of the new initiative that the Pentagon has now introduced Total Force Fitness, a services-wide program that splits overall fitness into eight categories: psychological, social, spiritual, environmental, behavioral, medical, physical, and nutritional. The "perfect soldier" that has been the Holy Grail of the military since wars have been fought is now seen to be not an emotionless robot with the demeanor of a mighty oak but a hyper-aware, sensitized human who understands how to control his emotions, a reed, if you will, capable of bending and then springing back, no matter how much pressure is applied to it.

Studies carried out at the Naval Health Research Center's Warfighter Performance Lab in San Diego take fMRI brain scans and test the saliva and blood samples of the small minority of Navy SEALs who get through Hell Week. During the aptly named week six out of the twenty-four weeks total that constitute Navy SEAL training, the recruits are handed over to three instructors who rotate over twenty-four hours to subject their charges to the most physically and mentally uncomfortable conditions possible. Over five days they enjoy no more than fifteen hours sleep in total while being asked to push their bodies and minds to levels they've never been pushed to before.

It is the Navy SEALs' way of finding out the "best of the best" by pushing its recruits to their breaking point and then adding more physical, psychological, and mental pressure to take them beyond it. The principal goal is to identify the unique mental, psychological, and neurochemical makeup of the successful individuals and then study those who are successful and reverse engineer the process to replicate it in others.

The suggestion here, and it is an obvious one, is that instead of being born, great warriors can be made. Provided we understand the steps the naturals implement to make their minds perform a certain way, we can create the methodology to help others level up. The thinking is not unique to the military. Independently, but with overlapping results and approach, Olympic coaches are looking at how they can use the mental and psychological profiles of star Olympians, performers who are resilient to mental pressure, to help athletes perform at peak. And, on the business front, exceptional corporate leaders are being studied to analyze the skills they use so that great leadership can become something that is studied rather than an inherent skill that an individual possesses.

The formula is unique for each individual, the result of environment, learned behavior, and genetics. Top performers in any field are different. Their brains are different. They look at the world and see it in a way that is different from the way everyone else sees it. Snipers in particular see the relationships between objects, people, and situations. They see opportunities and the natural flow of dynamics they can use to their advantage. Where most people see problems, they see challenges they can overcome. They have this way of taking a longer view than anyone else and it is reflected in the decision-making process they employ when it comes to their missions. There are commonalities among all elite groups that are worth noting. Top performers in the military, like snipers and Navy SEALs, show neural patterns during fMRI scans that are similar to those of Olympic athletes and top baseball players. Because they are beginning to form a by now familiar list of skills and attributes that has been growing and becoming more detailed from chapter to chapter, it's worth itemizing them again to get the more granular picture that's emerging:

- **Analytical thinking.** The breaking down of problems into achievable goals.
- **Visualization.** Using mental imagery to visualize scenarios and their possible solutions in detail.
- **Self-control.** Managing to silence the distracting mental voice that tells us how we cannot succeed.
- **Positive thinking.** Learning to create small victories that lead to larger ones.

- **Situational awareness.** Knowing what's going on around us at all times.
- **Self-awareness.** Examining who we are and trying to understand why.
- **Pushing against comfort zones.** Striving to overcome physical, mental, or psychological limits.
- **Constant learning.** Acquiring new skills or new hobbies and honing existing ones.
- **Patience.** Learning to not rush unnecessarily as it leads to critical mistakes.
- **Tolerance of adversity.** Taking difficulties and challenges as they come.
- **Empathy.** Being able to see the point of view of others and imagine their situation.
- **A support network.** Having friends to reach out to in times of need.

The perfect warrior cannot be had without the perfect warrior mind and it seems the perfect warrior mind cannot be constructed in a vacuum. It takes the proverbial village to raise the child into the complex being that's capable of making good, critical decisions under pressure. It is that being that the military wants to send on Special Ops missions, baseball scouts want to discover in their trawling, Olympic coaches are hoping to find, and businesses court in the hope of attracting. That being is special, with a brain that places him or her at the very thin, tapering edge of the Bell graph of averages of human cognition.

THE SCIENCE: The fundamental tenet of neuroplasticity is that there are specific brain training activities that can alter the way different regions of the mind that are needed to help cope with stress and make rational decisions in chaotic situations communicate with each other.

MANAGING THE BRAIN

"All roads lead to Rome," the popular saying, is a corruption of the sentence, "A thousand roads lead men forever to Rome," which appeared in *Liber Parabolarum*, a manuscript published in 591. It placed Rome at the heart of a sprawling empire and showed that everything that happened in Rome and everything that happened outside it were inseparably joined by this communication network. Rome reacted to the events constantly taking place in its dominion, but Rome also actively influenced those places through its attention and passively shaped them by its very existence. This is the network effect at work. The moment you establish a line of communication between two points, you subtly change both. That is also true for the way the brain is affected by the mind.

The pathways through which the mind can reprogram the body are explained by affective neuroscience (the study of the neural mechanisms of emotion), interpersonal neurobiology (the study of mental health via the many different facets of living), and mindfulness (the state of being aware of the present). What changes us is the ability of the brain to change its internal architecture, to build more roads radiating out from Rome, if we go with my analogy, and to do that it needs to initially be aware of its own capability to do that. Mindfulness practitioners explain this by saying that meditation is all about "cultivating an awareness of awareness and paying attention to intention."

The brain changes in response to experience. This is true for all nervous systems. Even the tiny worm *C. elegans*, whose nervous system has just 302 cells in total, exhibits neuroplasticity in direct response to what it encounters. When the nervous system changes, there is often a correlated change in behavior. Higher organisms with complex nervous systems can also experience changes in psychological function. Learning, memory, addiction, maturation, recovery, conditioning, and transformation are all examples of behavioral change. Learning a new motor skill like using a sword or engaging in martial arts or learning to paint requires plastic changes in the structure of the cells that control the motor skill and the creation of new neural pathways in the brain to account for the new types of control that are being put in place.

The restructuring of the physical brain in direct response to the stimulus of the mind results in an intentionally created mental state. If we practice what we are doing over and over again (the repetition phase that is at the core of all complex activities, whether they are storming a machine gun or riding a bike), the experienced mental state becomes easier to attain. The physical changes in the architecture of the brain that make it possible become permanent.

Marines, snipers, SEALs, athletes, and musicians repeat things over and over again. They drill and they practice and drill and practice until some tasks become second nature. Then they are taught to observe themselves doing those tasks, to become aware not just of the physiological changes they experience but also the mental ones. Mindfulness provides us with control of our mental state. John Way, an Army Special Forces soldier who trained at Fort Bragg, explained in an interview how he was able to remain calm during ambushes and firefights with bullets wheezing around and explosions everywhere: "You see an explosion, and you don't let the overwhelming experience of the explosion get to you. You've got other stuff going on. Okay, those are explosions, but who's shooting and where's he at? You see the problem and you see the solution. You're able to break it down and focus, instead of everything just coming at you at once."

Other studies carried out by Naval Health Research Center scientist Douglas C. Johnson looked at SEALs using saliva and blood samples and fMRI brain scans that were compared to those of a control group of healthy males. The SEALs showed more activation in small areas of the brain found in both the left and right hemisphere called insula. Insula play a role in controlling emotion, pain, and self-awareness, and they anticipate stress and prepare the body for a fight-or-flight response. The changes in the insula are directly linked to the ability SEALs have to detect danger seconds faster than anyone else, which means they have more time to think and more time to act. This then makes even a reaction to a sudden threat an act of deliberate mental clarity despite the apparent chaos of the situation. Just like the top-flight baseball players we saw in chapter 3, situation recognition, deep in the mind, prepares the body for a response long before conscious thought kicks in.

There are other direct benefits to mindfulness training. Medical students who were put through a mindfulness meditation training program experienced improved empathy, and physicians in the same program reported a decreased burnout rate and enhanced attitudes toward their patients. These welcome results prove how mindfulness improves the ability to handle stress on the go and act just like the trained sniper: Adapt. Overcome.

THE BUSINESS CASE

If businesses did as much drilling, assessing, and perfecting as the military the world right now would be a massive corporate enterprise. Being in business would require as much training beforehand as the SEAL and marine recruits put in before they can become accepted in the ranks. We know this is not the case.

The military, obviously, has an advantage. There is a massive body of prior knowledge that is being kept alive through each regiment's history and traditions. New recruits do not have to learn by making the same mistakes. And before they even go in the field and face a firefight, they have been prepared for what to expect, taught drills to help them deal with the physical, mental, and psychological impact of it.

Yet, during Hell Week, Navy SEALs go through a training experience designed to make every person who experiences it say at some point, "I've had enough." Those that make it and become SEALs overcome that instinct. How do they do that? How do the men and women who successfully pass through this manage to endure the cold, the fatigue, the barked-at commands, the handling that's designed to break you mentally and psychologically, the hunger and the sleep deprivation and come out the other side? Ready to face the remaining eighteen weeks of Navy SEAL training (Hell Week is week six).

Alden Mills, a former Navy SEAL and now the CEO of a very successful fitness company, explains that the trick lies in dissociation. Not the kind of dissociation that needs the help of a psychologist but the kind of dissociation experienced when a trained mind can successfully compartmentalize discomfort, pain, hunger, even injuries and get the job it is tasked to do, done.

The Navy SEALS have a saying: "It doesn't matter, if you don't mind," and it is their way of codifying the arduous training that makes them capable of what to ordinary people seems like superhuman performance.

Snipers also train themselves to take hours of discomfort and can subject themselves to the incredible deliberation of motion that is so slow that it can take them hours to crawl across just a few yards of open ground. To achieve this they have to tame the impulses of their own minds, silencing everything to attain the focus they need to get a particular job done.

So, how is this done? How can every reasonable instinct be ignored, every logical response overruled to the point that the mind has zero problems and can focus just on what it has to do? Snipers and marine commandos use a variety of Eastern meditation techniques, some going back to the era of the samurai, to calm their minds, focus their thoughts, and prepare their bodies for what is coming. Even though not every sniper or Special Forces vet has been taught formal Eastern meditation techniques, every one of them has found his own path to practicing something similar on his own. One former SEAL sniper whom we shall call Jon went through the service before the current focus on mental toughness through Eastern meditation.

We talk among ourselves. It's tough. So we always looked for something to help us. You talk badass rep history's full of them. Ninja. Samurai. Spartans. They all had this work ethic. Hard work. No backing down. Keep your mind as clean as your body. We tried mantras. Seeing how they'd help. Before training. After, when we were bleary eyed with exhaustion. After some of the stuff we'd seen. Not everyone wanted to do it, but I found it helped. I listened to the silence of my own mind. It made me see sense. It's hard to explain. But I could see how things were right. Just by meditating like that. It kept me focused. It kept me sane.

Jon's account is important. His experience from before brain science came along and started to codify things provides a direct, connective link between modern-day warriors and warriors across all time. The truth is that the elite military warriors, refined as they may seem by intense training and fancy weaponry, are far from unique to our days. In ancient Sparta young boys had to endure beatings, fatigue, sleep deprivation, and standing under a cold waterfall to "toughen up." In what sounds remarkably like the Navy SEALs' Hell Week, samurai would put themselves through days with no or little food and hardly any sleep. They would train with the sword and practice unarmed combat techniques throughout that time, often undertaking arduous runs or walks through hostile territory. They would force themselves to endure cold baths and they would train in snow and ice to force their bodies to become subject to their will.

We have the tools today that allow us to see what's going on inside the human brain. We understand that the brain of an ancient Spartan warrior who was subjected to an extreme, lifelong regimen of training is no different from that of a samurai or a sniper or a Special Forces soldier or a corporate executive or any ordinary person who has been taught to activate particular neural pathways and think in very specific ways. What everything we have been looking at hinges upon is the degree of transfer that's possible.

There are two important concepts we need to work with which we shall examine a little more formally now. One is transfer and the other one is context. The two are linked. Transfer, as we saw briefly in chapter 6, is the ability of what's learned in one area to become applicable in another. Psychologists who study this examine whether snipers practicing a specific skill in a video game or a virtual reality setting have learned to apply the same skill in a real life setting. While the skill being trained may be the same and the scenarios of the virtual and real environments may be identical, the context is not. The virtual environment offers a different depth of sensory input, there are no accompanying smells or sounds, and there are few distractions, all of which can be present in the real world. Perhaps the biggest difference of all is the fact that the virtual world comes with a respawn option: fatal mistakes are never terminal. This is an element that is decidedly missing from any real-life scenario, and that alone introduces a number of psychological and mental stressors which cannot really be replicated.

To be sure, there are parameters that can be adjusted to make up for this perceived shortcoming of the virtual world. And we already know from the amazing outcome of US Airways Flight 1549 that you can learn to perform things you have never been specifically trained for. But it's not quite so simple. To better illustrate the point, consider *American Sniper* hero Chris Kyle, the man who was so cool under fire that the military ordered a battery of tests and psychological evaluations to be done on him when he got home from his tour of duty. Kyle tried his hand at the then newly released game *Call of Duty* while on base, back in Iraq. As he recounted in a later interview that appeared in the *New York Post*:

> *"The new* Call of Duty *came out, and we had the headsets and we hooked up our whole camp so we could be playing each other from our rooms. We were going online with satellites and everything.*
>
> *"I had a headset that one of my guys gave me, and I'm sitting there playing. And the same kid keeps killing me, and he was talking mad junk to me. I'm sitting there, and I'm getting pissed.*
>
> *"He's cussing and everything. Come to find out, he's like a twelve-year-old kid back in America. He kept killing me, and he's like, 'I'm going to slay you.'*
>
> *"Motherf--ker—when I get home, I'm going to sneak into your bedroom and I am taking you out. I'm a Navy SEAL!"*
>
> *And he's like:* "Whatever. You're in your mama's basement."

Imagine, the US Army's most feared sniper was being taken out by a kid. Context has a filtering effect that changes the way we perform. In a different setting that makes exactly this same point, consider how many elite athletes who've qualified for the Olympic Games choke in their first appearance. The combined effects of the moment, the setting, and its importance are too much for them to handle. Physically they may be ready but mentally they are not, and it is the mental component that needs to come together to complete the physical preparation.

When it comes to activity-specific performance, the components of peak performance that crop up from one sport or activity to another are virtually identical:

- Great eyesight (and remember how a large component of vision is mental)
- Good memory (snipers remember the particulars of their shots, baseball players can reel off the conditions of their home runs, baseball players know exactly the play that made each of their three-point shots possible)
- Great anticipation (Wayne Gretzky's explanation of skating to where the puck will be)
- Fast reaction time (elite performers across every field are microseconds faster in reacting than anyone in the control groups being studied)
- Excellent focus (when it counts all elite performers are able to switch from a broad attention span to a narrow one, that cuts out all distractions)

These are the five parts of the truly awake mind; its subconscious alert, busy activating the centers of the brain required to perform the physical action necessary, to make the critical decision that is required. There's a danger here of getting caught up in the physicality of elite athletes and soldiers, to think that the exceptionalism of Olympians and SEALs and snipers excludes the rest of us from attaining their mental abilities. But the skill set is relevant. Snipers and fighter pilots may require great vision but analysts and business planners need to be able to "see" trends from facts and figures. Because the human brain only has so many mental state configurations that reflect a state of peak performance, it stands to reason that it will be encountered whether one is dealing with insurgents behind enemy lines or sitting comfortably behind a desk, making critical decisions that will determine the fate of a business.

So now only the question of context remains to be settled: Is the ability to remain calm and think clearly under pressure totally transferable? Could a top-level sniper run a global corporation? Can elite athletes become great business leaders? Anecdotally snipers and Olympians do go into consulting, public speaking, and own-brand product lines, so the unofficial answer would be "I guess so." But we need more than just guesses here. The aim of this book is not so much to uncover the overlaps between all the different activities people engage in and then connect the dots between them to draw a picture of the mind's ability to perform at seemingly superhuman levels. That would be pointless. Everything uncovered, documented, itemized, and explained is designed to give us a chapter-by-chapter skill set to work upon, improving our own capabilities, acquiring new ones, changing our mind-set so that we are no longer ruled by circumstances, we are no longer blindly reacting to events around us and are capable of taking positive action to make our own decisions and control our own destiny.

Two studies carried out independently of each other, one at the Brain Mind Institute in Lausanne, Switzerland, overseen by Leila Overney and colleagues, and the other at the department of psychology of the Sapienza University of Rome, headed by Salvatore Aglioti, studied the cognitive abilities, executive decision-making, and reaction time of elite tennis players and basketball players, respectively. The intention was to discover whether their exceptional on-court skills were still available to them off-court, and whether they enjoyed a unique advantage in contexts outside their own sport.

They put each group of athletes through a battery of tests designed to establish a baseline for their sporting and cognitive abilities and then tested how they performed in a totally different setting. The results provided research-based evidence that showed that some cognitive abilities are, indeed, sport-specific, while others like visual attention, the ability to cut out distractions and focus on what is currently relevant to the task at hand, balanced decision-making, and cool-headedness are entirely transferable.

This may also be the dividing line between so-called hard and soft skill sets. The tennis players tested, for instance, were three times better than other athletes at picking out a tennis ball in a tennis-related setting but scored the same as everyone else when the setting was changed to something generic. Sports-specific cognitive abilities are "hard." They come with the specific knowledge of what is involved (much like snipers know their rifles, their ballistic signatures, the capability of the ammunition they use in different weather temperatures, and so on). But skills like the ability to switch quickly from broad visual attention where you are tracking several different variables at once to narrow visual attention where tunnel vision takes over is a "soft" skill that develops with practice, visualization, and experience.

The bottom line is that there are only so many ways the human brain can function. The limitations of our neural physiology become the bridging point that links all these different areas of activity together and becomes the part that dispels the myth of impossibility for the many who do not actively participate in them. None of us will become a great tennis player or an elite basketball player by watching the games on TV. For that, we have to participate and we need to have some physical criteria such as strength and height. But all of us can learn to recognize strategic openings in a game play and the dynamics of a match which allow better decisions to be made just by watching.

The way the warrior mind works, the way trained sniper minds work is similar to the way any elite mind delivering peak performance works and it is something we can all learn to imitate.

THE LEGO PRINCIPLE

LEGO bricks are pure magic. All the pieces clip together the same way. You can use different-sized pieces to create anything, from a *Star Wars* light saber to a WWII aircraft carrier and each project, large or small, starts off the same way: with the clipping together of a few LEGO bricks. The LEGO bricks themselves are pretty mundane. Just different colored pieces of plastic of various sizes clipping together with a patented connecting system. The true magic is the outcome. Entire cities have been built to scale using LEGO bricks. You can even build an M107 sniper rifle using them. Yet they are all built out of the same little bricks.

The point is that the final product, grandiose and exciting as it may be, is only possible because of the methodical, intentional, and directional clicking together of the LEGO bricks that are the fundamental building blocks.

Snipers and elite soldiers use the same modular approach to problem solving. Whether we are facing a critical decision at work, a relationship-defining moment, or a personal crisis that requires a life-changing decision, we can all benefit from clearer

Fig 9.1 SWAT marines army M107 sniper assault rifle gun weapon 1:1 scale.

thinking by applying a devastatingly simple three-step process that becomes the gateway to silencing the noise of the mind:

Step 1: Sit down
Step 2: Shut up
Step 3: Count your breaths up to one hundred

It seems simple (it is) but it provides a basis for building discipline and self-control. This was a form of meditation that was developed to help the battle-hardened elite swordsmen of Japan's past, the samurai, to prepare to lay their lives on the line. It is now practiced by high-level business executives in Japanese multinational corporations and constitutional figures in the Japanese federal government.

It is an instant primer. A mental trigger for activating mental calmness. But let's get even more specific. When it comes to successfully responding to challenges and developing the mind-set that allows us to respond so that we load the outcome to our favor there are ten very specific, granular steps we can learn to apply:

- Set goals for mental as well as physical skills.
- Set goals that are specific and measurable.
- Set a target date for completion of those goals.
- Set goals that are difficult but realistic.
- Set short-term, intermediate, and long-term goals.
- Set goals for practice as well as for applying in a real-life situation.
- Set goals that are positive (like "achieving X by this date") as opposed to negative (like "losing my cool less often").
- Remain flexible enough to adjust goals as needed.
- Write the goals down on paper.
- Emphasize performance goals over outcome goals (such as winning).

Visualizing and self-affirmation are very powerful tools in planning your life and responding to a challenging situation. There are two very specific examples from two very different walks of life that we can look at for inspiration:

At Planet Hollywood in New York City, there is a handwritten letter hanging on the wall that martial artist and actor Bruce Lee wrote to himself. It's dated 1969:

*I, Bruce Lee, will be the first highest paid Oriental superstar
in the United States. In return I will give the most exciting per-
formances and render the best of quality in the capacity of an
actor. Starting 1970 I will achieve world fame and from then
onward till the end of 1980 I will have in my possession
$10,000,000. I will live the way I please and achieve inner har-
mony and happiness.*

    Bruce Lee, Jan. 1969

In the finals of the 100-meter men's race in the 2016 Olym-
pics in Rio de Janeiro, world record holder and fastest man on
Earth, Usain Bolt was chasing longtime rival Justin Gatlin. Bolt,
wary of a false start that might disqualify him from the race, was
out of the blocks even slower than usual. Gatlin, a sprinter who
many felt was technically perfect, had come off flawlessly from
the start and was already ahead.

What happened next has been well documented. Bolt, seemingly unfazed, picked up his pace, unfurled his legs, and secured
his place in Olympic history having won the gold medal in the
100-meter men's race in three consecutive Olympic Games. But
it's Bolt's comment reported in the *New York Times* afterward that
is of note here. As he raced to catch his rival, Bolt could easily
have panicked. The 100-meter race is brutally unforgiving. It's
over in less than ten seconds, which means that mistakes that cost
microseconds can make all the difference. The margin for error
in your executive decision-making in that race is precisely zero.
This is what Bolt said about what he was thinking as Gatlin ac-
celerated away from him: "I told myself, 'Listen, don't panic. Take
your time, chip away, and work your way back in.'"

Bolt, indeed, caught Gatlin just past the halfway mark and, with less than 50 meters of racetrack to go, soundly beat him. His comment, however, is like he had all the time in the world and infinite space to correct his slow start. Both Bruce Lee and Bolt exhibit, in their approaches, the very traits that govern cool-headed responses to a challenge. A measured approach, great visualization, an exceptional work ethic, belief in themselves and their abilities, and the determination to succeed.

THE SNIPER SKILL ACQUISITION LIST

In this chapter you learned:

- Preparation requires experience not just thinking about something, but also trying to do it.
- Every problem has a solution. We just need to identify the problem correctly and devise a way to deal with it.
- The brain can be trained to be better focused and more positive. It takes persistence, patience, and time.
- Snipers are masters of methodology. Devise the one that will work for you and stick with it.
- Practice awareness of your thoughts and actions. Understand your own motivation for doing something, every time.

Success doesn't necessarily come from breakthrough innovation but from flawless execution. A great strategy alone won't win a game or a battle; the win comes from basic blocking and tackling.

—NAVEEN JAIN

10

Structure: Learn to Choose the Right Strategy for Maximum Adaptability When the Stakes Are Really High

THE TWO SNIPERS had been circling each other for three days now. Each was the pinnacle of personal commitment to their craft; both were at the very top of their profession, the products of a war that had already claimed millions of lives. Now they were reduced to fighting over a small patch of land, the life of each held as the ultimate prize for success.

One of them, flown in specially from Berlin by the Wehrmacht, was Major Erwin König, a decorated officer of the German army, a man who had become head of a sniper school and who had, in a very short time, made his presence felt to the enemy. The other was the legendary Vasily Zaytsev, the boy from the Urals who'd grown up with a rifle. He was the morale booster of the beleaguered Soviet army that was desperately trying to hold Stalingrad and the man who would eventually be credited with 225 confirmed kills, eleven snipers among them.

Now they were locked in battle together. Tethered by their

mutual knowledge and expertise, trapped by circumstances beyond their control in a cat-and-mouse game that would only end when one of them was dead. Each move they made, each decision they took, each calculated choice became a deadly game play on the chessboard called Stalingrad.

Anyone who's seen the fictionalized encounter between Major Erwin König and Vasily Zaytsev in the hit movie *Enemy at the Gates* realizes two things: First, what a hellish place Stalingrad was at that moment in history, how cheap human life had become. And second, the critical role played by snipers from the Soviet side in halting the German advance into the city.

Military historians have cast some doubt on the veracity of the encounter between König and Zaytsev. There is little official paperwork to support the existence of the former and the story of the latter has some credibility gaps. But war is such a chaotic situation that they cannot entirely discount it either. Regardless of its veracity, what *Enemy at the Gates* manages to authentically convey is the mental aspect of a sniper hunting a sniper.

In the battle between equals wits, intelligence, and the ability to think creatively and make the right decisions play a far greater role in ensuring success than being able to shoot straight or have a great sniper rifle. Sniper battles allow us to peel off the mystique surrounding how snipers think and actually deconstruct the modular way they piece together the information they get in order to make the decisions they make.

Because so much of the work is mental every weapon in a sniper's arsenal comes into play. Empathy is required to help you get into the mind-set of the other sniper. You want to determine: Who? Where? When? Why? Because all of it matters, when it comes to information, both human intelligence (what other people are saying and doing, and the way they are behaving) and signal intelligence (information that can be supplied independently or intercepted) are important.

The point that has been constant throughout this book is that everything matters, nothing can be overlooked, and the sniper's skill is found in his ability to recognize what's important quickly and deliver relevant signals from the general noise of data his senses report and his brain processes. There are four things snipers do that are completely applicable to businesses of all types:

- **Do their homework**—Snipers spend hours and sometimes days collecting all available information about their mission or the area where they will be deployed in. This is understandable. When they are operational they will be expected to put context and meaning to what they see and without accurate, real-world information they will be unable to interpret what they see correctly in order to make the right decision.

- **Choose a vantage point**—Snipers will almost always be in an elevated position. Higher vantage points give broader points of view that allow more of the picture emerging before them to be seen. This is the mental equivalent of taking a step back in real life, in a business context, and gaining some perspective that may affect the judgment being made.

- **Choose timing**—Snipers do not allow circumstances to dictate their actions. They are deliberate in everything they do, even when they are under immense pressure. They exercise precision and cultivate deliberate calmness.

- **Keep their cool**—Even when under pressure snipers know

that nervousness, an elevated heart rate, and shaky hands can make them miss the best-aimed shot. So they practice keeping their cool by devising personal strategies that help them control their emotions and maintain their detachment. Business is always about passion and it is personal, but decisions should never be made emotionally.

Illustrating the highly structured approach one sniper, hunting another, would deploy, Daniel Kearns, a former US Marine with sniper training, explained on Quora, the question-and-answer Web site, how a trained operative thinks in order to get into the mind-set of the sniper he's hunting. The process, he explained, starts even before the decision is made to engage the enemy sniper. You need to determine right from the start aspects of his identity. Is he, for instance, an outsider brought in for the

Fig 10.1 Sniper hero of the Soviet Union, Vasily Zaytsev (left) in Stalingrad, December 1942.

task or is he a local with great shooting skills? Is he a pro doing a job or is he a fighter who's home on "leave" and is moonlighting out of conviction?

> *Where is he? Obviously the key. But more than just his hides and shooting positions. Where does he sleep? Does he live with the local fighters and move into position?*
>
> *When does he operate? Does he move into position at dawn and shoot at dusk?*
>
> *Why? Shoot one soldier per day? Draw assets from another base in preparation for an attack on that base? Restrict the movements and observation of this forward operating base (FOB) perhaps in preparation for a large body of soldiers moving through the area?*
>
> *These questions will not all be answered, but the more information the better.*

Kearns describes the complexity of skills that are required to create the detailed picture required for a successful outcome. Data comes in from every direction with the sniper-hunter having to pull in HUMINT (human intelligence) as well as SIGINT (signal intelligence) in order to better understand his quarry. Locals, for instance, may let something slip in conversations on the radio. Relatives may say something about someone being back home on leave or in hiding.

Even then the job is not done. The sniper-hunter will have to rely on the assistance of other snipers needed to watch possible firing positions and rally points that the hunted sniper may be using in order to narrow down the field of activity and determine the best plan of counter-action.

Obviously, the mind that can approach a situation in such a structured, precise, methodical manner creates a very granular picture of the reality it observes. It creates the kind of mind-set that in a business environment provides a clear, competitive advantage.

> **THE SCIENCE:** The brain that perceives itself at risk activates specific neurobiological responses that govern the choices that are made and directly influence the decision-making process. There are conditioning techniques that can mitigate the brain's natural response and the body's instinctive reaction and they then confer a natural competitive advantage.

THE BRAIN AT RISK

We have never quite understood the nature of fearlessness nor the chemistry of bravery. We have always suspected that it takes a very special type of person to be a hero. Someone who comes from a different kind of background or a different set of experiences. Literature shows heroes being created through the crucible of tribulation and internal suffering. The intimation is that they are not quite like us. This may not be as true as we thought, but neither is it entirely false.

Every hero has a brain. That brain has an internal architecture that is identical to any other brain. While every brain is unique in terms of the neural connections it creates for itself and the knowledge it stores within it, it is the architecture that makes it possible to function in the first place, and the way the architecture works in particular brains, like a hero's for instance, can be scanned and mapped.

The reason all this is relevant to us is because we need to understand why snipers are so cool under pressure and how we can become like them. Typically in order to better understand the sniper mind and its workings we need to go outside it and beyond it. Way outside it, as it turns out to be as we look at Alex Honnold, acclaimed as the greatest-ever climber in the free solo style, meaning he ascends without a rope or protective equipment of any kind. Alex is so seemingly fearless that he has his own verb: *to honnold*, usually written as *honnolding*. Its meaning is given as to stand in some high, precarious place with your back to the wall, looking straight into the abyss below you. To face fear head on, literally.

Alex's exploits have turned him into a legend in the free climbing community and an oddity among climbers everywhere. His apparent lack of fear has made him the target of much speculation, not least by neurobiologists eager to understand if his internal wiring is as different as rumors suggest.

The cognitive neuroscientist who has spent the most time running scans on Alex Honnold's brain is Jane Joseph, who in 2005 was one of the first people to perform fMRIs on high sensation seekers hoping to understand why their brains led them to choose intense experiences, accepting the risks associated with them. While frequently this kind of internal wiring in the brain leads to self-destructive behaviors such as drug use, alcohol addiction, out-of-control gambling, and compulsive, unsafe sex,

Fig 10.2 Alex Honnold is perhaps the greatest free solo climber of all time. He climbs alone and without the assistance of any rope. During a climb he may spend as long as twelve or more hours in what climbers call the Death Zone, dangling from heights from which a fall would be fatal.

with Honnold, Jane Joseph sought to discover how exactly the mind can regulate the body's responses so that the pursuit of extreme experiences does not become catastrophic.

During tests where Honnold was subjected to sensory stimuli while in an fMRI scanner his amygdala, the brain's center for interpretation of stimuli and threat response, was examined for a response. What Jane Joseph discovered is that Honnold is capable of an extreme form of what snipers call "arousal control." He feels fear just like any other person, but instead of his amygdala triggering reflexive reactions and activating the higher processing centers of the brain which kick in for us to feel fear, his frontal cortex was able to calm it down.

Compared with a control subject of similar interests and inclination, Honnold showed just how extraordinary he really is by displaying zero brain activity during the arousal stage of the tests. He also displayed zero brain activity during further tests that tested the reward system of his brain. According to the fMRI scanner he really had no sense of fear, none at all, which outwardly may help explain his preternatural calm when he is hanging by his fingertips above a drop that's 2,000 feet (609.6 meters) high.

But this is not how Honnold himself describes his sensations. He has always felt fear. In a climbing career that now is over twelve years old and with hundreds of difficult climbs under his belt, he has also explained how he did and still does thousands of easy climbs. By starting ropeless climbing early in life and pushing himself through the difficulties he faced on each climb, he trained himself to have confidence in his own ability to overcome challenges and control the anxiety he felt while climbing.

While self-taught, this was no different in effect from Hell Week experienced by Navy SEALs, the "selection" undergone by the SAS, or any sniper training course that pushes its recruits past their limits in incremental stages and habituates them to extreme danger and mental pressure in its "stress inoculation" phase.

Honnold describes the mental resilience he developed as "mental armor." He learned to be mentally tough by repetition, challenging himself each time to get past his comfort zone by building up on small successes and learning from small failures. It is a recipe that is by now familiar to us. The military trains snipers the same way, building them up in skill, confidence, identity, and ability until they appear to be as superhuman in what they do as Alex Honnold.

There is one more element to both fearlessness and bravery and it has to do with memory. We've already seen just how much of a role memory plays in sniper training. The ability to observe clearly and retain detail is drilled into sniper recruits from very early on. Remembering scenarios and playing them out, mentally, including covering all the negative outcomes that need to be avoided, is something that Honnold also shares with snipers. Just like snipers and their logs, Honnold keeps a detailed climbing journal in which he revisits his climbs and makes note of what he can do better. He even visualizes each difficult climb in detail, including losing his grip, falling and ending up on the ground, broken, bleeding, and far from any possible help, to help him feel comfortable with them mentally before he tackles them physically.

At the University of Texas at Austin, the head of the Monfils Fear Memory Lab, Marie Monfils, has also spent time looking at Honnold and his exploits. Memories, she's explained in interviews, are not consolidated and unchangeable, cast in stone and filed by the brain in some archive, as thought of in the past. Instead, memories, even fearful ones, are subject to reinterpretation. Each time they are revisited, they are seen through the filter of additional knowledge, skill, and experience. A memory that may have been fearful because we did not know how to deal with it at the time can be turned into a positive one as we become better at handling the kind of problem it represents. Once fearful memories that filled us with anxiety can be turned, in this fashion, into fearless ones.

Adding additional data in this area is a group of rhesus monkeys at the department of neuroscience at Washington University in St. Louis. Rhesus monkey brains have similar architecture to human ones, which makes them easy to study when it comes to testing risky behavior. It turns out that when it comes to thrills and spills rhesus monkeys are not any wiser than humans. Given a choice between a small amount of juice or a fifty-fifty chance of receiving either double that amount of juice or nothing at all, they consistently chose to gamble in the hope of getting a higher reward short term than to go for the sure thing. And that despite the fact that, over time, the amount of juice received under either condition would be the same.

Ilya Monosov, who is assistant professor of neuroscience at the university, published this study in the *Journal of Neuroscience*, explaining that at the moment of choice the rhesus monkeys, who'd been wired to a portable fMRI, exhibited neural activity in the part of the brain called the ventral pallidum. The ventral pallidum is associated with the calculation of the value of a stimulus and the control of dopamine, a neurotransmitter that also makes us feel good. Monosov believes that as "the ventral pallidum inhibits dopamine neurons, suppression of this area during risky behavior may increase dopamine release."

The study also found that neurons in a nearby brain area called the medial basal forebrain became most active after the monkeys made a risky choice but before they learned the outcome of their choice. That part of the brain provides input to a wide network of cortical brain regions involved in learning and memory. Feeling uncertainty over an outcome leads not just to learning new things but also to retrieving stored memories as the brain tries to find reassuring scenarios in its store of knowledge.

Uncertainty then can be managed by more actively resorting to knowledge and memories, and everything we fear can be overcome through a managed, persistent, incrementally escalating exposure to the source that creates the fear in the first instance. The decisions we make are then less likely to be influenced by environmental conditions, impulses, or emotions. We can learn to be better versions of who we are, and make better executive decisions by using the tools of learning, memory, and awareness of our own actions, to gain a more balanced perspective.

THE BUSINESS CASE

"Why did the chicken cross the road?" This is a riddle joke that's been the opening of many a stand-up comedian doing the night-club circuit. It is also a leading question inviting answers which expose an individual's belief system. Stand-up comedians use it because it provides a hook for a follow-up with some very telling real-world implications. Let me explain.

In the absence of any other information, the obvious, rational answer to the question of the chicken's motivation is "to get to the other side." Yet this reveals a mode of thinking called constructivism. Grounded in logic, constructivism accepts that the environment creates structure and that the world is largely deterministic. Causality then flows from external conditions to executive decisions. The chicken *had* to cross the road in order to get to the other side so that must also be its sole motivation.

At first this may seem overly restrictive. It means all of our choices, all of our decision-making is rationally predetermined by the environmental circumstances we find ourselves in and the limitations those circumstances impose. This is not the case exactly. While constructivism defines the operating parameters we are in, each time, there is always room for the ideas and actions of an individual to shape the landscape they find themselves in by redefining its inherent limitations. This is called reconstructionism.

Craig Harrison, who we encountered in chapter 1, and Matt Hughes, in chapter 4 made choices and took actions that overcame the obvious limitations dictated by their environment, the capability of their equipment, and the particulars of their circumstances. Harrison's record-beating shot and Hughes's curving of the bullet were the result of the interjection of human decision-making in what would otherwise be a cut-and-dried deterministic scenario.

In the popular video game *Tetris* where various geometric shapes fall from the top of the screen and need to be manipulated by the player so that they form a perfect, solid line, the possibilities are determined by the shapes that appear, the speed at which they drop, and what is already on the baseline, but everything else is created by the executive decision-making, experience, and skill of the player.

When Apple first looked at bringing out the iPhone, the company was operating in a landscape dominated by BlackBerry, whose phones were famous for their tactile, responsive physical keyboards. In a perfectly rational, deterministic world, Apple would have assessed the strengths and weaknesses of the dominant player and would have set out to achieve a competitive advantage by differentiating itself either through a premium price or a lower cost. Logically it should have brought out either slicker, more expensive phones with physical keyboards that beat the BlackBerry on looks or produced similar-looking ones that were cheaper to produce, undercutting its rival on price. It would then have aligned its value chain accordingly, creating manufacturing, marketing, and human resource strategies in the process.

On the basis of these strategies, financial targets and budget allocations would have been set. The approach would have created a market front for it where it would have dug in against the bigger, very successful Research in Motion (RIM), which then owned the at the time iconic BlackBerry brand. The stage would have been set for years and years of incremental improvements as RIM and Apple subtly repositioned themselves in response to each other's initiatives.

This is not, however, as we all know, what Apple did. Steve Jobs exhibited many of the traits that go with the mind-set of the trained sniper ("Adapt. Overcome."). Each problem that cropped up as part of the iPhone project helped usher in ever more creative solutions, and at no point did Jobs permit anyone to waver from the "mission" of bringing the iPhone to the market.

The way we make decisions, particularly in a business setting, is something that has been theorized about and hyperanalyzed, probably, since the first turnip changed hands for some money across a stall in a medieval town square. This is why it's a good opportunity to now formalize a little of our knowledge of the systems we employ. This isn't so much a prescriptive approach that creates a new set of restrictions for us as a more broad-based look at how decisions are arrived at in some situations. It's meant to both sensitize us to the processes we implement when we make a decision and make us aware of the more formal theories surrounding those processes so that we can feel more empowered when we employ them and more confident when we challenge them, overrule them, or simply ignore them.

SIX APPROACHES TO DECISION-MAKING

The ingredients of any decision-making process, boiled down to their absolute basics are simple enough: A problem presents a timeline within which something must be done about it, there is a set of outcomes for successful resolution and a set of outcomes for an unsuccessful resolution. In order to achieve the outcome we want we require specific resources. There are always limitations we have to work with. Somehow we must make all this work to our advantage.

Well, as we move through the steps of considering the problem, formulating possible solutions, and projecting the outcome we employ some very specific models of decision-making:

- **The Classical Approach**—This is the application of choices based on previous data and experience. This is usually the most immediate form of decision-making we bring to bear on a problem. Snipers keep track of every shot they make. Olympic athletes, star basketball and baseball players, and (as we saw with Honnold) exceptional climbers all keep detailed logs of their activities. This means that they have a detailed body of information that becomes the immediate backdrop against which a first decision can be made. Situation analysis then provides all the other elements that may affect the decision. This approach necessitates specific behavioral patterns from us: the keeping of detailed notes (or some means of actually getting hold of relevant information and data) and the using of a relatively good memory to go over, analyze, and learn from each of our past successes and failures. It takes for granted that we are totally into what we do to the extent that we think about it, internalize the lessons we learn, and use them to build better ways of dealing with a similar problem each time.
- **The Human Resource Approach**—Here, human nature is

302 • THE SNIPER MIND

a key element in every decision-making process. It will affect us as we are making the decision (which is why we need to be aware of it), but it will also affect the behavior of all other participants in the scene. As key decision-makers we will need to be aware of all this and we have to become capable of factoring human nature into the desired outcomes we seek. Snipers study people carefully. They have a clear understanding of the way people behave in particular situations and this becomes a layer of metadata they use as additional signals to aid in their decision-making. This requires a high degree of empathy. Business decisions or, indeed, any kind of decision that does not employ some empathy in the process misses out critical aspects that only complicate matters afterward. This is the classic head-versus-heart dilemma. Neither of these two approaches is exclusive of the other. An awareness of the benefits and vulnerabilities that each brings is key to establishing when to use one or the other. Studies carried out by the department of psychology at Saint Mary's University, in Halifax, Nova Scotia, showed that the best decision makers know exactly when to appeal to the head and when to appeal to the heart by being aware of both processes.

- **The Quantitative Approach**—The moment a decision has been made, its implementation requires specific steps which create a methodology. This is where decision trees and situation analysis figure heavily. Knowledge, information, and the ability to understand how everything falls together become key in the choices that will be made, the potential outcomes and pitfalls, and the advantages and disadvantages. During training, snipers are required to perfect their camouflage and evasion skills by carrying out stalks in which the "enemy" already knows they are coming. It teaches them to make critical decisions under the pressure of a ticking clock and in less than ideal conditions. They learn to use the elements that are in place, creating decision trees that make use of everything they have to work with in the most creative manner possible in order to achieve their mission. All too frequently, the quantitative approach is used in business environments to itemize what is missing from a resource list of requirements and to justify why something cannot happen as opposed to finding ways to make it happen.

- The Systems Perspective—This is a formalization of the LEGO principle we first saw in chapter 9. A sniper's every mission, just like every marketing campaign, every new organizational initiative, is made up of many moving parts and each of those moving parts has its own structure, its own milestones, and its own specific tipping point. It is only by breaking everything down into segments and identifying the bottlenecks and the points where a decision can create divergent outcomes that a project can be turned into a manageable set of actions. Bruce Lee was a master at employing this approach in planning his life and deciding just what he should do in the present in order to help attain his future goals.

- The Contingency Approach—Nothing ever goes according to plan. Business and Special Forces missions seem to share the same sensitivity to initial conditions. The multitude of external factors that need to fall in place for something to go smoothly also increase the likelihood of things going wrong. Being prepared for just such contingencies is a mind-set that needs to be cultivated. It is no accident that snipers, Special Forces operatives, Olympic athletes, elite baseball and basketball players, and solo rock climbers use detailed visualization where they go through not just the positive aspects of the task lying ahead but also the negative ones, seeing exactly what might go wrong and how they could deal with it. By being prepared for the worst, they are best positioned to take advantage of every opportunity that presents itself and, when things really do not go according to plan, they are also best prepared to deal with the challenges.

- **The Technological Advantage Approach**—Sometimes better equipment is all that's required to give us a strong competitive advantage. This is a quick win that we should always be ready to recognize. The famed seventeenth-century samurai Miyamoto Musashi wrote in *A Book of Five Rings*, his partially allegorical treatise on strategy: "Like a soldier, the carpenter sharpens his own tools. He carries his equipment in his tool box, and works under the direction of his foreman. He makes columns and girders with an ax, shapes floorboards and shelves with a plane, cuts fine openwork and bas reliefs accurately, giving as excellent a finish as his skill will allow. This is the craft of the carpenters. When the carpenter becomes skilled, he works efficiently and according to correct measures. When he has developed practical knowledge of all the skills of the craft, he can become a foreman himself." Knowing what to use, when, and where is always part of our skill set as experts.

THE FOUR PILLARS OF MENTAL STRENGTH

Mental strength can be developed. The brain is a muscle that can be trained. Mental strength, as we saw with Alex Honnold or any SEAL undergoing Hell Week, does not require a blocking out of emotions. Quite the opposite. It requires us to embrace our emotions; become aware of them, understand them, and then manage them by placing them in a context that gives real meaning to why we resist them.

Holding back tears at a friend's funeral is not a mark of strength. It is an act of denial that may come back to haunt us. Across the entire spectrum of elite human activity there are four specific elements that can rightly be called the four pillars of mental strength:

- Setting goals
- Mental visualization
- Positive self-talk
- Arousal control

Each of these, depending on context, has a number of separate segments. It is however, the apparent simplicity of what makes us mentally strong that makes it possible to actually become so.

However, what is it that keeps us at it? When even building mental strength requires strength, what is it exactly that can guarantee that we don't falter? What is it we can do to make sure that we come back again and again and do the things we have to do in order to keep moving forward?

The American philosopher and psychologist William James had this to say:

> *Compared with what we ought to be, we are only half awake. Our fires are damped, our drafts are checked. We are making use of only a small part of our possible mental resources . . . men the world over possess amounts of resource, which only exceptional individuals push to their extremes of use.*

The entire body of William James's work can be summarized in his quest to answer two simple questions: First, what are the types of human abilities? And second, how can the average person go about achieving them? We now know that physical and cognitive skills go hand in hand. That the mind is woven throughout the body, that you can't do a push-up, throw a punch, swing a baseball bat, or take a rifle shot without your brain doing something amazing.

James was interested in understanding the differences between those who go on and achieve what they set out to do and those who feel that, somehow, the load is too much, the path too difficult, and they give up. Trying to answer the same questions, researchers from the University of Pennsylvania and the University of Michigan looked at West Point cadets as they undergo the grueling initiation of their first summer on campus, known as "Beast Barracks."

Tracking almost two and a half thousand individuals across two classes and categorizing their aptitude into skill sets such as SAT scores, leadership potential score, physical aptitude exam, and so on, the researchers discovered that the most accurate predictor of success across all participants studied was what they called "grit." They went on to write in the *Journal of Personality and Social Psychology* that:

> *We define grit as perseverance and passion for long-term goals. Grit entails working strenuously toward challenges, maintaining effort and interest over years despite failure, adversity, and plateaus in progress. The gritty individual approaches achievement as a marathon; his or her advantage is stamina. Whereas disappointment or boredom signals to others that it is time to change trajectory and cut losses, the gritty individual stays the course.*

In other words, those who succeeded displayed stamina over speed or strength. A willingness to stay the course and not give up, undergo a change of heart or show a willingness to opt for an easier path. The researchers used the "big five" model of personality traits to help classify the cadets:

- Openness to experience
- Conscientiousness
- Extraversion
- Agreeableness
- Neuroticism

In each combination of traits it was grit that became the decisive factor for success. When it comes to developing the right mental attitude there are three things we have been preparing for throughout this book: Developing good habits. Not worrying about things we cannot control. Doing some form of exercise frequently.

THE SNIPER SKILL ACQUISITION LIST

In this chapter you learned:

- The four things snipers do that every businessperson can copy.
- The road to exceptional performance under pressure is paved by perseverance and incremental attempts.
- There are specific models that describe the decisions we make. An awareness of them allows us to create the right structure for our decision-making and avoid the obvious traps.
- The four pillars of mental strength help us build mental resilience against stress and adversity.
- Grit is the "magic sauce" that helps us turn into exceptional people.

The emotional brain responds to an event more quickly
than the thinking brain.
—DANIEL GOLEMAN

11

Feeling: Harness Feelings and Use Emotional Intelligence to Build Winning Strategies Like a Navy SEAL

SCOUT SNIPERS ARE THE EYES, the ears, and, often, the trigger finger of their commanders. They operate at the very edge of the Marine Corps' military capabilities, securing pathways, gathering intelligence, and, when the need arises, providing overwatch.

Ramadi, in central Iraq, is a city that's about 68 miles west of Baghdad and 31 miles west of Fallujah, all of which put it smack bang in the center of the insurgency hot zone during the Iraq War. For scout sniper Tim La Sage, deployed with the 2nd Battalion, 5th Marine Regiment, it became the place where, while on a 3:00 a.m. mission targeting the cousin of Abu Musab al-Zarqawi, a militant Islamist from Jordan, he almost lost his life:

We were moving into an alley a couple blocks away, "bumping across" we call it. Two guys had been sent ahead to provide cover. I think they had been spotted, because somebody was waiting as we crossed a street where an IED was placed. We had gotten really good at spotting these; but this one we didn't see. We were running across the street when they detonated it. It was a huge blast. Two of my teammates, one to my right and one to my left, were killed. It was a mess.[2] At the end of this, I could put a beer can through my thigh. I lost all the muscle and fiber in my leg.

His account is one of fighting while sustaining injuries that would have put most men out of action, helping comrades injured even more seriously than himself and desperately fighting back the enemy, editing out the fear, the pain, and the despair, and maintaining battle effectiveness until help arrived and he and those he guarded could get out of there.

The way snipers are trained to "suck it up"—code for containing their emotions when under pressure—is the stuff of legend. One of the serving snipers I interviewed was Ryan G. and he had a very interesting take on this ability:

You know it's gonna be shitty. You're in the mix. When they're training you they watch to see what you do. You know you can stop at any time. Just give up and drop out. But if you want it, you know in your head that you are not gonna quit, no matter what, because you are there to be the person you want to be. So the only way to get you out is if they make things bad enough to kill you and you know they ain't gonna do that. Which is not what it's like when you're active. You're always under fire or in a really bad position where one wrong move can really cost you. So you blank everything out. The weather, the

---

2. Editor's note: Out of the eight people in LaSage's unit, seven would earn the Purple Heart.

fatigue, the fear. There is nothing. You focus on what you're there to do: save lives. Your decisions will make someone die, others live. You're like God with a scope. So you let your mind take everything in, let your fear ride out, focus on your breathing, listen to your heartbeat. And you do what you have been trained to do because you are the edge of the sword.

What's interesting in his account is that Ryan, consciously or unconsciously, is using a mix of physical and mental tools to acknowledge and control his emotions. In his account of how he has been trained to control what he is feeling, for instance, he mentions both situational awareness (a cognitive analysis approach) and identity (the Know Thyself dictum). He cleverly subverts the system when he says that during training he knows that he cannot be allowed to die so the fear he feels is unjustified. He is willing to go all the way because he knows he is safe. Then he demonstrates the transfer of that training to a live situation when death can be just a second away. He is able to compartmentalize it completely, using the controlled breathing techniques he has been taught, calming himself down and visualizing the motivation for what he does to help keep him focused. He doesn't block emotion. He acknowledges it. Then he simply rides it out because he knows that is better than letting it control him.

In his account he demonstrates his ability to activate what psychologists describe as three very distinct elements that are key to self-development:

• **Self-Awareness**—The ability to recognize and understand personal moods, emotions, and drives, as well as the effect they have on others.

- **Self-Regulation**—The ability to control or redirect disruptive impulses and moods and adapt to changing circumstances. This is defined in the by now familiar dictum that is drummed into every trained sniper ("Adapt. Overcome.").
- **Internal Motivation**—A passion to do what he does for internal reasons that go beyond status and external rewards.

Such is the power of the trained sniper mind that it appears to supersede normal human differences among trained snipers. It creates a solid, unwavering line connecting snipers of all nationalities, all cultures, and throughout all times. The ability to use their minds in a particular way draws mental parallels and creates psychological twins of people who outwardly could not be more different.

For instance, consider how Thomas Plunket, a nineteenth-century Irish soldier serving in the British 95th Rifles during the Napoleonic Wars, becomes the sharpshooting twin of Carlos Norman Hathcock II, the part Native American marine sniper in Vietnam who crawls over 1,500 yards to shoot a high-ranking enemy officer.

In 1809, at the Battle of Cacabelos, a minor incident in the wider conflict of the Napoleonic Wars, Plunket shot the French Général de Brigade Auguste-Marie-François Colbert at a range of around 2,000 feet (600 meters), using a Baker rifle. Plunket had run forward to make this shot. Before returning to his own lines he reloaded and shot down Colbert's aide-de-camp, Latour-Maubourg, who had rushed to the aid of the fallen general, proving beyond doubt that the first shot had not been a fluke; the deaths were sufficient to throw the pending French attack into disarray, an early documented instance of both the "one shot, one kill" and "one shot can change history" doctrines snipers have learned to apply.

The connecting thread of history doesn't stop there. Francis Pegahmagabow, an Ojibwa warrior with the Canadians who was the most effective sniper of World War I, is credited with killing 378 Germans and capturing 300 more, which makes him appear to be an earlier version of Vasily Zaytsev, the farmboy from the Urals who served with Russia's 62nd Army in World War II.

Such are the similarities in mentality, disposition, and approach that, stripped of their national identity, removed from their place in time, you could take any top sniper anywhere, list their attributes, and you'd be forgiven for thinking you're describing the same person. There is a reason for this. Just like one Olympic athlete, reduced to the essentials of his craft that enable him to perform at that elite level, is indistinguishable from another, so does the sniper mind band together all those who are trained to think in a certain way.

The strength and power of a fully developed sniper mind comes from the ability to harness and control feelings and emotions constructively, creating an empowering, motivational platform from what most people would be demoralized and demotivated by. It's no mean feat. It means being able to grope into the empty space from which despair should normally spring and manage to pull out hope.

In what sounds like a plot pulled straight out of the *Rambo* franchise, in the cinematic vista of our mind's eye we see a man standing alone, hungry, cold, possibly wounded. His equipment is outdated. His ammunition is running low and against him is arrayed an entire enemy army, advancing his way. History offers many such examples, and the Winter War between the Soviet Union and Finland readily provides us with one.

In 1939, the Soviet Union under Joseph Stalin launched an invasion of its neighbor, Finland, deploying twelve divisions (about 160,000 men) against the much smaller country. In what came to be known as the Battle of Kollaa, the Finns were outnumbered, by 125 to one, with at one point just thirty-two of them defending a territory against over four thousand Soviet troops.

Simo Häyhä was a sniper on the defending side, serving under the 6th Company of JR 34. His involvement in the Winter War was extraordinary. With his Mosin-Nagant M91 rifle, he would dress in white winter camouflage, and carry with him only a day's worth of supplies and ammunition. While hiding out in the snow, he would then take out any Russian who entered his killing zone. Häyhä preferred to use iron sights on his gun instead of scopes, as scopes had a tendency to glare in the sunlight and reveal his position. While he may sound like an "ordinary" sniper, this was far from the case: over the course of one hundred days during the winter he racked up over five hundred kills, earning him the nickname "The White Death." The Soviets feared him so much that they mounted numerous counter sniper and artillery attacks to get rid of him, all of which failed miserably.

Despite gaining around 22,000 square miles of Finnish soil, the Soviets lost the Winter War, with one million of their original 1,500,000 troops having been killed by the defending Finns. A Russian general later remarked that the land they had conquered was "just enough to bury their dead."

Just thirty years later and over 5,000 miles (8,000 km) away, another sniper by the name of Ed Eaton would find himself part of a helicopter night mission over Vietnam. The Viet Cong shot

Fig 11.1 Simo Häyhä after being awarded with the honorary rifle model 28.

down his chopper resulting in most of the men aboard being injured with near fatal wounds. His friend and mission leader Major Mike Perkins got the worst of it, being pinned down under the helicopter and unable to get out. With the downed helicopter still under attack, Ed Eaton buttoned down his emotions and got to work. He would later say that since he had the least amount of injuries he felt it necessary to protect his fellow soldiers.

Climbing atop the wreckage and using a combination of his sniper rifle, damaged by the crash, and an M16, Eaton used his sniper's night sights to spot two separate groups of Viet Cong descending upon them from over 500 yards away. Without pausing to consider how open he was to their return fire he traded accurate, precision fire with both groups, forcing them to take cover and slow their descent to his location. The use of the two guns made the enemy believe that Ed was more than one man. Even more impressively, after Eaton got the hang of the damage to his sniper rifle, he adjusted to its aiming flaws and began taking enemy guys out one at a time.

He kept up his fire long enough for help to arrive. When a pair of helicopters came through to rescue the men, Major Perkins, whose injuries were too much for the ride, opted to stay and was given a grenade for suicide in case of capture. The choppers were about to leave when Ed asked to remain with his friend because he did not want him dying alone out there with no hope for survival. With time running out, the chopper pilots had to take off, leaving the pair on the battlefield with Ed holding off even more enemy soldiers with limited ammunition, as they descended upon him from their positions.

It was a seemingly hopeless situation. One which Eaton, in a clear parallel with the actions of Master Sergeant Gary Gordon and Sergeant First Class Randy Shughart in Mogadishu, during the *Black Hawk Down* incident, did not expect to survive. During a brief respite in the firing he told his friend that he would keep his last two bullets for them so they would not be captured alive.

Incredibly, despite his wounds, dwindling ammunition, and the hopelessness of his situation, Eaton managed to pin down the approaching enemy long enough for a second rescue party to arrive and airlift him and his wounded friend to safety.

Reading about the exploits of snipers, listening to them as they recount moments of exceptional bravery and heroism in a matter-of-fact way, we realize that when culture, nationality, and time become irrelevant, then what we have come to recognize as the signature attitude of the sniper mind has to be the product of specific training applied on otherwise ordinary minds. And a significant part of that training revolves around recognizing, harnessing, and making better use of emotional intelligence.

THE SCIENCE: Understanding emotions, managing them effectively, and using them in thinking and reasoning helps with cognition, task performance, and social relationships.

THE FOUR BRANCHES OF EMOTIONAL INTELLIGENCE

If emotions are not to be shut off but acknowledged, managed, directed, and utilized, what is the skill set that will help us do that? In order to understand what we need, we must acknowledge that we are, on the whole, appalling communicators but excellent worriers. Because most of us are so deeply wrapped in our insecurities, we communicate as little as possible. At the same time we are constantly engaged in an exhausting game of guesswork, trying to decode the hidden meaning and intent lying behind the equally sparse communication of those around us.

Our insecurities drive us. Our fears control us. We try to hide the first and deny the second and it is exhausting us. Our communication suffers not because we cannot communicate but because we don't know how to communicate without giving away the fact that we feel inside that we are weak and everyone is out to get us.

Before we look at how this can be solved, it is important to understand that an improvement in how we use emotional intelligence cannot take place outside our awareness of the context in which emotional intelligence exists in the first place. If we are unaware of social norms, cultural conventions, and the societal constructs that arise around them, our judgment is likely to be flawed and our assumptions will be wrong. Our decision-making and subsequent actions will also then be flawed and wrong.

So it appears we cannot realistically divorce emotional intelligence from social interaction. And we cannot separate social interaction from critical decision-making and the actions we engage in. If anything, there is a growing body of work that shows that emotional intelligence accounts for what we perceive as individual differences in abilities. It is the reason one star athlete succeeds over another when on paper they are evenly matched, and why one SEAL recruit quits when others who may not be as smart or physically gifted do not.

The proposed framework for looking at the qualification and measurement of emotional intelligence in individuals relies on four distinct branches:

- How we perceive emotion
- How we use emotion to facilitate thought
- How we understand emotion
- How we manage emotion

The Yale Center for Emotional Intelligence, a nonprofit research organization among whose partners is the Air Force Research Laboratory, acknowledges on its Web site that "emotions drive learning, decision-making, creativity, relationships, and health." Each of the four branches is integrated differently within each individual's psychological makeup. The development of each branch is directly related to some of the fundamental differences in a person's ability to reach critical decisions based upon the way he thinks from what he sees. For instance, both the perception and expression of emotion and the capacity of emotion to enhance thought are relatively separate areas of information processing. A male soldier seeing a crying baby will react differently to the information than will a mother or a nurse, even though they each see exactly the same tabloid playing out in front of them.

Research carried out by the Carnegie Institute of Technology showed that 85 percent of our financial success is due to skills in "human engineering." Personality, the ability to communicate, how we negotiate, and our style of leadership are more important than technical ability or intelligence, which they found accounted for only 15 percent of success.

When emotional intelligence is about the interactions of the person in a social setting, what is important becomes more obvious. Sociologists, psychologists, and neurobiologists now consider the context in which social interaction takes place to be the filter which allows the brain to understand what is relevant signal and what is distracting noise from all the information it processes. The skills that emotional intelligence is made of then fall into two distinct categories: personal competence and social competence.

Personal competence is composed of self-awareness and self-management. Social competence is made up of social awareness and relationship management. These four skills together are the entire measurable skill set emotionally intelligent people possess.

How these affect perception and how perception is affected by them in turn is something social psychologist Emily Balcetis has made her life's work to find out. What she has to say ties in neatly with all the small, persistent pieces we've been putting together all along our journey in this book.

THE VISION THING

In chapter 2 we saw in German photographer Simon Menner's work the importance of vision and perception and the awareness that trained snipers develop. *Seeing* is frequently used as a synonym for *understanding* in everyday English. And seeing is the primary channel through which the brain collects information to understand the world around it.

Snipers develop an intuitive understanding of the environment they are in and how it looks. As their mental skills advance, they become masters at inserting themselves in it without interrupting any of its patterns and drawing attention to themselves. They also develop a detailed understanding of how visual information is processed, becoming adept at interrupting the process via which the brain of an outside observer latches onto their hiding place.

Every step we've taken so far along this journey has looked at the skills a trained sniper mind possesses and asked the question "What if?" What if there is a way to develop those same mental skills without having to give up your job, abandon your life, and sign up to the army to train as a sniper?

We've seen one piece of evidence after another that shows that the brain only has specific channels for processing information and specific systems for doing things. Because of that, transfer, the ability to take skills learned in a simulated environment and apply them in real life, allows us to emulate many of the things the trained sniper mind is capable of. Along the way we've picked up skills and tips on how to become more aware, more mindful, capable of greater control over our bodies and emotions, more focused and determined.

All of it, of course, requires some effort. None of it comes easy. But there is a clear, documented path between what the brain does and what the body then becomes capable of doing. There is a clear, documented path between what the body does and how it then affects the capabilities of the mind. If there is one overall vital lesson we've learned as we read through the incredible accounts of trained snipers, it is that there is no real division between body and mind. The two are one. We can, for the purposes of study, reduce them into specific, differentiated, organic components, but that no more shows us their true function and integration into the whole of our being than taking apart the tires of a sports car and studying the chemical formula for galvanized rubber would reveal to us about the capabilities of the vehicle they once belonged to.

So, little tweaks, the small things we do in our daily lives as a result of all the things we've learned, have the ability to change the paths our lives take and where we eventually end up.

Two research scientists now come to add not just more evidence but also two tips that can help us achieve almost instant improvements in our mental and physical performance. Typically, in their studies, they identify traits that trained snipers routinely apply and they highlight structure in approach and thinking that the military has long worked to instill in its recruits. Untypically, they show how anyone can achieve them.

The first researcher is Emily Balcetis, who's an assistant professor at New York University and whose work on perception and cognition is drawing more and more attention. In her 2006 thesis, "Motivated Visual Perception," which contained the subtitle, "How We See What We Want to See," Balcetis examined how motivations constrain perceptual processing and highlighted three distinct ways in which the mind affected the body and vice versa:

- **Wishes bias the resolution of visual ambiguity**—In other words our expectation of what we want to see leads us to interpret what we see. This ties in directly to what we already know about how snipers use the environment around them to enhance their ability to take action and to hide by priming the mind. It relates to all the findings we have looked at regarding baseball players and other elite athletes. It helps explain how states of mental alertness can alter physical outcomes.

- **We can be taught to reduce cognitive dissonance which then changes perception and helps in the regulation of psychological states**—Trained snipers who accept hardship and difficulty as part of the mission display exactly this characteristic. Typically, what Balcetis's research uncovered was that by priming ordinary individuals to feel good about themselves (the positive self-talk that SEALs and elite Special Forces soldiers use), ordinary men and women not only perceive a difficult task as being easier, but they also perceive the effort required to complete it as being more manageable and much easier even when in actual fact they are working harder than ever.

- **We can be taught to narrow the focus of our attention on an object of desire and actually bring about the outcome we want as a result**—Snipers become masterfully adept at focusing their attention on the task at hand, excluding all distractions and engaging their minds fully in completing the task. Balcetis's research shows that this is not a sniper-exclusive trait. It is a capability, much like all the others we have looked at in this book, which anyone can develop. Excitingly, it is so simple to affect that it is like a small mantra of reaffirmation that can produce almost instant results.

What Emily Balcetis discovered was that the amount of visual information that we can focus on at any given time is relatively small when compared to what is actually available to us:

What we can see with great sharpness and clarity and accuracy is the equivalent of the surface area of our thumb on our outstretched arm. Everything else around that is blurry, rendering much of what is presented to our eyes as ambiguous. But we have to clarify and make sense of what it is that we see, and it's our mind that helps us fill in that gap. As a result, perception is a subjective experience, and that's how we end up seeing through our own mind's eye.

The connection between the mind and body happens through the way the brain sees rather than what the eyes see, and perception has the ability to neurochemically change the way the body performs through the activation of hormones and neurotransmitters. By taking ordinary people of various physical capabilities and priming them to think of themselves as capable and highly motivated to get fitter, Balcetis was able to illustrate that they showed considerable, measurable improvements in their physical and cognitive abilities when measured against a control group that had not been given the same priming.

Her analysis of the performance-enhancing differences showed that:

- People who committed to a manageable goal that they could accomplish in the near future, who believed that they were capable of meeting that goal, and who really thought they could accomplish it, performed better by almost 30 percent when compared to people who did not engage in this structured way of thinking and acting coupled with a strong sense of self-belief. Trained snipers are, of course, conditioned to believe in their capabilities. The US Marines drum into every recruit the sense of their own capabilities, teaching them to "walk tall" because they know that it leads to better judgment calls, better decisions, and better positive outcomes in the battlefield.

- Focus changes our subjective experience but it also changes the objective outcome of our performance. Being "in the zone," being mindful, being aware of our environments and everything we do makes the brain perform differently. This is then translated into improved, measurable performance at a cognitive and physical level in the real world.

- We can all teach ourselves to see the world differently through our mind's eye by training our brains to work in a more structured, controlled way and controlling the seemingly random pull-and-push of our emotions.

Emily Balcetis's simple tip for achieving all of this? It's a four-word mantra that allowed ordinary people that had never been trained by the military in their lives to exhibit enhanced performance in their daily tasks. What is it?

EYES ON THE PRIZE

That's all. A reminder to stay focused. To keep one's mind away from distractions, to engage fully with what is happening, to believe that one's capability is not restricted just by what one thinks he or she can physically do. To believe in one's ability to reduce even the most complex task into small, manageable steps that leads to the reward.

Mao Zedong, who became one of the founding fathers of the People's Republic of China, popularized the saying, "A journey of a thousand miles starts with a single step" as the Red Army began its military retreat (known as The Long March) that would begin his ascendancy to power. He adapted it from an earlier saying by sixth-century-BC Chinese philosopher Lao Tzu, which states: "Do the difficult things while they are easy and do the great things while they are small. A journey of a thousand miles must begin with a single step."

"Eyes on the Prize" is an intellectually elegant reminder to focus on what is really important to us. It acts like a mission statement that constantly filters the relevance of what we think and what we do. Tempting as it is to oversimplify things a little and present the reminder to stay focused as a trigger for our "software" to kick in, it doesn't quite work like that. Self-awareness, focus, and self-affirmation not only activate the "software" that runs us but they also change the "hardware," which in turn creates new opportunities for the software to control.

Sounds complicated? It is, until Amy Cuddy, social psychologist at Harvard University, explains it and then it becomes simple. Much of Cuddy's life's work has been spent on analyzing the impact of nonverbal behavior in communication. Her research examines how this type of behavior influences those on the receiving end (obviously), but she also looks at how nonverbal behavior influences the person who uses it.

In this regard Cuddy's work is different from most research being done in this field. It breaks away from the popular examination of power poses and how they affect the observer and looks at how the physical poses we assume change the chemistry of our brains and, over time, even our internal wiring so that from a neurobiological point of view we become different people.

In her many talks and research publications, Cuddy has provided evidence on how our minds change our bodies and our bodies then change our minds. She has amassed an impressive body of evidence showing that self-affirmative power poses and gestures that establish a sense of confidence in ourselves and make us feel more in control, even when we are not, are mirrored by chemical changes in the body which boost testosterone and reduce the levels of cortisol, the stress hormone, allowing us to be calmer and capable of thinking more clearly under stress. This also affects our ability to make critical decisions when they matter the most.

As Cuddy explained in her TED Talk on the way the minds of those who feel powerful affect their bodies and the way their bodies, in turn, influence their minds:

> I'm talking about thoughts and feelings and the sort of physiological things that make up our thoughts and feelings, and in my case, that's hormones. I look at hormones. So what do the minds of the powerful versus the powerless look like? So powerful people tend to be, not surprisingly, more assertive and more confident, more optimistic. They actually feel they're

going to win even at games of chance. They also tend to be able to think more abstractly. So there are a lot of differences. They take more risks. There are a lot of differences between powerful and powerless people. Physiologically, there also are differences on two key hormones: testosterone, which is the dominance hormone, and cortisol, which is the stress hormone.

Notice the part where those who feel less stress because their bodies produce smaller amounts of cortisol when they are under stress are better able to control their emotions and think in a broader context.

Cuddy's research findings mirror those of Lee Ann Harker and Dacher Keltner from the University of California, Berkeley, who analyzed college yearbook photographs to mine positive emotions and then correlate them with life and career outcomes thirty years later. What is impressive in the Harker and Keltner study is that the correlation of positive emotions to positive career and life outcomes much, much later appeared to be independent of looks and IQ skills.

Essentially, as Cuddy makes clear, "our bodies change our minds and our minds can change our behavior, and our behavior can change our outcomes." To all those who say, "Fake it, till you make it," Cuddy has this to say: "Fake it, till you become it." This makes sense. Because the brain does not have a "fake" and a "real" mechanism for expressing emotion and controlling the way it affects our thinking, faking it, over time, leads to incremental changes in our brain's wiring that become permanent.

The way snipers train, with small, repetitive tasks designed to build up their confidence with small successes until they begin to truly feel the part, is the military's more formalized way of transforming ordinary men and women with ordinary doubts, fears, and uncertainties, into highly motivated, focused professionals who are capable of performing at an exceptionally high level.

This is, as it happens, exactly what businesses have always wanted to achieve with their staffs.

THE BUSINESS CASE

Outwardly American Express and the United States Air Force have nothing in common. Yet, coming into the twenty-first century, both organizations suffered a common attrition problem. The United States Air Force was seeing a high level of first-year recruit turnover, leading to a waste of resources and a shortage of good pilots. American Express was also seeing a high level of attrition in customer-focused sales associates, with many failing to make the grade after a short time on the team. It too was experiencing a waste of valuable resources and a drop in customer numbers.

To counter their problem, both organizations turned to emotional intelligence as a marker and approached the issue in a similar way. In order to quantify the levels of personal and social competence of their people, they put each of them through a fifteen-point assessment:

- Self-regard
- Emotional self-awareness
- Assertiveness
- Independence
- Self-actualization
- Empathy

- Social responsibility
- Interpersonal skills
- Stress tolerance
- Impulse control
- Reality testing
- Resourcefulness
- Problem solving
- Optimism
- Happiness

Unsurprisingly, those who scored high in both personal and social competence in each organization went on to also become the best recruiters and sales associates, respectively. There is a clear, persistent pattern between the "soft skills" that snipers learn to develop and the positive outcomes they achieve using the "hard skills" they are trained in as part of their job. The same applies, as evidenced by the example with American Express, with business.

Successful commercial organizations succeed in the tricky task of human communication within their internal structures. They manage to make their employees feel included, needed, and valued. When employees understand the role they play and its relevance to the bottom line, they begin to act with the dedication and focus of trained elite soldiers: they become mission-specific in their work and keep in mind the outcome they expect. Their eyes are very much on the prize.

In the transfer of skills, experience, and knowledge that takes place from military training to a commercial setting, there are seven personal qualities that stand out that lead to better decision-making and positive outcomes. Every successful sniper has them.

Altogether they form the seven key requirements at the core of every elite performance under difficult conditions.

THE SEVEN KEY REQUIREMENTS

One British sniper, whom we shall call Ed, who served with the Royal Marines in Iraq and Afghanistan explains the motivation that drives elite performers in this unique group of men:

I joined the army because it was all I could do. Did my time for a while and then trained to become a Royal Marine sniper. I did one tour of duty in Iraq and then I was in Afghanistan ranging with the Brigade Reconnaissance Force before things became as bad as they are now and I retired due to an injury sustained in combat. The conditions we were in were rough. Patrols were always potentially dangerous. My second tour was hell. Yet I miss it. I miss the sense of camaraderie with the lads. The knowledge that we had each other's backs which is hard to find outside the army. I have thought since. A lot. Why? What drives us. When you're a sniper the world looks different. Places become potential hiding holes. Social settings are awkward because your brain is constantly assessing the threat level and it's hard to dial it back. It took me three years to start settling down after I came back. To feel normal again. Why a sniper? Because we all want the same thing. All of us. We never say it. Not to anyone else. Not even ourselves. But we want it. To be the best. The very best we can ever be. We hold this gun and we look through the sights and we feel everything else fade away. All that remains then is the gun, the target, the shot,

the decisions you will make. The world stops for everything else.
We are alone in it then and things make more sense. I wanted,
always, to just be the best I could ever be.

To count, to matter, to understand, to have a purpose that gives the world meaning are values businesses have long been searching for. Some of them, like Zappos for instance, the shoes, apparel, and eyewear company owned by Amazon, have managed to achieve it by establishing organizational principles within the company that are very similar to the horizontal command structure of the Special Air Service (SAS).

Others, like the John Lewis Partnership in the United Kingdom or W. L. Gore & Associates (the makers of the Gore-Tex brand), have created complex internal communication structures designed to help keep everyone within the organization engaged, responsible, and accountable.

When we map the sniper mind's toolbox directly onto what would be required in a business setting seven key requirements emerge as core:

- **Excellent task capability**—Anyone running a business has to have an encyclopedic understanding of it. A software entrepreneur, for instance, must understand the capabilities and limitations of code even if he cannot code himself. A linen retailer would need to know everything there is about linen that makes his business different from anyone else's and is relevant to his customers. A writer who doesn't understand his genre will never be able to rise in his or her career irrespective of how well he or she can write. Task capability is job-specific. It requires an understanding of the hard skills that make a person competent to do their job and it requires a commitment to keeping that skill set current.

- **Great people skills**—Even if you're working on your own from home, there will be some tasks that will require you to reach out to peers, competitors, or suppliers. Those who do not have people skills that allow them to navigate these issues successfully will stumble unnecessarily. Successful relationship building requires many soft skills, such as empathy, that are key to social competence and offer a better way to function in social groups.

- **Emotionally stable**—Emotional self-awareness, impulse control, and arousal control are as key to enterprise as they are to snipers in the field. Properly harnessed emotions can aid in motivation, clarity of thought, and decisiveness of action. Self-knowledge and a keen sense of mission and identity are as crucial to today's business executives working in a fluid, challenging, and changing marketplace as to a sniper working on a mission with variables he cannot control, a ticking deadline, and the pressures of successfully completing his task.

- **Smart and keenly observant**—Knowledge, experience, and good observation skills are critical to helping a mind that needs to make a decision fast by picking the best one from all the available choices that present themselves in the circumstances. In business, just like on the battlefield, intelligence, observation, and the ability to "put two and two together" are elements that can lead to success. Snipers constantly hone their observation skills and they constantly work on and update their store of knowledge. Successful businesses evolve because the people inside them evolve, which, in a sense, is very much like the creed of trained snipers: "Adapt. Overcome."

- **Situational awareness**—No sniper goes into any situation with his eyes shut or his mind asleep. For a businessperson this skill translates into a close understanding of industry trends and the dynamic pressures that are in play. The vision in our heads (our mind's eye that Balcetis talks about) is what gives us the edge when it comes to dealing with adversity, demonstrating resilience, and exhibiting flexibility, ingenuity, and innovative thinking.

- **Good at picking directions**—Critical decision-making in business, life, and the military is about choosing paths in decision trees. Whether you are deciding where to travel over enemy territory or are setting annual directives for the e-commerce department, you will require the ability to decide with clarity and conviction and not get lost or be distracted by details. The implicit theories and beliefs we develop as individuals are key to how we then behave in complex situations.

- **Patience**—Patience requires self-awareness, critical thinking, and focus. It requires the ability to use a host of soft and hard skills, including exercising impulse control and arousal control to defer gratification in order to get the job done right. Of all the soft skills that snipers are taught this is the one they learn to prize the most in retrospect. Being patient allows them to be calmer and make better decisions under pressure. It's the "keeping of one's head" that Rudyard Kipling was on about in "If—."

Stanford University psychologist Carol Dweck has conducted research which shows that success in business and life comes down to mind-set. Those who maintain an open, learning, ever developing outlook and use positive reinforcement to help themselves stay positive do better in life and enjoy successful careers. Using emotional intelligence, the ability to reflect inward and constantly reassess where we are has become the modus operandi apparently of those who achieve measurable success in today's very challenging world.

THE SNIPER SKILL ACQUISITION LIST

In this chapter you learned:

- Emotional intelligence is the "secret sauce" that enhances every set of hard skills.
- There are four branches to emotional intelligence which allow us to understand how to develop it.
- How we see the world is critical to our decision-making processes.
- There is a simple directive we can give to ourselves to help us clarify our thinking, focus better, and make better decisions.
- At a basic level businesses today face the same challenging, fluid conditions that snipers meet in the field and they demand the same knowledgeable, adaptive approach that snipers have been taught to apply.

*Obstacles are those frightful things you see when you
take your eyes off your goal.*
——HENRY FORD

12

Performance: Build Perfect Outcomes from Improbable Situations by Learning How to Overcome Every Obstacle

WHEN YOU'RE A PERSON HOLDING a rifle, even if that rifle is the L42A1 sniper rifle, a Drummond Class corvette is a fearsome sight to behold. At 260 feet in length it is almost as long as a football field and it weighs 1,320 tons at full load, about as much as 721 Jeep Cherokees piled on top of each other. Its upper deck bristles with armaments including four MM38 Exocet anti-ship missiles, a 100 mm/55 Mod.1968 dual purpose gun, twin Bofors 40 mm L/70 AA guns, two 20 mm Oerlikon AA guns, two .50 cal Colt M2 machine guns, and two triple 324 mm ILAS-3 tubes (WASS A-244S torpedoes). It has enough firepower to mount an effective antiaircraft role and simultaneously defend or attack coastal fortifications.

By comparison the L42A1 is just 3 feet 6 inches in length and weighs 9.7 pounds. Its 7.62 millimeter caliber has a ten-round magazine and an effective range of just 800 yards. Based on the Lee-Metford rifle of 1888, it was the Royal Marines and RAF

Fig 12.1 ARA Guerrico in 2005 at Mar del Plata naval base.

Regiment sniper rifle from 1970 until 1985, when it was retired as being insufficiently powerful for a modern battlefield. Pictures of it show that with its now quaint wooden stock it looks more like a hunting rifle than an instrument of war.

In an engagement that lasted ten weeks in 1982, Argentina and the United Kingdom went to war against each other in the South Atlantic over two British overseas territories: the Falkland Islands and South Georgia and the South Sandwich Islands. The conflict began on Friday, April 2, 1982, when Argentina invaded and occupied the Falkland Islands (and, the following day, South Georgia and the South Sandwich Islands) in an attempt to establish the sovereignty it had claimed over them. It was in the invasion of South Georgia that a war corvette would be pitted against a sniper rifle in a desperate struggle for supremacy.

Fig 12.2 The L42A1 sniper rifle looks more like the kind of starter gun you buy for Christmas than the fearsome instrument of war it is.

The struggle began when on April 3, 1982, Argentine forces landed on South Georgia. The island used to be a whaling station, now fallen into disuse. The only command post there was Shackleton House, part of the buildings of the British Antarctic Survey station, overlooking King Edward Point, the capital of the island and also the port below it. It was manned by a detachment of twenty-two Royal Marines, among them Command Sergeant Major Peter J. Leach, who was the platoon's sniper, armed with the L242A1 sniper rifle.

The Royal Marines had arrived there a few days earlier and had dug in, preparing to defend the island from the Argentine military. When it became apparent to the Argentinian commander that the marines were putting up too much of a spirited defense to allow his troops to move from the harbor where they'd been air-dropped via helicopter to the station, he called in the corvette, the *Guerrico*, to move in to join the battle and quickly settle the matter. The ship's commanding officer, Captain Carlos Luís Alfonso responded swiftly, steering the *Guerrico* into the cove and preparing to engage the Royal Marines, but he had to operate at low speed because of the presence of thick kelp patches near the point. Nevertheless, Captain Alfonso crept into position and his crewmen readied their weapons: 20-millimeter guns mounted on both the port and starboard sides of the ship, a twin 40-millimeter mount just aft of the bridge, and the ship's primary armament, a turret-mounted 100-millimeter gun on the forward deck.

The combat report of the engagement gives an almost minute-by-minute account of what happened next:

> At 11:55 a.m. the starboard 20-millimeter gun opened fire on King Edward Point, but it only got off two rounds before mal-functioning. One minute later the twin 40-millimeter mount opened fire, but it did not manage much better: the left barrel failed after just four shots, and the right barrel's extractor failed after only five. Then at 11:59 a.m., when the ship was approximately 550 meters from the point, the Royal Marines opened fire. Machine gun fire began striking Guerrico. Bullets shattered the starboard window of the bridge and penetrated the ship's radio shack. As the gunners on the twin 40-millimeter were attempting to clear their jams, marine Steve Parsons had a clear shot at them with his L4A4 Bren gun. He aimed center-mass on one of the crewmen and fired an opening burst, but it fell short. Seeing the splash of the rounds, Parsons elevated his point of aim, and fired again with short, controlled bursts. Bullets from his Bren struck the mount, wounding two and killing Petty Officer Patricio Guanca.

The corvette's battle-readiness was under question and this evened the odds a little as the ship moved against the dug-in marines. As all the action was going on the ship's 100-millimeter main gun fired one round, but then experienced a failure of its loading mechanism as a result of accumulated salt deposits that there had been no time to clean after the ship's rough crossing to reach South Georgia quickly from the Argentina mainland.

While the gun's crew struggled to get the loading mechanism running again, one of the Royal Marines fired another light anti-tank weapon (LAW) rocket that hit the turret, exploded, and jammed its elevation mechanism.

Then Royal Marine Dave S. Combes fired a shot from the squad's other anti-tank weapon: the L14A1 84-millimeter Carl Gustav recoilless rifle. The shell streaked toward its target at 800 f.p.s., skipped once on the surface of the water, ricocheted into the ship's hull, and exploded.

The explosion ripped a hole in the corvette's starboard side. Within minutes of entering the narrow point the *Guerrico* passed behind the buildings of the British Antarctic Survey station and out of the field of fire of the marines. In a matter of a few minutes, the corvette had taken over one thousand rounds that had impaired its fighting capability. It had suffered casualties in its crew and had a hole in its side, and all from an infantry unit of Royal Marines who were lightly armed. But the battle was far from over.

Shallow waters on either side of the narrow channel that the *Guerrico* used to approach King Edward Point had prevented the ship from maneuvering, and this meant that Captain Alfonso was irreversibly committed to entering the cove. He continued ahead with a gaping hole in his starboard side from the anti-tank weapon hit.

Although the first round had not gone to Captain Alfonso's advantage he knew that a warship gives you an incredible advantage

Fig 12.3 This photograph shows King Edward Point and the buildings of the British Antarctic Survey station as they appeared in November 2008. Shackleton House once stood on the narrow plateau directly beyond the red roofs at right.

regardless. A graduate of the Argentine Naval Academy's class of 1958, he had served previously aboard the cruiser *Belgrano*, the minesweeper *Chaco*, and the destroyers *Buenos Aires* and *Rosales*, so he was neither inexperienced nor reckless. His decision to run the gauntlet again was a measured calculation. Believing it to be the best course of action, Captain Alfonso cleared the bridge and gave the order to once more go past the command point where the Royal Marines lay waiting.

As the plume of smoke indicated that the *Guerrico* was about to return, the Royal Marines braced themselves. At that point, thirty-seven-year-old Command Sergeant Major Peter J. Leach left his position from the dug-in defenses in the grass outside and ran into Shackleton House. Once inside, he climbed the stairs to the second floor and rushed down the hall to the end of the building facing Grytviken. Then, using the butt of his rifle, Leach broke out the glass of a corner window and dragged a table into the middle of the room, creating a handy sniper platform for himself. By 1982, Leach had been in the service for nineteen years and was a veteran of combat tours in Borneo, Northern Ireland, and Cyprus. In that moment of crisis his decision-making process was in high gear. He had calmly assessed the situation and was looking to do what snipers do best: act as force multipliers.

Lying on the table on the second floor, the sergeant major took aim directly on the approaching ship's bridge. By then, the *Guerrico* was once again facing the channel and closing on King Edward Point. A moment later, as the other Royal Marines began hammering away at the ship for a second time, Sergeant Major Leach began firing carefully aimed shots at the vessel. He directed his opening rounds at the five windows across the front of the bridge. At this point, only Captain Alfonso, the helmsman, and the quartermaster were manning that station as glass began to shatter all around them. The three men were forced to crouch down behind the ship's structures to avoid being struck by the rapid succession of accurate shots coming from Leach's sniper rifle. The effect was crucial. With its 100-millimeter gun stuck due to the rocket fire it had received, Captain Alfonso was hoping to use the ship to aim the weapon. But that required standing at the bridge and relaying precise direction to the engine room in conjunction with the gun's crew.

With the bridge taking in lethal sniper fire, this was now out of the question.

As the *Guerrico* moved behind the cover of the buildings of the British Antarctic Survey station the Marines had to disengage

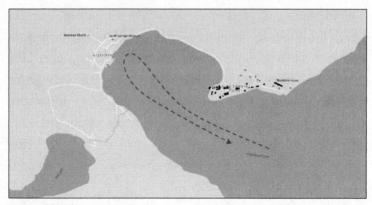

Fig 12.4 King Edward Cove. The dotted line shows the path taken by the *Guerrico*. The boxes show the defense positions taken by the Royal Marines and the cross on the left of Shackleton House indicates the position initially occupied by Command Sergeant Major Peter J. Leach.

their fire but Sergeant Major Leach, who no longer had a shot, seized that opportunity to run to another vantage point from which he could see the ship again. He took up another firing position and resumed harassing firing at the *Guerrico*, this time at the three windows on the port side of the ship's bridge. There was more glass being shattered and deadly bullets flying as Leach rained down more well-aimed sniper fire on the quartermaster, the helmsman, and Captain Alfonso. Then the *Guerrico* came out from behind the British Antarctic Survey station buildings, and the rest of the Royal Marines opened up once again. They raked the ship from stem to stern with another barrage of automatic weapons fire, and Dave Combes launched a second 84-millimeter round from the light anti-tank weapon. That round slammed into the *Guerrico*'s Exocet anti-ship missile launcher, knocking it out of commission. During the last few moments, as the ship retreated out of small-arms range, Leach moved to yet another window on the second floor of Shackleton House, and threw a few parting shots at the *Guerrico* as it limped past King Edward Point. In just fifteen minutes of combat a warship had gone from being an intimidating, well-armed presence to being a damaged hull, listing to one side as it retreated from the soldiers. Leach's precision firing at the bridge of the ship had blinded it during the crucial moments when it could have brought its big guns to bear and blasted the marines' positions, and it had most likely demoralized its crew with the proximity of well-placed lethal sniper fire.

Despite their victory over the warship, the Royal Marines still had to contend with the Argentinian soldiers on the ground and casualties of their own. In the end it was the latter that decided it for them. In order to get medical aid for wounded comrades they surrendered. They were transported to Argentina and repatriated soon after. The war would end not long after that with Britain declared the victor.

For his role in keeping the warship busy and ineffective during those critical moments in what is now called the Battle of Grytviken, Sergeant Major Leach was awarded the Distinguished Service Medal.

If there ever was an instance of building positive outcomes out of an improbable situation and incredible odds the moment Sergeant Major Leach took on a warship armed with a sniper rifle has to be it. It was not just a case of David versus Goliath. It was a case of flesh and blood versus a mountain of steel. Just how this kind of mental fortitude can be applied to other situations is part of a special kind of science.

THE SCIENCE: There is a neural basis to the attentional networks we employ as adults which is directly linked to the training we subject ourselves to and the habits we create and then put into effect.

IT'S ALL ABOUT ATTENTION

Throughout this book we have seen numerous instances of elite athletes and elite soldiers and they all share the same characteristics: the activation of neural pathways in their heads allow them to "see" what is going on, to perceive it, at a deeper level, much earlier than their conscious brains become aware of it.

Adding to all those instances comes one more body of research using fMRI techniques that quantifies everything we've been through to this point. Namely that the ability to do extraordinary things begins with the development of attentional networks in the mind. We cannot do something if we cannot first perceive it. To perceive it we have to be able to sense it and evaluate it in the context of our activities. The paradox is that deep perception and subliminal sensing take place well below the conscious threshold of our minds.

We saw in the University of California's Social Cognitive Neuroscience Lab study that social media posts that go viral are powered by the deep belief their creators have in their value to their intended audience.

There are deep implications in all this on how we capture someone's attention in a commercial context like the Web, when even our own conscious attention levels can mislead us. The implication is that anyone in business is responsible not just for their own development but also for the development of their audience. The connections and conversations that take place then happen in a shared, possibly even cocreated, space. This constitutes what we would formally call a framework, an organized system connecting those who sell, in our example, with those who buy. Both subgroups constituting the whole. Both subgroups engaged in a journey of mutually beneficial development and change.

Researchers from the department of psychiatry at the Mount Sinai School of Medicine in New York, and the department of cognitive neurology at the University Hospital Aachen in Germany, looked at fMRI scans of adults and children between the ages of eight and twelve and discovered that "behaviorally, children exhibited a numerically smaller alerting effect and significantly larger invalidity (reorienting) and interference (executive control of attention) effects." In other words younger brains did not yet have in place the complex neural pathways that allowed their brains to focus on the things that mattered to them easily.

The researchers discovered that children had to think harder and use up a lot more parts of the brain to make sense of information that adult brains found easier to absorb and react to. The researchers also noted that:

Functional group differences overlapped with structural group differences in gray matter volume in particular within the frontal polar areas. The data suggest that there is a transition from functional yet immature systems supporting attentional functions in children to the more definitive adult networks and that the differences observed may reflect both developmental changes in cognitive strategies and morphology.

As we get older and, arguably, wiser our brains develop both functionally (that is, the mental heuristics we employ to create lightning-fast reactions to specific stimuli) and structurally (we have more complex, associative networks in our brains, borne out of practice and experience).

We've sort of circled back. This is the area Amy Cuddy and Emily Balcetis have mapped so well with the brain and body engaged in a dance of constant change as one feeds back to the other and each responds to the signals it receives. The fMRI research on the importance of attentional networks within our brains highlights the power of self-awareness to change how we think, what we think, and who we become.

If we truly want to be able to make decisions that make us proud in moments that define us, we need to understand how we fit in the context of our personal reality and what contribution our skill set can make to the moment.

THE BUSINESS CASE

Michael Janke, former Navy SEAL sniper and current chairman of Silent Circle, an encrypted communications company, has frequently answered questions openly on Quora about the skill set overlap between CEOs and snipers. In a 2012 exchange, he also explained how being a sniper provides you with a set of complementary skills that any CEO would give their eyeteeth to possess. These include being able to support your team and make sure they perform their very best; to subdue your ego; to be able to cut distractions out so that getting to your goal becomes possible; to deal with rapid change without being fazed by it or giving in to panic; and to use the motto of every sniper: "Adapt. Overcome."

> *The ability to not have an ego in the game at hand and not make the mission, goal or success, "about me," but rather about everyone else. To use your power only when the moment is required . . .*

This is again the transfer of skills from one setting to another. Mark Divine, another former Navy SEAL and now a leadership coach, says, "Many SEALs are average guys, but they learn an unusual level of discipline and a different way of thinking, looking at the world and achieving their goals." When all the elements of elite military training and mental conditioning are working together, there is virtually no situation which cannot be handled to provide a positive outcome.

To get things done, to keep their eyes on the prize, trained snipers use a four-step approach that is drummed into them during training until it becomes second nature:

- Plan
- Execute
- Reassess plan
- Execute

This is a rhythm of working that combines the best of achievement motivation and aggression with the best of judgment and forethought. In many ways this is how snipers teach themselves to operate. Trained operatives, snipers especially, know that in every mission they undertake there will be a multitude of details, each of which will be a problem of some kind. Some of them will be due to external factors (the terrain, the weather, the people, the day) which the sniper can do nothing to affect. Others come because of mission issues (the difficulty, changes in plans, unforeseen circumstances). The point is that nothing is like the movies where the sniper is tasked with his mission and he then has to simply go ahead and heroically execute it. The small obstacles always get in the way.

One small obstacle is perhaps easy to overcome. Two will also be dealt with swiftly. Three become part of a problem-solving pattern. If the small obstacles keep accumulating, however, ordinary people stop, their task becomes "impossible," their focus is drained, and their determination wanes. You then get a myriad of excuses surfacing. To the average person each of these appears "good enough" to not follow through with what they have to do, to abort their plan, to fail their "mission."

Snipers and elite Special Forces operatives also experience the same cognitive load as details accumulate, changes are made, and plans often need to be adjusted on the fly. The difference between them and everyone else is that they have trained themselves to successfully deal with this accumulation of details. They have developed the personal strategies that allow them to successfully face each difficulty, overcome it, and make it part of a success pattern rather than a perceived accumulation of events that will cause them to fail.

Like most things that snipers and Special Forces operatives are trained to do, this too, is a mental trick. It requires strategies that take into account human psychology and positive thinking. It demands the ability to successfully compartmentalize discomfort, editing it out of the picture as deferred gratification demands focus on the task at hand first.

Faced with an issue, snipers use their training to break down a task into its particular areas through a relatively straightforward four-step process:

- Identify the problem.
- Formulate a plan of action to tackle it.
- Evaluate it.
- Reformulate it if necessary.

These then become the primary tools for taking stock and regaining control of complex situations that often appear to be spiraling out of control. While the methodology is simple, the application is not. While business life is every bit as challenging as the military, the differences in the details of each theater of operations is sufficient to frequently cloud the benefits of transfer of skills. As a result an opportunity is lost.

Reduced to basics both business and the military operate in the same way. They both worry about future outcomes and they both crave control over the present. They both believe that by controlling the present better they can reduce the uncertainty of the future.

CRAVING CONTROL

At the former Yale Center for Anxiety and Mood Disorders at Yale University, Douglas Mennin used to spend a lot of time listening to people's worries about the future and then studying the neural pathways of their brains. He believes that worry, the negative thoughts we all have about the future, evolved as a constructive problem-solving behavior that provides us with a competitive advantage. Those who succeed in adequately preparing for a future event succeed in surviving and become more successful.

In the modern world, however, our brains can go on a loop with worry creating three different responses: overthinking, avoidance of negative outcomes, and inhibition of emotions. While these may sound like highly desirable approaches, here's what usually happens to us: Because we are highly intelligent, the analytical parts of our brains refuse to believe that too much of a good thing may not be even better. So we believe that by overthinking and fretting over every detail, we are achieving greater control of the future and reducing its uncertainty.

Instead, excessive worry (the thought-driven aspect) overloads us cognitively, which leads to a feeling of being incapable of managing a situation. This then links our worry with anxiety (the emotional element). So instead of thinking more analytically, overthinking and anxiety overstimulate the fear processing areas in our brains, releasing more of the stress hormone cortisol but without offering any outlet as the imagined threat is imaginary.

Reeling under a double whammy for which we can produce no action plan, both our mental and physical functions overload. Our brains experience confusion and uncertainty, their higher cognitive functions become disrupted, and our bodies are overwhelmed with cortisol.

Normally, worry would galvanize us. It would prepare us mentally for the typical flight-or-fight response, and the mental planning and visualizing we've done would make us confident of our ability to deal with the future. But this is not what happens.

Brain scans show that worriers exhibit increased activity in areas of the brain associated with executive functions, such as planning, reasoning, and impulse control, hindering rather than helping those processes, and because they are worrying and their brains are overstimulated and preoccupied, they miss signs of actual danger.

Because our brains try to protect themselves from the constant stress of worrying they dial down our emotional responses to stimuli. As a result our excess fretting reduces activity in the sympathetic nervous system in response to a threat. This branch of the nervous system normally allows our bodies to react quickly to impending danger by accelerating breathing and also increasing heart rate to oxygenate muscles for fight or flight.

Researchers now believe that the brain activity in non-anxious people may be evidence of an "early subconscious warning mechanism," which keeps them cool, calm, and collected. And they are better able to deal with complex adversity.

Historically, the military has always been better than businesses at training its people how to achieve this. It has been the one organization that acknowledges the importance of soft skills. It is the military which has also created a structured approach to acquiring them, practicing them, and sustaining them. When businesses do invest in acquiring similar skills by investing, for example, in corporate retreats that promote the building of leadership skills and inward reflection, they fail to provide a structured, supportive framework to help maintain them afterward. The few exceptions to this, like Zappos and W. L. Gore & Associates, only prove the rule.

So, where do we go from here? In the best possible world, businesses will begin to adapt in order to overcome the multitude of challenges facing them today. They will begin to truly invest in their people and prize each one as an individual with a fully developed role, contributing to the bottom line. They will begin to foster mindful engagement with work and full participation. They will train, develop, and shelter their people the same way as the military does.

It won't happen any time soon. We are still in a command-and-control world where bottom-line politics and short-term profits determine the day. And though businesses often like to borrow freely from the language of the military, calling their staff "troops" and describing work as "being in the trenches," they are unlikely to truly shift mentality quickly, not because they do not really want to but because they cannot move fast enough.

Large, global businesses will change slowly because change is costly and it is frightening and those caught up in it resist it. Smaller businesses will move way faster, but they usually tend to use larger businesses as a benchmark to emulate because they see their size and manpower and market share and think that their model of governance is what they should be aiming for. So they end up giving up, very quickly, the things that make them competitive in the first place: their close-knit sense of community, their sense of shared purpose and common mission, and their agility in bringing it about.

While this may not sound too hopeful, I would not have written this book if I did not already see signs of change. The marketplace is unforgiving. It demands mindfulness, responsibility, initiative, accountability, intelligence, and flexibility. It demands, in short, the highly adaptive behavior of the trained sniper's mind. Businesses that fail to heed the call will find themselves falling increasingly behind. Both businesses and the military accept that they now require skills that cannot be mass produced and individuals that are not easy to find.

This calls for people who can consistently and persistently employ and use adaptive thinking. In "Special Warfare Study," a commissioned report written for the US Army, adaptive thinking is defined as

> consisting of competencies such as negotiation and consensus building skills, the ability to communicate effectively, analyze ambiguous situations, be self-aware, think innovatively, and critically use effective problem solving skills. Each of these competencies is an essential element of leader development training for the US Army Special Forces.

We now need business people with warrior mind-sets not because business has become any more competitively difficult than at any other time in the past, but because, just like in war, the landscape has shifted. Armies no longer array themselves in rows in front of each other firing blind volleys in a massed body of men, victory belonging to those with the biggest guns, the most bodies, and the fewest casualties. Businesses can no longer rely on the power of their advertising budgets and the glossiness of their packaging to convince a shifting, fragmented, and intelligent audience to buy from them.

Modern armies and modern businesses act in an environment that has them dealing directly with their competitors, building bridges and relationships with the people they intend to help, and winning hearts and minds in order to win the battles that will lead to the winning of the "war." Both the military and businesses now need to redefine "victory" and reimagine success.

Because the complexity of each of us as individuals is a microcosm of the world around us, the first battle we fight which we need to win is always with ourselves. Everything we have learned in this book is equally applicable to one person living his life, running a business, carving a place for himself in the world, as it is for a start-up, a small business, or an international conglomerate.

The US and British armies have so recognized the value of the sniper mind that they have begun a pilot program intended to train all their active troops to have sniper mind skills: reconnaissance, observation, critical thinking, and, of course, sharpshooting.

Today, in business, we are in dire need of corporate warriors that will embrace and then fully live the warrior mentality. Business, just like sniping is, above all, a mind game.

There remain but few more dots to join. One of them is: How do we prepare ourselves to recognize and adequately respond to the psychological traps that lie ahead of us? There are traps and issues for which there can never be adequate training.

Brett Steenbarger, who's written a book on the psychology of trading on the stock exchange called *The Psychology of Trading: Tools and Techniques for Minding the Markets*, points out how sniper skills are desirable for cool-headed decision-making when it comes to trading:

> *One of my favorite posters in my office is of a military sniper in the field, peering out from ground cover. The caption beneath the picture reads, "The sniper's greatest weapon is a sharply honed intellect. He combines a mastery of stealth, situational awareness, ballistics and precision shooting skills into one of*

the most lethal weapon systems to ever strike fear into the enemy."

If the sniper became too aggressive and excessively bored with sitting in the field waiting for the right shot, he might leap from his cover and begin spraying the enemy with fire. Most of the shots would probably go wild, and the out-of-control sniper would quickly be located and mowed down.

No, the sniper waits for the ideal shot: "stealth" and "situational awareness" are essential tools of the trade. Being a sniper means combining aggression with exquisite self-control and judgment. It is controlled aggression.

Interestingly Steenbarger uses a four-step pattern to create a rhythm of work not unlike that of the trained sniper:

Plan. Trade. Reassess plan. Trade: It's a rhythm that combines the best of achievement motivation and aggression with the best of judgment and forethought.

AVOIDING AND EVADING PSYCHOLOGICAL TRAPS

The American Psychological Association has played a key part in developing credible responses to threat assessment. The aim of the Threat Assessment Plan (TAP) is to identify a potentially dangerous situation, or the moment when things begin to go wrong and begin its containment long before it develops into something bigger.

For project managers, CEOs, and entrepreneurs, this is a mission-critical skill. All too often great projects, excellent marketing campaigns, and brilliant product development plans go awry because small details that were either ignored as being of no consequence or were simply completely overlooked, give rise to circumstances that can derail everything.

In my opinion, a classic example of this was when Google, which had an excellent relationship with the former European Union competition commissioner Joaquín Almunia, seemingly failed to recognize that his successor was entirely different and was unlikely to rubber-stamp the report of her predecessor. Indeed facts show that, once Margrethe Vestager took over, Google found itself in one anti-competition probe after another, with suggestions being that the search engine's behavior in Europe was unfairly promoting its own products and harming consumer interests as a result.

Did Google executives slip into a culture of relaxation where they believed they had done enough to prevent any issues arising in the EU and derailing their plans and the smoothness of their operations there? It is always easier to read things in hindsight and while this is pure conjecture on my part, it is likely, especially when we take into account the fact that up to that point things had been going smoothly and there were no red flags to immediately create an alert situation. Could they have avoided it by approaching it differently right from the start? Again, this is conjecture, but given the amount of talent and raw brainpower available to the company, the answer from my perspective is yes, they could have.

The principle is simple enough to be taught to anyone on the fly and robust enough to be adaptable in almost any kind of situation and organization. The principle is simple enough: nothing takes place in a vacuum. Nothing is instant and sudden.

It consists of three steps, called functions:

- **Identify**—In order to identify a potential threat people need to know when, how, and where to report concerns and what criteria to use. This requires clear thinking, great communication, and the establishment of common frameworks within the community or organization. For this stage to succeed, engagement with the people involved is a must.
- **Assess**—The next step in a threat assessment is gathering and evaluating information from multiple sources. That involves planning, coordination, and cooperation of everyone involved. It requires the acknowledgment of common goals and the development of specific skill sets so that everyone involved is operating more or less at the same level.
- **Manage**—More often than not, an assessment reveals a manageable underlying issue that needs to be handled. Tact, intelligence, critical judgment, and initiative are all called upon at this stage.

Like everything else we looked at here, the apparent simplicity of the statements hides a wealth of details.

We live in a world where approximations and generalizations no longer serve us very well. Warfare, medicine, business, sports science, and health are becoming increasingly personalized affairs. They are but the tip of the iceberg. The question that's facing us as we stand with our backs against the wall, looking out is, "How?" How can we make sense of it all? How can we make the right decisions at the right time? How can we ensure that we do not falter when we most need not to?

In every chapter in this book we saw how others do it. We

looked at what science tells us about the new skills and how they affect us. We learned how to apply what army snipers, Rangers, Green Berets, and Navy SEALs are learning to apply.

In all of these we take steps forward that, incrementally, improve us. We become better versions of ourselves. It is not easy. But "easy" has never served us well. Every time something was easy, we only deferred the price that would eventually have to be paid, the cost that would inevitably apply.

In Frank Herbert's award-winning sci-fi series that has become known as the *Dune* books, one of the characters blithely reminds herself that "too much knowledge never makes for simple decisions."

This has been a journey of knowledge so you can learn to make better decisions, not simple ones.

THE SNIPER SKILL ACQUISITION LIST

In this chapter you learned:

- Where we divert our attention determines what we think is important to us.
- Our brains and the executive decisions we make are only as good as our functional and structural makeup.
- Worry does not set us free and it doesn't even prepare us for the future.
- Navy SEALs use a simple four-step process to tackle each situation they face, as it arises.
- In business, as in personal life, the processes we apply to minimize threats is the same. Only the scale will be different.

AFTERWORD

The world is gripped by sniper-mania. The box office success of *American Sniper*, which chronicles the life of the late Chris Kyle, has made being a sniper sexy again. Yet, despite the popularity of the idea, snipers are still regarded with a sense of suspicion and a sense of mistrust. The very things that make them special also make them different, and being different singles them out from the fold.

The military annals are full of instances of incredible bravery and sacrifice displayed by snipers in action. The data we have on their careers confirms what we already know about them. As fighting units they are among the most effective in any armed force and always have been so. As people they appear to be exceptional in their humility, disposition, and ability to perform well under pressure.

Snipers also appear to be exceptional in their performance. They are the ultimate product of a fusion of soft and hard skills that is really hard to find. As such, they are capable of enduring extremes of cold and heat, hunger and thirst. They are incredibly aware of their surroundings, supremely confident in their own abilities, and singularly focused on the task they have to perform. There are countless instances throughout the literature of war where a single sniper, embarking on a secret mission, the details of which he would find out en route, would have to improvise, operate beyond any hope of support from his own side, and yet still manage to carry out his mission and then, even more incredibly, return home unharmed, even though the enemy he left behind was agitated and actively looking for him.

It is this superhuman aspect of the sniper, alongside the obviously awe-inspiring capability to hit targets accurately from miles away, that most captures our attention. Yet, now we also have a body of evidence that shows us how the brain works. We know that being exceptional does not have to be rare. We've learned that being focused and effective, capable of harnessing the power of the mind to focus attention and complete a difficult task on time and to a high level of performance, need not be the preserve of those who have undergone simulated torture, who have endured near drowning, who have gone for days with little food and little sleep, while being subjected to cold and being tormented by fatigue. All of these are elements of Fort Bragg's sniper training school and are encountered during the infamous Hell Week, about a fifth of the way into sniper training.

All of these methods and physical trials, hard as they may sound, are just tools. They are the tools the army has traditionally used to help it shape the minds of its men and unlock their potential. There are other ways. And it is the army that has actually, again, pioneered them.

Snipers can do what they can because of their brains. If we know anything about the human brain, it is that it is incredibly powerful. Its uniqueness lies in the fact that it can be taught to do virtually anything. When neuroscience gives us the ability to peer deep into the brain's workings and actually see it in action, we realize that it is possible to learn to replicate its mental states. It is possible to be taught to achieve almost anything we can imagine: the single-minded focus of a sniper looking to hit a target over a mile away, the calmness of a Buddhist monk lost deep in meditation, the contemplation of the balance of the forces of the universe, the concentration of a fighter pilot juggling the instrument panel and complex conditions to land his plane on an aircraft carrier in the middle of an ocean.

What the data is showing us is that when we replicate those mental states, we are possessed of abilities that are very similar to those who exhibit those mental states.

There are two things that are true in our world and which will never change: First, the world is made up of data. Data has the capability to show us an underlying picture we did not even know existed.

Second, everything in the world is interconnected. We are now beginning to see just how firm those connections are even when the links are not apparent.

The world we are in right now is challenging. Things are changing extremely quickly; what was true yesterday may not be so today. We are required to be flexible in our approach, adaptive and adaptable in our mentality, responsible in our disposition. We need to be capable of displaying critical thinking under pressure, and to always be learning in our lives. We are, in short, being asked by our challenging times to be nothing less than exceptional.

The Sniper Mind is a book about how to be exceptional. It is a book about how to be more than the sum of our parts by understanding how our brains work, what makes them work better, and how to actually achieve that improvement. Snipers do exceptional things in their careers not because they have been trained (though that obviously helps), nor because they have been ordered to, but because they understand the world and their place in it and feel duty-bound to do what no one else can.

It is the same here, with you. Armed with such empowering knowledge, capable now of more than anyone else around you, you are required to step up, you are being asked to do the exceptional things that no one else can, making difficult business decisions and critical choices that no one else can. Success in business does come with its own rewards, but that is no longer enough. Success in business is now a requirement, because business is deeply embedded in the fabric of our world and the fiber of our societies.

What we do, now, as businesspeople, team leaders, project managers, CEOs, entrepreneurs, and even as ordinary people making life-changing decisions, has the potential to change our world in small but important ways. Our cumulative actions are part of a greater change. A much bigger shift. It is happening, because of us. Because of who we are, because of what we have become.

That is real power. Use yours wisely.

ACKNOWLEDGMENTS

No book is ever the product of one person. This one is no different. My agent, Pam Harty, and her colleagues at the Knight Agency deserve my thanks for their faith in me, the hard work they put in, and the constant support I receive. My gratitude also goes to Jeff Leeson and Rachel Livsey from Benson Collister for their ideas, suggestions, encouragement, and enthusiasm. They both played an instrumental role in the birth of this book.

Pam Adger, Greg Ryals, Nelson Brown, Michael Mason, Self-DefenseTraining47 (Adam from DARABEE's The Hive), and Korellyn (also from DARABEE's The Hive) helped with ideas, articles, suggestions, encouragement, and their virtual presence when I needed assistance. A special thanks must go to Martin Shervington, whose suggestion for the title proved, once again, his brilliance. Michel Reibel, former sniper and current digital innovation driver, also deserves a special mention for his candor when it came to his experiences, drive, and focus, and for proving the point when it comes to how a trained sniper mind helps you rise above the fold. To avoid turning this page into another book, I will say a big "Thank you!" to all my friends in Google+ who were there for me when my brain, mushy from research, groggy from sleeplessness, and tripping from long hours of writing, would lead me down paths of the interwebz that maybe I shouldn't have spent that much time exploring. Your wit, intelligence, patience, humor, and conversation provided the oxygen from which all these thoughts written here were born—you all know who you are. For Simon Menner, photographer extraordinaire and a man with a highly developed social conscience, I reserve a special thanks here. He truly deserves it. The two Ns in my life made sure I at least got enough food, if not sleep, and attention when I was flagging and preserved my sanity throughout the process of writing yet one more book. To both I owe a gratitude that goes beyond words.

I've worked with editors in one capacity or another all my adult life. Marc Resnick stands out from the pack with his extraordinary patience with me; he made me feel really happy to be working with him.

APPENDIX I

KIM'S GAME

Rudyard Kipling saw more direct conflict and observed the impact of British imperialism more than most British subjects of his time. An Englishman who'd been born in Bombay, he became steeped in the lore and traditions of both cultures and, as a result, went on to straddle both in a way that few writers, journalists, and poets have managed to do since.

In 1900 he started the serialization of a multicultural spy story that also touched upon enlightenment through Kim, one of its characters. In the book, the boy, who was destined to become a master spy, plays a game called the Jewel Game. This game has since been renamed Kim's Game.

Originally, Kim's Game was played by the Boy Scouts, Girl Scouts, and Girl Guides. It has since been adopted for the training of snipers at the United States Marine Corps' Scout Sniper Instructor School in Quantico, Virginia, as well as sniper schools at Camp Lejeune, Camp Pendleton, and in Hawaii.

The reason the game is so effective is because it trains the eyes to observe and the mind to remember things. Memory plays a key part in situational awareness, and the brain is like a muscle. The more you train it the better it gets. Situational awareness is key to understanding the environment a person finds themselves in. By understanding the environment better, there is also better understanding of all the options available as well as potential threats.

Snipers and Special Forces operatives know that they need to be able to remember a turn they took two hours earlier or the writing on a sign they passed in the dark and while hunched over, carrying a load. The importance of details observed earlier in the day can play a critical role in decisions they have to make late in the evening.

In their December 21, 2001, edition, *The Wall Street Journal* profiled US Marine Sergeant Christopher G. Jacox about the rigors of working as a military sniper. Heavily trained military specialists, snipers are able to coolly pick out their targets and hit them from as far as one mile (1,609 meters) away, even during heavy fighting.

As part of their job, snipers are trained to work and survive behind enemy lines and collect tactical intelligence on their missions, which means remembering tiny details of what they see. "A discarded tin can might indicate something about food supplies and morale. A bunch of cans might suggest the size of the enemy force," the article explained. "Every little thing counts," added Sergeant Jacox in the article.

To train the mind to work like that requires the same methodical, gradual, and persistent approach that marks sniper training in general. Kim's Game is perfect for that, and it can be adapted to take into account almost any scenario. In one variation of it favored by Navy SEALs, people playing it have to do so while all around them between ten and twenty people shout at them, pelt them with objects, and generally go out of their way to create a distraction.

The game's players have to not only concentrate on what they are doing but also cut out all the distractions going on around them so that they do not mess up their play.

But what is Kim's Game? It is simplicity itself. On a tray, you place a number of objects of different size, texture, and origin. In the book, the game used jewels and semiprecious stones of differing colors, cuts, and sizes. Snipers are trained using objects like bullets, pens, paper clips, and so on.

Once you've placed those objects on the tray, you give your players (usually two at a time) just sixty seconds to memorize them. They can touch the objects, handle them, taste them, do whatever they want to them in that time. Then you cover the objects with a cloth or a handkerchief and the two players have to recite what they saw on the tray. The person with the most correct items wins.

The point of the game as played by scout snipers, of course, is much deeper than a win. Scout snipers are trained not just to observe but also to remember. The game may start with just a few objects on a tray, but soon the number of objects expands while the time the trainee sniper has to observe everything is reduced and, frequently, the gap between observing and reporting becomes longer and longer. After playing for a while, it is not unusual for a trainee to be given just half a minute to memorize twenty or thirty objects. He then has to undergo a full day's training and studying and, at the end of the day, he is still expected to be able to recite the objects he'd seen briefly at the beginning of the day.

Typically, the training gets more and more complicated, but snipers' minds also get better and better at it. Being able to take in details, keep them in mind, and remember them even if there are a dozen distracting noises or events going on at the same time are all critical components of the fearsome weapon that is a trained sniper's mind.

Consider just how important that could be, however, in a business environment where distractions abound and those working are still expected to be able to pay attention to every relevant detail in order to deliver great executive thinking. Or how useful such an ability would be during delicate business negotiations when tiny observed details may give vital clues on how to behave in order to get to the desired outcome.

Kim's Game is played with real-life objects because, usually, those being trained are most likely to have to deal with real-life objects. But instead of items on a tray, it can be easily converted to items on a screen, on a slide (as in a PowerPoint presentation), and so on.

Advanced variations of the game use what has been observed to force the person who is being trained to use critical thinking under stress. For instance, they can be asked to explain the importance of a photograph or give the length of a pencil instead of the fact that there was a pencil. They can be asked to recall the name on a business card or the color of a car shown in a photograph. The point is that the game is infinitely adaptable, easy to set up, and delivers real results.

Owners of iPhones can download a digital version of Kim's Game at the app store: https://goo.gl/Of9la2. There is an online version of this at http://goo.gl/k0RytX which is, however, a little limited in scope.

Depending on how tough on yourself you really want to be, you can try to play Kim's Game when you have only had four hours' sleep. You could try and do it after a really tough day at work, when you are mentally exhausted, or after a really hard workout when your eyes are blurry with fatigue.

APPENDIX II

MINDFULNESS MEDITATION TECHNIQUES

If you have never meditated before, you probably have a lot of unlearning and new learning to do. Your perception of meditation is probably influenced by fiction books and the movies. You probably think you need to be super-flexible and already some kind of Jedi Knight to be able to do some weird mind tricks. Rest easy. It's not like this at all.

If you are familiar with meditation because you have done some in the past, then this appendix is probably redundant for you. All you need is a spot on the floor to sit on and some quiet "me time" in your head. And then go straight to the last step in this section.

If you are a mindfulness meditation virgin, relax. This is not going to hurt at all. Find a chair if you cannot sit cross-legged on the floor (or are going to be too self-conscious doing so) and sit on it until you are comfortable. Hold your body upright but don't stiffen up and don't slump. Instead, let your body find its own comfortable upright position. Let the soles of your feet touch the floor and let your arms fall on your lap, palms facing upward, hands completely relaxed. Keep your hands fairly close to your pelvis so there is no drag pulling you forward. The point is to find a natural balance to this so that you are not having to tense in any way to maintain the position.

We are going to do this incrementally. We are going to learn to meditate mindfully the same way snipers learn to do the amazing things they do: by taking many little steps, often.

Step 1: Once you have your relaxed position, use a kitchen timer or an app on your phone that counts time down, and set either to just three minutes. Close your eyes. Sit there and focus on your breathing. Feel it come into your body and then out again. Just focus on the breath coming in as you breathe in and then the breath going out as you breathe out. That's all. Do this once a day for a week or until you feel you can do it without becoming self-conscious or having to struggle with yourself to maintain the focus. Once it becomes comfortable, increase the timer to five minutes and repeat the process daily until five minutes also becomes a comfortable time. Keep doing this, increasing the timer incrementally in two- or three-minute segments until you can maintain this for a full twenty minutes.

Step 2: Once you have mastered focusing on your breathing, the next step is to improve your concentration. Set the timer again for three minutes and this time, as you are sitting there with your eyes shut and your body perfectly balanced and relaxed, concentrate on your breathing in and your breathing out to the exclusion of everything else. Do not allow any other thought to enter your head during this time and if any does focus on your breathing. It is actually a pretty hard thing to do, so keep the times short and, just like before, keep at it until you feel yourself getting better and better, at which point you can increase the length of time on the timer. The goal, once again, is to get to a full twenty minutes of this. Do not get frustrated if it takes you some time to get there, that's perfectly normal. Meditating mindfully is a skill. Like everything else, it takes time to develop. Be patient and give yourself that time; it truly is not a race.

Step 3: In step three we add to the complexity of what you focus on while meditating mindfully. You can now hold the pose, breathe in and out, and focus on your breathing for twenty minutes. So, set the timer again to three minutes, and this time focus on an awareness of your body as you breathe in and out. Feel how you sit, what your feet feel like. Notice the coolness or warmth of the air on your skin. Become aware of your environment and your body within that environment. Feel the sensations being produced and know what they mean, while all the time focusing on your breathing. This is a mental juggling act because the temptation is to all of a sudden rush everything, destroy your concentration, and feel like you're back at square one. Again, be methodical and patient. Start with three minutes and incrementally, over a week or two, bring the time up to five, then eight, then ten, and keep on increasing the time in these small baby steps until you can, once more, focus on your breathing and be totally aware of your body and the environment for a full twenty minutes.

Step 4: Find the tension in your body. When you sit there, breathing in and out, taking in how your body feels, you will become aware of where the tension in your body is. Maybe it is in your shoulders or your back or your legs or your lower abdomen. Set your timer to three minutes again. You are now focusing on your breathing, being aware of your body and your environment, and also scanning your body for tension. Once you have spotted that tension practice releasing it, smoothing it out with your mind. Slowly imagine it to be like a ball of tangled up string and what you are doing is untangling it, a little bit at a time. Again this takes time to perfect. Practice the incremental step method, slowly increasing the time you spend like this once you become totally comfortable with the previous allotted time. The goal, once again, is to be able to spend twenty minutes in a state where you are aware of your breathing, your environment, and your body, and your mind can roam over your body and release the tension felt there.

Step 5: Start with the timer set to just three minutes again. Sit comfortably as you have done throughout all these steps. Now, as you focus on your breathing, are totally aware of your body and the environment, and are releasing any tension you might be aware of in your body, follow your thoughts as they arise. This is probably the hardest thing to do because your mind will throw up all sorts of ideas alongside associated thoughts and feelings. Rather than ignoring them, you need to trace them, connect with them, follow each one until the next one arises and overtakes it. This is not about suppressing the colorful and seemingly chaotic way your brain thinks, it is more about embracing it fully. This may take some time to perfect so be patient. Allow yourself time to master it as you have done throughout all the other steps in this sequence. Do not get frustrated or lose your focus. Once you can comfortably follow your thoughts in a three-minute period without losing track of your breathing or how your body feels or what is happening around you, try increasing the time to five minutes and then eight and then ten. Keep on increasing the length of time you mindfully meditate until you get to twenty minutes. Then you're done!

When your mindfulness becomes powerful, your concentration becomes powerful, and when you can fully concentrate you have the chance to control the way your thoughts arise and the way you make decisions based upon what you perceive and how you feel.

APPENDIX III

GIVE THE GIRL A GUN

The two soldiers of the Red Army approached the scene of battle with caution. Despite the apparent look of carnage and the dead bodies strewn all around the battlefield, the idea of "trust nothing and no one" had been drummed into them by months of fighting the retreating German army.

Just 1.9 miles from the East Prussian village of Ilmsdorf, the area they were now entering had been subject to intense fighting, a reflection of the redoubled, desperate efforts of the German army to hold firm against the Soviets. It was January 27, 1945. Just two weeks earlier the Red Army had begun its East Prussia Offensive, a major move that would push the German army into a retreat, all the way back to Berlin.

The carnage that greeted the two Soviet soldiers as they slowly advanced on the remnants of a Red Army artillery gun was evidence of the desperation felt by the former aggressors in the closing months of the Second World War. Their eyes took in the lifeless, twisted bodies, victims of big gunfire from the German side. They then alighted on what at first sight appeared to be a mass of soot and dust and intermingled body parts. It was two bodies propped against the broken, damaged Soviet big gun. One of them was slightly moving.

The dead one was an artillery captain who had taken a fragment to the head. There was hardly any blood from the wound so his death must have been almost instant. The other one was recognizably female. She had short blond hair pulled back in a ponytail. Her face, angular with youth, was covered in soot and dust. She had been trying to shield the wounded captain when the shells struck. Shell fragments had sliced her open across the stomach and chest. Her hands were clutching her wounds, desperately trying to stop the flow of blood. The ebb of life was leaking out of her. To the two men who found her she was instantly recognizable despite her state.

She was Roza Shanina, just twenty years old and already a legend in the Red Army. She was attached to the 184th Rifle Division and, as a sniper, had fifty-nine confirmed kills to her name.

No book is ever gender neutral. Whether the author chooses to acknowledge the historically inherent gender inequality by using a masculine or feminine pronoun when creating the imaginary character that stands for the ideal reader, or worse, chooses to blithely pretend it doesn't happen by using the generic *they* does not mitigate the fact that gender neutrality is a myth and inequality continues to exist.

In putting this book together I have drawn, almost exclusively from the male gender. War stories, in their many details, feature men. Those hundreds of snipers who responded to my request for interviews were all men. The detailed accounts of the past regarding snipers have been heavily male-centric.

Yet, as this appendix highlights with its beginning, women snipers do exist. The Soviet Army, during World War II, was so hard-pressed for manpower that it drew from every part of its population. Women made it to the front lines and female snipers were there.

As the literature of the time pointed out, in temperament, patience, perseverance, and persistence, they were perhaps better suited to the task of sniping than many of their male colleagues. So why are there not more instances of them? The reason is perhaps best answered by the story of Azi Ahmed, a British woman who between 1999 and 2002 trained with the SAS, the British elite regiment of supersoldiers, who use selection, their dreaded program, to sift through recruits for the most promising candidates.

Ahmed, just 4 feet 11 inches tall and weighing 98 pounds, made it through a modified version of the grueling physical SAS training, only to be denied any recognition of the fact when the program she was part of was axed as the issue of women serving on the front lines or, as in this case, behind enemy lines was too politically contentious to be allowed to continue.

Until now, the male-dominated debate of women in war has been an issue of protection rather than training, female weakness instead of capability. We all know it is wrong. The British army, in a direct acknowledgment of its flawed policy, has now allowed women to serve in combat positions once again. The Pentagon has similarly opened all front-line positions to women. We would like to think this change is because these organizations have finally realized just how wrong discrimination is and how a lack of diversity robs them of vital talent and crucial skills, but that's not why they have decided to reexamine their policies and rule that women can, after all, be fighting fit.

The reason lies in the fact that the nature of combat itself has changed. Where in the past it could require more brawn than brain, perhaps it has now become a highly skilled game of technology, superior training, mental fitness, psychological aptitude, adaptation, and flexibility. The greatest weapon, again, has been acknowledged to be the human brain.

From a neurological point of view, we know today that a male brain shares more commonalities than differences with a female one. Neurologically, gender is more fluid than we can comfortably contemplate. Modern training methods have closed the physical capability gap between men and women. The differences that still remain are more cultural artifacts than gender-specific obstacles thrown up by nature.

So, this book, while it draws heavily from the extensive literature that featured men as snipers, is really more about their brains than their muscles. Everything that goes into making a trained sniper mind in a man can also create one in a woman. The same applies in business. Diversity is happening in our time, albeit more slowly than we would want it to.

In reading this book, taking in all the incredible feats of male snipers, consider that we shall soon have tales of incredible feats performed by female snipers like Roza Shanina and Lyudmila Pavlichenko, a World War II Ukrainian Soviet sniper who, with 309 confirmed kills, is considered to be one of the top military snipers of all time.

Before we even get there, however, we should have many more instances of women outthinking and outperforming men in mission-critical positions in business because they have minds trained like snipers.

APPENDIX IV

BE WATER

An appendix, in a book, is defined as the section at the end of the book that gives additional information on the topic explored in the contents of the text. It is there to enrich, educate, possibly even delight the reader, adding fresh dimensions and greater depth to the subject he has been reading about, which had it been included in the main text, could have quite possibly derailed the book itself, diverting from its intent.

Nothing quite derails a conversation or even an idea easier than Bruce Lee. The pop culture baggage his name has accumulated over the years, the many reinterpretations he has been subjected to, plus his kickass on-screen persona and his undoubtedly innovative approach to martial arts, have created such a multidimensional personality that there was simply no way anything pertaining to him could have been introduced in the book that would not have required an entire chapter to unpack.

The same is true of this appendix. But the requirement to be brief forces us to focus upon Bruce Lee's achievements through the prism of the sniper's mind, asking what it is exactly that Lee has to contribute to this very particular conversation.

"In order to control myself I must first accept myself by going with and not against my nature," Lee wrote in *Bruce Lee: Artist of Life*, a compilation that is part biography, part philosophical treatise, part documentation of his thoughts. Lee's approach of accepting the current conditions and rising above them, being situationally aware and exercising arousal control, is something that resonates with snipers undergoing their specialized training.

The particular passage where Lee explains how he had an epiphany that subsequently allowed him to develop as a martial artist and become who he became is particularly telling:

> *After spending many hours meditating and practicing, I gave up and went sailing alone in a junk. On the sea I thought of all my past training and got mad at myself and punched the water! Right then—at that moment—a thought suddenly struck me; was not this water the very essence of gung fu? Hadn't this water just now illustrated to me the principle of gung fu? I struck it but it did not suffer hurt. Again I struck it with all of my might—yet it was not wounded! I then tried to grasp a handful of it but this proved impossible. This water, the softest substance in the world, which could be contained in the smallest jar, only seemed weak. In reality, it could penetrate the hardest substance in the world. That was it! I wanted to be like the nature of water.*
>
> *Suddenly a bird flew by and cast its reflection on the water. Right then I was absorbing myself with the lesson of the water, another mystic sense of hidden meaning revealed itself to me; should not the thoughts and emotions I had when in front of an opponent pass like the reflection of the birds flying over the water? This was exactly what Professor Yip meant by being detached—not being without emotion or feeling, but being one in whom feeling was not sticky or blocked. Therefore in order to control myself I must first accept myself by going with and not against my nature.*

In a precursor to one of Lee's most famous speeches about the nature of water, mental resilience, and his admonition for the perfect fighter to "be like water," Lee quoted directly from Lao Tzu in his book:

> *Nothing is weaker than water,*
> *But when it attacks something hard*
> *Or resistant, then nothing withstands it,*
> *And nothing will alter its way.*

Sometimes it's these small things that stick in the mind and make a real difference when it counts the most.

APPENDIX V

ENTER THE SNIPER MIND

For a long time now I have sought escape from mental pressure in the fictional, kill-or-be-killed world of *Uncharted*. It's a good game I play badly despite my more than ten thousand hours there, primarily because for me it's a way of decompressing while I let other thoughts percolate in my head. As a result I am not 100 percent present in the game and, to the chagrin of my teammates (because I use the multiplayer option to play online), I can occasionally appear to be playing for the other team rather than my own.

I have changed a little. Well, quite a lot actually. During my research for this book I came across the studies looking at the effects of *transfer*, the ability of the brain to learn a skill in a virtual environment and then transfer that very same skill to a different context in the offline world.

It changed my approach to online gaming, particularly as some of the best practical advice regarding snipers, the art of sniping, and the preparation for an intense sniping mission came from anonymous users inhabiting online gaming forums.

In the course of researching this book, not only did I change my own behavior and strategy when paying *Uncharted*, but I learned to make better use of "dead space"—areas where one is naturally hidden from view—to approach the enemy faster. My observation skills became sharper as I became more mentally immersed in the game, and my overall mind-set changed, allowing me to remain calmer under pressure, like in the zany moments when all hell breaks loose. I am now a better player and, even more important, I can actually see myself improving, which before was simply not happening.

If you want to experience a little of what it's like to be in a fast-moving, unpredictable environment against an enemy just as determined and intelligent as you, *Uncharted* is one game I recommend wholeheartedly. I also recommend *The Last of Us*. Like *Uncharted*, it places you in a virtual world where you have to fight for your life. Unlike *Uncharted*, it would appear to require a PhD in group dynamics and a hyperawareness of tactics and strategy.

Just in case you have time to also do a little mission-tasking and get a feel for what it's like to be a sniper, I recommend *Sniper Elite III: Shadow Warrior*, probably one of the most painstaking strategy and weapons games available to play and, when played at its most advanced level, one that provides a very accurate simulation of what it's like to be a sniper.

For a flavor of what war looks like these days, its messiness, boredom, unpredictability, and basic principles that strip the actions of soldiers from ideals, patriotism, politics, and ideology and make them just about survival and support of their friends next to them, I unreservedly recommend the two feature film documentaries by American journalist Sebastian Junger, *Restrepo* and *Korengal*. In writing this book I watched them both several times. It gave me fresh respect for and real insights into the men who find themselves in combat.

BIBLIOGRAPHY

1 SEEKING A COMPETITIVE ADVANTAGE

Armstrong, Neil. "SAS: Who Dares Wins—8 tips on how to pass the brutal Special Forces selection test." *The Telegraph,* October 19, 2015. http://www.telegraph.co.uk/culture/tvandradio/11939959/Do-you-have-what-it-takes-to-join-the-SAS.html.

"Avoiding Pain and Embracing Pleasure." *Psych Central.* https://psychcentral.com/news/2009/12/28/avoiding-pain-and-embracing-pleasure/10424.html.

Burke, Claire. "Theo Paphitis: Too Many Startups Fail." *The Guardian,* July 8, 2014. https://www.theguardian.com/small-business-network/2014/jul/08/theo-paphitis-startups-dragons-den.

Wood, Geordie. "The Sadness and Beauty of Watching Google's AI Play Go." *Wired,* March 11, 2016. https://www.wired.com/2016/03/sadness-beauty-watching-googles-ai-play-go/.

"World's Longest Sniper Kill Shot Ever Recorded in History." YouTube video, 6:13, posted by KandyTV, April 30, 2014. https://www.youtube.com/watch?v=zcqULBT8tLo.

2 CHOOSING THE BATTLEFIELD

Anderson, David L. "Introduction to the Science of Vision." *Consortium on Cognitive Science Instruction,* 2006. http://www.mind.ilstu.edu/curriculum/vision_science_intro/vision_science_intro.php.

"Cognitive neuroscience of visual object recognition." *Wikipedia.* Accessed

September 12, 2015. https://en.wikipedia.org/wiki/Cognitive_neuro science_of_visual_object_recognition.

Graham, Steven, and Jiaying Jiang, Victoria Manning, Ayna Nejad Baladi, Koh Zhisheng, Shan R. Salleh, Xavier Golay, Yeh Ing Berne, and Peter J. McKenna. "IQ-related fMRI Differences During Cognitive Set Shifting." *Cerebral Cortex* 20(3) (2010): 641–49. https://academic.oup.com/cercor /article-abstract/20/3/641/420968/IQ-Related-fMRI-Differences -during-Cognitive-Set.

Hall, Peter, and Martin Owen. "Simple Canonical Views," a published abstract presented at the British Machine Vision Conference 2005. http:// www.robots.ox.ac.uk/~phst/BMVC2005/papers/264/paper.pdf.

Hesketh-Prichard, H. *Sniping in France*. Kirkland, WA: Tales End Press, 2012. http://www.talesendpress.com/2012/07/sniping-in-france-by-h -hesketh-prichard.html.

Hong, Wei, and Allen Yang Yang, Kun Huang, and Yi Ma. "On Symmetry and Multiple-View Geometry: Structure, Pose, and Calibration from a Single Image." *International Journal of Computer Vision* 60(3) (2004):241–65.

Just, Marcel Adam, and Augusto Buchweitz. "What Brain Imaging Reveals About the Nature of Multitasking." *Oxford Handbooks Online*, November 2014. http://www.oxfordhandbooks.com/view/10.1093/oxfordhb/9780 199842193.001.0001/oxfordhb-9780199842193-e-4.

Majaj, Najib J., and Ha Hong, Ethan A. Solomon, and James J. Dicarlo. "Simple Learned Weighted Sums of Inferior Temporal Neuronal Firing Rates Accurately Predict Human Core Object Recognition Performance." *Journal of Neuroscience*, September 30, 2015. http://www.jneurosci.org /content/35/39/13402.short.

Mather, George. "Chapter 9: Shape and object perception." *Foundations of Sensation and Perception, Second Edition*. London: Psychology Press, December 2008. http://www.psypress.co.uk/mather/resources/chapter .asp?chapter=09.

Menner, Simon. "Simon Menner: Camouflage." Accessed January 12, 2015. http://simonmenner.com/pages/Camouflage2016.htm.

Min, Patrick, and Joyce Chen, and Thomas Funkhouser. "A 2D Sketch Interface for a 3D Model Search Engine." *SIGGRAPH 2002 Technical Sketch*, July 2002. http://dl.acm.org/citation.cfm?doid=1242073.1242151.

Obdržálek, Štěpán, and Jiří Matas. "Object Recognition Using Local Affine Frames on Distinguished Regions." From proceedings at the 13th British Machine Vision Conference, 2002. http://www.bmva.org/bmvc/2002 /papers/134/full_134.pdf.

Palmer, Stephen, and Eleanor Rosch, and Paul Chase. "Canonical Perspective and the Perception of Objects." In *Attention and Performance IX*. Hillsdale, NJ: Lawrence Erlbaum, 1981: 135–51.

Perrett, D. I., and M. H. Harries. "Characteristic Views and the Visual Inspection of Simple Faceted and Smooth Objects: Tetrahedra and Potatoes." In *Perception* 17 (1988): 703–20.

Peters, Gabriele, and Barbara Zitova, and Christoph von der Malsburg. "How to Measure the Pose Robustness of Object Views." In *Image and Vision Computing* 20 (2002):341–48.

"Solid Snake." *Wikipedia*. Accessed January 12, 2016. https://en.wikipedia .org/wiki/Solid_Snake.

Trafton, Anne. "How the Brain Recognizes Objects." *MIT News*, October 5, 2015. http://news.mit.edu/2015/how-brain-recognizes-objects-1005.

"Welsh Marksman Bends Shot to Kill Iraqi Rifleman." *WalesOnline*, April 5, 2003, updated April 1, 2013. http://www.walesonline.co.uk/news/wales -news/welsh-marksman-bends-shot-kill-2487044.

3 THE RIGHT TOOLS FOR THE JOB

"Battle of Mogadishu (1993)." *Wikipedia*. Accessed September 12, 2015. https://en.wikipedia.org/wiki/Battle_of_Mogadishu_(1993).

Cohen, Elliot D. "How to Be Empathetic." *Psychology Today*, May 17, 2015. https://www.psychologytoday.com/blog/what-would-aristotle-do /201505/how-be-empathetic.

Coughlin, Jack, and John Bruning R. *Shock Factor: American Snipers in the War on Terror*. New York: St. Martin's Griffin, 2015.

Epstein, Robert. "The Empty Brain. Your Brain Does Not Process Information, Retrieve Knowledge or Store Memories. In Short: Your Brain Is Not a Computer." *Aeon*, May 18, 2016. https://aeon.co/essays/your-brain -does-not-process-information-and-it-is-not-a-computer.

Kringelbach, Morten L., and Kent C. Berridge. "The Neuroscience of Happiness and Pleasure." *Social Research*, Summer 2010. https://www.ncbi .nlm.nih.gov/pmc/articles/PMC3008658/.

Nummenmaa, L., and H. Saarimäki, E. Glerean, A. Gotsopoulos, R. Hari, I. Jääskeläinen, and M. Sams. 2014. "Emotional Speech Synchronizes Brains Across Listeners and Engages Large-Scale Dynamic Brain Networks," *Neuroimage* 102 (November 2014):498–509. http://www .sciencedirect.com/science/article/pii/S1053811914006466.

Öngür, D., and J. L. Price. "The Organization of Networks Within the Orbital and Medial Prefrontal Cortex of Rats, Monkeys and Humans." *Cerebral Cortex* 10 (March 2000):206–19. https://www.ncbi.nlm.nih.gov /pubmed/10731217.

Panksepp, Jaak. "Toward a General Psychobiological Theory of Emotions." *Behavioral and Brain Science* 5 (1982):407–22. https://www.cambridge .org/core/journals/behavioral-and-brain-sciences/article/div -classtitletoward-a-general-psychobiological-theory-of-emotionsdiv/B 09ABA6E2B1333EFFBD687253617E698.

Peelen, Marius V., and Anthony P. Atkinson, and Patrik Vuilleumier. "Supramodal Representations of Perceived Emotions in the Human Brain." *Journal of Neuroscience* 30 (2010):10127–34. http://www.jneurosci.org /content/30/30/10127.short.

Saarimäki, Heini, and Athanasios Gotsopoulos, Iiro P. Jääskeläinen, Jouko Lampinen, Patrik Vuilleumier, Riitta Hari, Mikko Sams, and Lauri Nummenmaa. "Discrete Neural Signatures of Basic Emotions." *Cerebral Cortex,* April 29, 2015. https://academic.oup.com/cercor/article/26/6/2563 /1754140/Discrete-Neural-Signatures-of-Basic-Emotions.

"Takuan Sōhō." *Wikipedia*. Accessed February 10, 2016. https://en.wikipedia .org/wiki/Takuan_S%C5%8Dh%C5%8D.

Weinberger, Sharon. "Brain training moves from battlefield to boardroom." BBC, November 18, 2014. http://www.bbc.com/future/story/20121024 -from-battlefield-to-boardroom.

4 SMARTS

Anderson, C., and J. A. Horne. "Placebo Response to Caffeine Improves Reaction Time Performance in Sleepy People." *Human Psychopharmacology* 23 (2008):333–36. doi:10.1002/hup.931.

Boaler, Jo. "When You Believe In Yourself Your Brain Operates Differently." Online posting. Accessed January 12, 2016. https://www.youcubed.org /think-it-up/believe-brain-operates-differently/.

Draganich, Christina, and Kristi Erdal. "Placebo Sleep Affects Cognitive Functioning." *Journal of Experimental Psychology: Learning, Memory, and Cognition,* 2014. https://www.apa.org/pubs/journals/features/xlm-a00 35546.pdf.

Epstein, David J. *The Sports Gene: Talent, Practice and the Truth About Success.* New York: Vintage Digital (Kindle edition), 2013.

Gallego, Jelor. "Most Accurate Map of the Brain To Date Reveals 97 New Regions." *Futurism,* July 22, 2016. https://futurism.com/most-accurate -map-of-the-brain-to-date-reveals-97-new-regions/.

Hart, Thomas G. *The Dynamics of Revolution: A Cybernetic Theory of the Dynamics of Modern Social Revolution with a Study of Ideological Change and Organizational Dynamics in the Chinese Revolution.* Stockholm: Stockholm University, 1971.

Hopkins, Cameron. "Jeff Cooper: Father of Modern Pistol Shooting." *American Rifleman,* May 18, 2011. https://www.americanrifleman .org/articles/2011/5/18/jeff-cooper-father-of-modern-pistol -shooting/.

Levit, Kenneth J. "The CIA and the Torture Controversy." *Journal of National Security Law and Policy* 1 (2005):341. http://jnslp.com/wp-content /uploads/2010/08/05_Levit_Master_c.pdf.

Mason Oliver J., and Francesca Brady. "The Psychotomimetic Effects of Short-term Sensory Deprivation," *Journal of Nervous and Mental Disorders* 10 (2009):783–85. https://www.researchgate.net/publication/38011659 _The_Psychotomimetic_Effects_of_Short-Term_Sensory_Deprivation.

Mayer, Jane. "Counterfactual: A Curious History of the CIA's Secret Interrogation Program." Book review in *The New Yorker,* March 29, 2010.

McCoy, Alfred. *A Question of Torture: CIA Interrogation, from The Cold War to The War on Terror.* New York: Henry Holt, 2006.

Meek, James G. "U.S. Officials Slam Dick Cheney's Claim that Waterboarding 9/11 Mastermind 183 Times Was a 'Success'" *New York Daily News.* April 22, 2009.

PhysOrg. "Believing Is Seeing: How Mindset Can Improve Vision." *Medical Xpress,* May 2, 2010. https://medicalxpress.com/news/2010-05-believing -mindset-vision.html.

Stern, Eric K. *Crisis Decisionmaking: A Cognitive Institutional Approach.* Stockholm: Swedish National Defence College, 2003. https://www.fhs.se

/Documents/Externwebben/forskning/centrumbildningar/Crismart
/Publikationer/Publikationsserier/VOLUME_6.PDF.

Stewart, Scott. "A Practical Guide to Situational Awareness." *Stratfor,* March 14, 2012. https://www.stratfor.com/weekly/practical-guide-situational -awareness.

Sun, Y., and Y. Zhang, N. He, X. Liu, and D. Miao. "Caffeine and Placebo Expectation: Effects on Vigilance, Cognitive Performance, Heart Rate, and Blood Pressure During 28 Hours of Sleep Deprivation." *Journal of Psychophysiology* 21 (2007): 91–99. doi:10.1027/0269-8803.21.2.91.

Tippett, Krista. "Ellen Langer: Science of Mindlessness and Mindfulness." *On Being,* September 10, 2015. http://www.onbeing.org/programs/ellen -langer-science-of-mindlessness-and-mindfulness/.

Tombaugh, Tom N. "A Comprehensive Review of the Paced Auditory Serial Addition Tests (PASAT)." *Archives of Clinical Neuropsychology* 21 (2006): 53–76. doi:10.1016/j.acn.2005.07.006.

5 SCIENCE

"US Airways Flight 1549 New York City Hudson River Crash" YouTube video, [43:02], posted by Mayday Air Crash Investigation, March 21, 2016.

Fleming, Mike Jr. " 'Star Wars' Legacy II: An Architect of Hollywood's Greatest Deal Recalls How George Lucas Won Sequel Rights." *Deadline,* December 18, 2015. http://deadline.com/2015/12/star-wars-franchise -george-lucas-historic-rights-deal-tom-pollock-1201669419/.

Harris, A. W. "Making Decisions Under Duress." *Journal of Law and Social Sciences,* July 2012. http://dl6.globalstf.org/index.php/jlss/article/view /967.

Ingersoll, Geoffrey, and Robert Johnson. "This Intense Training Course Makes US Marine Scout Snipers the Deadliest Shots on Earth." *Business Insider,* February 4, 2015. http://www.businessinsider.com/this-intense -training-course-makes-us-marine-scout-snipers-the-deadliest-shots -on-earth-2015-2.

Larsen, Amber. "Military Special Operations: Do You Have the Mental Fortitude to Make It?" *Breaking Muscle.* Accessed January 12, 2016. https:// breakingmuscle.com/learn/military-special-operations-do-you-have -the-mental-fortitude-to-make-it.

Munir, Kamal. "The Demise of Kodak: Five Reasons." *Wall Street Journal,*

February 26, 2012. http://blogs.wsj.com/source/2012/02/26/the -demise-of-kodak-five-reasons/.

Olson, Samantha. "Your Gut Feeling Is Way More Than Just a Feeling: The Science of Intuition." *Medical Daily,* March 12, 2015. http://www .medicaldaily.com/your-gut-feeling-way-more-just-feeling-science -intuition-325338.

Rubin, Ben Fox. "Amazon's Prime Day Breaks Single-Day Sales Record." *CNET,* July 13, 2016. https://www.cnet.com/news/amazons-prime-day -breaks-single-day-sales-record/.

Szalavitz, Maia. "Making Choices: How Your Brain Decides." *Time,* September 4, 2012. http://healthland.time.com/2012/09/04/making -choices-how-your-brain-decides/.

"US Air Cockpit Audio Tapes 'We're Gonna Be in the Hudson.'" YouTube video. Posted by Speakmymind02 on February 5, 2009. https://www .youtube.com/watch?v=JItbosItYZs.

"US Airways Flight 1549." *Wikipedia.* Accessed September 5, 2015.

Usborne, David. "The Moment It All Went Wrong for Kodak." *Independent,* January 19, 2012. http://www.independent.co.uk/news/business /analysis-and-features/the-moment-it-all-went-wrong-for-kodak -6292212.html.

Van der Linden, Sander. "Science of Speed Dating Helps Singles Find Love." *Scientific American,* March 1, 2012. https://www.scientificamerican.com /article/shopping-for-love/.

6 MIND

Anderson, Cameron, and Adam D. Galinsky. "Power, Optimism, and Risk-Taking. *European Journal of Social Psychology* 36 (2006): 511–36. http:// citeseerx.ist.psu.edu/viewdoc/download?doi=10.1.1.378.8398&rep =rep1&type=pdf.

Anderson, J. R. *Rules of the Mind.* Oxfordshire, UK: Psychology Press (Taylor & Francis Group), 1993.

———and J. G. Greeno, P. K. Kline and D. M. Neves. "Acquisition of problem solving skill." In *Cognitive Skills and Their Acquisition.* Edited by J. R. Anderson. Hillsdale, NJ: Lawrence Erlbaum, 1981.

Ashford, Susan J., and Ruth Blatt, and Don VandeWalle. "Reflections on the Looking Glass: A Review of Research on Feedback-Seeking Behavior in

Organizations." *Journal of Management* 29 (2003):773–99. http://www
.sciencedirect.com/science/article/pii/S0149206303000795.

Atkinson, R. C., and R. M. Shiffrin. "Human Memory: A Proposed System
and Its Control Processes." In *The Psychology of Learning and Motivation:
Advances in Research and Theory (Vol. 2).* Edited by K. W. Spence and
J. T. Spence. New York: Academic Press, 1968.

Blenko, Marcia W., Michael C. Mankins, and Paul Rogers. "The Five Steps
to Better Decisions." *Bain & Company,* August 6, 2013. http://www.bain
.com/publications/articles/the-five-steps-to-better-decisions.aspx.

Brenner, Lyle. "A Random Support Model of the Calibration of Subjective
Probabilities." *Organizational Behavior and Human Decision Processes* 90
(2003): 87–110. http://bear.warrington.ufl.edu/brenner/papers/brenner
-obhdp2003.pdf.

Briñol, Pablo, and Richard E. Petty, Carmen Valle, Derek D. Rucker, and
Alberto Beccera. "The Effects of Message Recipients' Power Before
and After Persuasion: A Self-Validation Analysis." *Journal of Personality and Social Psychology* 93 (2007): 1040–53. https://www.uam.es
/otros/persuasion/papers/2007%20JPSP%20Power%20SV.pdf.

Camerer, Colin F., and Robin M. Hogarth. "The Effects of Financial Incen-
tives in Experiments: A Review and Capital-Labor-Production Framework." *Journal of Risk and Uncertainty* 19 (1999):7–42. http://link.springer
.com/article/10.1023/A:1007850605129.

Cansler, David C., and William B. Stiles. "Relative Status and Interpersonal
Presumptuousness." *Journal of Experimental Social Psychology* 17 (1981):
459–71. https://www.researchgate.net/publication/223413944_Relative
_status_and_interpersonal_presumptuousness.

"Carlos Hathcock (Hunting the Cobra and the Suicide Mission)." YouTube
video, Posted by TheInferno, May 11, 2014. https://www.youtube.com
/watch?v=kTAYQHVJUDI&index=2&list=PLcqLaVm4XGbTz74cn
GufBSeGttMZ8ilWj.

Carpenter, Patricia A., Marcel Adam Just, and Peter Shell. "What One
Intelligence Test Measures: A Theoretical Account of the Processing in
the Raven Progressive Matrices Test." *Psychological Review* 97 (1990):
404–31. http://repository.cmu.edu/cgi/viewcontent.cgi?article=1727&
context=psychology https://www.ncbi.nlm.nih.gov/pubmed/2381998.

Chambers, John R., and Paul D. Windschitl. "Biases in Social Comparative

Judgments: The Role of Nonmotivated Factors in Above-Average and Comparative-Optimism Effects." *Psychological Bulletin* 130 (2004):813–38. http://www.communicationcache.com/uploads/1/0/8/8/10887248/biases_in_social_comparative_judgments-_the_role_of_nonmotivated_factors_in_above-average_and_comparative-optimism_effects.pdf.

Chase, W. G., and H. A. Simon. "The Mind's Eye in Chess." In *Visual Information Processing*. Edited by W. G. Chase. New York: Academic Press, 1973.

Davidson, Richard. "Change Your Brain by Transforming Your Mind." https://nccih.nih.gov/news/events/lectures/SES16. May 13, 2016.

Gino, Francesca, and Don A. Moore. "Effects of Task Difficulty on Use of Advice." *Journal of Behavioral Decision Making* 20 (2007):21–35. http://www.hbs.edu/faculty/Publication%20Files/06-019.pdf.

Gino, Francesca, and Maurice E. Schweitzer. "Blinded by Anger or Feeling the Love: How Emotions Influence Advice Taking." *Journal of Applied Psychology* 93 (2008):1165–73. https://faculty.wharton.upenn.edu/wp-content/uploads/2014/06/GinoSchweitzer-JAP-2008.pdf.

Gino, Francesca, and Jen Shang, and Rachel Croson. "The Impact of Information from Similar or Different Advisors on Judgment." *Organizational Behavior and Human Decision Processes* 108 (2009):287–302. http://www.sciencedirect.com/science/article/pii/S0749597808000903.

Gladding, Rebecca. "This Is Your Brain on Meditation." *Psychology Today*, May 22, 2013. https://www.psychologytoday.com/blog/use-your-mind-change-your-brain/201305/is-your-brain-meditation.

Gonzalez, Cleotilde, and Javier F. Lerch, and Christian Lebiere. "Instance-Based Learning in Dynamic Decision Making." *Cognitive Science*, 2003. http://repository.cmu.edu/cgi/viewcontent.cgi?article=1031&context=sds.

Klein, Gary. *Sources of Power: How People Make Decisions*. Cambridge, MA: MIT Press, 1998.

———Judith Orasanu, Roberta Calderwood, and Caroline E. Zsambok, eds. *Decision Making in Action: Models and Methods*. Santa Barbara, CA: Praeger (ABC-Clio), 1993.

Lazar, Sara W., and Catherine E. Kerr, Rachel H. Wasserman, Jeremy R. Gray, Douglas N. Greve, Michael T. Treadway, Metta McGarvey, Brian T. Quinn, Jeffery A. Dusek, Herbert Benson, Scott L. Rauch, Christopher I. Moore, and Bruce Fischl. "Meditation Experience Is

Associated with Increased Cortical Thickness." *Neuroreport*, November 28, 2005. https://www.ncbi.nlm.nih.gov/pmc/articles/PMC1361002/.

"The Offensive Mindset," *Tactical Paintball Sniper*, May 28, 2010. http://tacticalpaintballsniper.com/psychology/the-offensive-mindset/.

Posner, Michael I. *Chronometric Explanations of Mind*. New York: Oxford University Press, 1986.

———and S. E. Peterson, P. T. Fox, and M. E. Raichle. "Localization of Cognitive Functions in the Human Brain." *Science* 240 (1988):1627–31. https://www.researchgate.net/publication/19867429_Localization_of_cognitive_functions_in_the_brain.

———and Steven E. Petersen. "The Attention System of the Human Brain." *Annual Review of Neuroscience* 13 (1990):25–42. http://cns-web.bu.edu/Profiles/Mingolla.html/cnsftp/cn730-2007-pdf/posner_petersen90.pdf.

Reynolds, Gretchen. "How Meditation Changes the Brain and Body." *New York Times*, February 18, 2016. https://well.blogs.nytimes.com/2016/02/18/contemplation-therapy/?_r=0.

Romulo, Chris. "8 Ways to Develop a Warrior Mindset." *Muay Thai Authority*, January 7, 2016. http://muaythaiauthority.com/8-ways-to-develop-a-warrior-mindset/.

Ryan, Richard M. "Control and Information in the Intrapersonal Sphere: An Extension of Cognitive Evaluation Theory." *Journal of Personality and Social Psychology* 43 (1982):450–61. https://selfdeterminationtheory.org/SDT/documents/1982_Ryan_ControlandInfo_JPSP.pdf.

Schneider, Walter, and Richard M. Shiffrin. "Controlled and Automatic Human Information Processing: 1. Detection, Search and Attention." *Psychological Review* 84 (1977):1–66. http://psycnet.apa.org/psycinfo/1977-20305-001.

Schulte, Brigid. "Harvard Neuroscientist: Meditation Not Only Reduces Stress, Here's How It Changes Your Brain." *Washington Post*, May 26, 2015. https://www.washingtonpost.com/news/inspired-life/wp/2015/05/26/harvard-neuroscientist-meditation-not-only-reduces-stress-it-literally-changes-your-brain/?utm_term=.a0c6bfadd3f8.

Schunn, Christian D., and Dieter Wallach. "In Defense of Goodness-of-Fit in Comparison of Models to Data." Unpublished manuscript (2002), Pittsburgh, PA.

See, Kelly E., Elizabeth Wolfe Morrison, Naomi B. Rothman, and Jack B. Soll. "The Detrimental Effects of Power on Confidence, Advice Taking, and Accuracy." *Organizational Behavior and Human Decision Processes*, 2011. http://web-docs.stern.nyu.edu/pa/ksee_power_advice_taking.pdf.

Selst, Van. "Chapter 4: Ethical Decision Making." *Fundamentals of Cognitive Psychology* (Ronald Thomas Kellogg, ed.). Beyond Self (n.d.): n. pag. Web.

Shapiro, Shauna L., Gary E. Schwartz, and Ginny Bonner. "Effects of Mindfulness-Based Stress Reduction on Medical and Premedical Students." *Journal of Behavioral Medicine* 21 (1998): 581–99. http://mindfull awyerconference.org/pdf/art-98Behaviormed-Shapiro.pdf.

Shear, J., and R. Jevning. "Pure Consciousness: Scientific Exploration of Meditation Techniques." In *The View from Within* (189–209). Edited by F. J. Varela and J. Shear. Thorverton, UK: Imprint Academics, 1999.

Sherwood, Ben. "Ultimate Stress Test: Special Forces Training." *Newsweek*, February 13, 2009. http://www.newsweek.com/ultimate-stress-test -special-forces-training-82749.

Simon, H. A. *Models of Man: Social and Rational*. New York: John Wiley & Sons, 1957.

———and Yuichiro Anazai. *The Theory of Learning by Doing. Models of Thought (Vol. II)*. New Haven, CT: Yale University Press, 1979.

Smith, Edward E., and John Jonides. "Working Memory: A View from Neuroimaging." *Cognitive Psychology*, June 1997. http://www.sciencedirect.com /science/article/pii/S0010028597906587.

Stanley, Elizabeth. "Cultivating the Mind of a Warrior." *Inquiring Mind*, Spring 2014. http://www.inquiringmind.com/Articles/CultivatingMind OfWarrior.html.

Tart, Charles T. *Living the Mindful Life*. Boston, MA: Shambhala, 1994.

Wass, Sam V. "Applying Cognitive Training to Target Executive Functions During Early Development." *Child Neuropsychology*, March 4, 2015. https://www.ncbi.nlm.nih.gov/pmc/articles/PMC4270409/.

Wolkin, Jennifer. "How the Brain Changes When You Meditate." *Mindful*, September 20, 2015. http://www.mindful.org/how-the-brain-changes -when-you-meditate/.

7 FORTITUDE

Anwar, Yasmin. "Pulling An All-Nighter Can Bring on Euphoria and Risky Behavior." *Berkeley News*, March 22, 2011. http://news.berkeley.edu/2011/03/22/pulling-an-all-nighter/.

Aw, Ben. "4 Ways to Acquire Navy Seals' Mental Toughness." *Scientific Brains*. Accessed February 12, 2016. http://scientificbrains.com/4-ways-to-accquire-navy-seals-mental-toughness/.

Barch, D. M., and T. S. Braver, L. E. Nystrom, S. D. Forman, D. C. Noll, and J. D. Cohen. "Dissociating Working Memory from Task Difficulty in Human Prefrontal Cortex." *Neuropsychologia* 35 (1997):1373–80.31. https://www.ncbi.nlm.nih.gov/pubmed/9347483.

Bonnet, M. H., and D. Arand L. "We Are Chronically Sleep Deprived." National Center for Biotechnology Information. U.S. National Library of Medicine, n.d. Web. January, 12, 2016. https://www.ncbi.nlm.nih.gov/pubmed/8746400.

"The Brain from Top to Bottom." Online blog. Accessed March 10, 2016. http://thebrain.mcgill.ca/.

BrianMac Sports Coach. "Stress Management." Online. Accessed May 25, 2015. https://www.brianmac.co.uk/stress.htm.

Carpenter, Patricia A., Marcel A. Just, and Peter Shell. "What One Intelligence Test Measures: A Theoretical Account of the Processing in the Raven Progressive Matrices Test." *Psychological Review* 97(3) (1990):404–31. http://psycnet.apa.org/?&fa=main.doiLanding&doi=10.1037/0033-295X.97.3.404.

Evans, Lisa. "What 3 Companies Are Doing to Keep Employees Healthy." *Entrepreneur*, March 15, 2013. https://www.entrepreneur.com/article/226041.

"Famous Sports Quotes." *QuoteMountain*. Accessed May 20, 2015. https://www.quotemountain.com/quotes/sports/famous-sports-quotes.

Fiez, J. A., and E. A. Raife, D. A. Balota, J. P. Schwarz, M. E. Raichle, and S. E. Petersen. "A Position Emission Tomography Study of the Short-Term Maintenance of Verbal Information." *Journal of Neuroscience* 16 (1996):808–22.

Frey, Peter W. *Chess Skill in Man and Machine*. New York: Springer-Verlag, 1977.

Johnson, Warren R. *Science and Medicine of Exercise and Sports*. New York: Harper and Brothers, 1960.

Jones, J. Graham, and Lew Hardy. *Stress and Performance in Sport*. New York: John Wiley & Sons, 1990.

Newell, Allen. *Unified Theories of Cognition*. Cambridge, MA: Harvard University Press, 1990.

Schumacher, Gerald. *To Be a U.S. Army Green Beret*. St. Paul, MN: MBI Publishing, 2005.

"Selection Prep Program." Militaryathlete.com. Accessed May 20, 2010.

Sheikh, Anees A., and Errol R. Korn. *Imagery in Sports and Physical Performance*. New York: Baywood, 1994.

"Stress." Merriam-Webster. Eleventh edition, 2016.

"Strikeforce on American Forces Network." Timkennedymma.com. Accessed May 10, 2015.

Tod, David A., Rhys Thatcher, Michael McGuigan, and Joanne Thatcher. "Effects of Instructional and Motivational Self-Talk on the Vertical Jump." *Journal of Strength and Conditioning Research* 23 (1) (2009): 196–202. https://www.ncbi.nlm.nih.gov/pubmed/19130644.

Tri. "How to Be Mentally Tough Like a Navy Seal." *Examined Existence*. Accessed April 12, 2016. http://examinedexistence.com/how-to-be-mentally-tough-like-a-navy-seal/.

8 PREPARATION

Andersen, Charlotte Hilton. "New Study Shows Sleep Deprivation Can Increase Productivity at Work." *Shape*, March 24, 2015. http://www.shape.com/lifestyle/mind-and-body/new-study-shows-sleep-deprivation-can-increase-productivity-work.

Barker, Eric. "The Secret to Handling Pressure like Astronauts, Navy SEALs, and Samurai." *The Week*, August 19, 2014. http://theweek.com/articles/445438/secret-handling-pressure-like-astronauts-navy-seals-samurai.

Buettner, Dan. "The Island Where People Forget to Die." *New York Times Magazine*, October 24, 2012. http://www.nytimes.com/2012/10/28/magazine/the-island-where-people-forget-to-die.html.

Eriksen, Konstantin. "The Science of Epigenetics—How Our Minds Can Reprogram Our Genes." *Wake Up World*, 2012. http://wakeup-world.com/2012/03/26/the-science-of-epigenetics-how-our-minds-can-reprogram-our-genes/.

Eynon, N., J. R. Ruiz, J. Oliveira, J. A. Duarte, R. Birk, and A. Lucia. "Genes and Elite Athletes: A Roadmap for Future Research." *Journal of Physiology* 589 (2011):3063–70.5. https://www.ncbi.nlm.nih.gov/pubmed /21540342.

Gibson, William T. "Key Concepts in Human Genetics: Understanding the Complex Phenotype." In *Genetics and Sports* (Medicine and Sports Science). 54:1–10. Edited by M. Collins. Basel, Switzerland: Karger, 2009.

Kiss MAPDM, M. T. S. Böhme, A. C. Mansoldo, E. Degaki, M. Regazzini. "Performance and Sports Talent." *Revista Paulista de Educação Física*. 19(2004):89–100.2.

Komi, P.V., and J. H. Viitasalo, M. Havu, A. Orstensson, B. Sjodin, and J. Karlsson. "Skeletal Muscle Fibres and Muscle Enzyme Activities in Monozygous and Dizygous Twins of Both Sexes." *Acta Physiologica Scandinavica* 100 (1977):385–92. https://www.ncbi.nlm.nih.gov/pubmed /199045.

Martinuzzi, Bruna. "What's Empathy Got to Do With It?" *Networking Today*, October 2009. http://www.networkingtoday.com/article/What%E2% 80%99s%20Empathy%20Got%20to%20Do%20with%20It-1101.

Mednick, Sara. "Give it up for the down state-sleep." TED Talk. https:// www.youtube.com/watch?v=MklZJprP5F0. Accessed September 12, 2016.

Nezlek, J. B., and G. J. Feist, F. C. Wilson, and R. M. Plesko. "Day-to-Day Variability in Empathy as a Function of Daily Events and Mood." *Journal of Research in Personality* 35 (2001):401–23. http://jbnezl.people.wm.edu /Reprints/2001-J-Res-Pers-Empathy.pdf.

Pelusi, Nando. "Don't Harden Your Heart." *Psychology Today*, November 1, 2003. https://www.psychologytoday.com/articles/200311/dont-harden -your-heart.

Reis, H. T., and S. M. Smith, C. L. Carmichael, P. A. Caprariello, F. F. Tsai, A. Rodrigues, and M. R. Maniaci. "Are You Happy for Me? How Sharing Positive Events with Others Provides Personal and Interpersonal Benefits." *Journal of Personality and Social Psychology* 99 (2010):311.

Richards, Chip. "Four Ways to Reprogram Your Subconscious Mind." *UPLIFT*, June 2, 2016. http://upliftconnect.com/reprogram-subconscious -mind/.

Rilling, James K., and David A. Gutman, Thorsten R. Zeh, Giuseppe

Pagnoni, Gregory S. Berns, and Clinton D. Kilts. "A Neural Basis for Social Cooperation." *Neuron* 35 (2002):395–405. http://www.sciencedirect .com/science/article/pii/S0896627302007559.

Rodriguez, Tori. "Sleepy Brains Think More Freely." *Scientific American,* May 1, 2012. https://www.scientificamerican.com/article/sleepy-brains -think-freely/.

Russell, D. W. "UCLA Loneliness Scale (Version 3): Reliability, Validity, and Factor Structure." *Journal of Personality Assessment* 66 (1996):20–40. https://www.iscet.pt/sites/default/files/imce/ucla_loneliness_scale _version_3._reliability_validity_and_factor_structure.pdf.

Sallquist, Julie, and Nancy Eisenberg, Tracy L. Spinrad, Natalie D. Eggum, and Bridget M. Gaertner. "Assessment of Preschoolers' Positive Empathy: Concurrent and Longitudinal Relations with Positive Emotion, Social Competence, and Sympathy." *Journal of Positive Psychology* 4 (2009):223–33. http://www.tandfonline.com/doi/abs/10 .1080/17439760902819444.

"Sleep Problems Prevalent for Military Members Post-Deployment." *RAND Corporation*, April 6, 2015. http://www.rand.org/news/press/2015/04 /06.html.

Tucker, Ross, and Malcolm Collins. "What Makes Champions? A Review of the Relative Contribution of Genes and Training to Sporting Success." *British Journal of Sports Medicine* 46 (2012):555–61.4. http://bjsm.bmj .com/content/46/8/555.full.

9 RESPONSE

Aglioti, Salvatore M., and Paola Cesari, Michela Romani, and Cosimo Urgesi. "Action Anticipation and Motor Resonance in Elite Basketball Players." *Nature Neuroscience*, August 10, 2008. http://www.nature.com/neuro /journal/v11/n9/abs/nn.2182.html.

Blair, Gary Ryan. "Bruce Lee's 10 Million Dollar Goal." *Everything Counts.* Accessed April 12, 2016. http://www.everythingcounts.com/bruce-lees -10-million-dollar-goal/.

Kolb, Bryan, and Robbin Gibb, and Terry E. Robinson. "Brain Plasticity and Behavior." *Current Directions in Psychological Science*, February 1, 2003. http://journals.sagepub.com/doi/abs/10.1111/1467-8721.01210.

Marshall, Colin. "Oliver Sacks Explains the Biology of Hallucinations: 'We

See with the Eyes, But with the Brain as Well.'" *Open Culture,* August 16, 2016. http://www.openculture.com/2016/08/oliver-sacks-explains-the -biology-of-hallucinations.html.

Michelle W. Voss, Arthur F. Kramer, Chanddramallika Basak, Ruchika Shauurya Prakash and Brent Roberts. "Are Expert Athletes 'Expert' in the Cognitive Laboratory? A Meta-Analytic Review of Cognition and Sport Expertise." Harvard Business Review. N.p., n.d. Web. January 17, 2016.

Overney, Leila S., and Olaf Blanke, and Michael H. Herzog. "Enhanced Temporal but Not Attentional Processing in Expert Tennis Players." *PLOS ONE,* June 11, 2008. http://journals.plos.org/plosone/article?id =10.1371/journal.pone.0002380.

10 STRUCTURE

Ackerman, P. L., and E. D. Heggestad. "Intelligence, Personality, and In- terests: Evidence for Overlapping Traits." *Psychological Bulletin* 121 (1997):219–45. https://www.ncbi.nlm.nih.gov/pubmed/9100487.

Kukla, Robert D. "Metabolic Spinal Disorders in the Elderly." *Southern Medical Journal* 92(10) (1999):1037. http://sma.org/southern-medical-journal /article/metabolic-spinal-disorders-in-the-elderly/.

Neill, Conor. "Sun-Tzu's 5 Factors for Victory and 5 Attributes of a Leader." *Moving People to Action,* September 11, 2013. https://conorneill.com/2013 /09/11/sun-tzus-5-factors-for-victory-and-5-attributes-of-a-leader/.

Neisser, U., G. Boodoo, T. J. Bouchard, A. Wade Boykin, N. Brody, S. J. Ceci, et al. "Intelligence: Knowns and Unknowns." In *American Psychol- ogist* 51 (1996):77–101. http://differentialclub.wdfiles.com/local—files /definitions-structure-and-measurement/Intelligence-Knowns-and -unknowns.pdf.

Paulhus, Delroy L. "Measurement and Control of Response Bias." In *Measures of Personality and Social Psychological Attitudes* (Vol. 1: 17–59). Edited by J. P. Robinson, P. R. Shaver, and L. S. Wrightman. San Diego, CA: Academic Press, 1991.

Paunonen, Sampo V., and Michael C. Ashton. "Big Five Predictors of Academic Achievement." *Journal of Research in Personality* 35(1) (2001):78–90. http://psychology.okstate.edu/faculty/jgrice/psyc4333 /FiveFactorGPA_JRP.pdf.

Swanson, J. L. "Stability and change in vocational interests." In *Vocational*

Interests. Edited by M. L. Savickas and A. R. Spokane. Palo Alto, CA: Davies-Black, 1999.

Tangney, J. P., and R. F. Baumeister, and A. L. Boone. "High Self-Control Predicts Good Adjustment, Less Pathology, Better Grades, and Interpersonal Success. *Journal of Personality* 72(2) (2004):271–322.

Terman, Lewis M., and Melita Oden. "The Gifted Child Grows Up: Twenty-five Years' Follow-up of a Superior Group." In *Genetic Studies of Genius*, Vol. 4. Stanford, CA: Stanford University Press, 1947.

Tett, Robert P., and Douglas N. Jackson, and Mitchell Rothstein. "Personality Measures as Predictors of Job Performance: A Meta-Analytic Review." *Personnel Psychology* 44(4) (1991):703–42. http://onlinelibrary .wiley.com/doi/10.1111/j.1744-6570.1991.tb00696.x/abstract.

Tupes, Ernest C., and Raymond E. Christal. "Recurrent Personality Factors Based on Trait Ratings." *Journal of Personality* 60(2) (1992):225–51. http://onlinelibrary.wiley.com/doi/10.1111/j.1467-6494.1992.tb00973 .x/abstract.

Twenge, Jean M., and Liqing Zhang, and Charles Im. "It's Beyond My Control: A Cross-Temporal Meta-Analysis of Increasing Externality in Locus of Control, 1960–2002." *Personality and Social Psychology Review* 8(3) (2004):308–19. http://journals.sagepub.com/doi/abs/10.1207 /s15327957pspr0803_5?journalCode=psra.

11 FEELING

Abel, Ernest L., and Michael L. Kruger. "Smile Intensity in Photographs Predicts Longevity." *Psychological Science,* April 2010. http://www.jstor.org /stable/41062245?seq=1#page_scan_tab_contents.

Barrett, L. F., and P. Salovey, eds. *The Wisdom in Feeling: Psychological Processes in Emotional Intelligence*. New York: Guilford Press, 2002.

Brackett, Marc A., and John D. Mayer, and Rebecca M. Warner. "Emotional Intelligence and the Prediction of Behavior." *Personality and Individual Differences* 36 (2004):1387–1402. http://unh.edu/emotional_intelligence /EI%20Assets/Reprints . . . EI%20Proper/EIbrackett_mayer_warner .pdf.

Fredrickson, Barbara L. "What Good Are Positive Emotions?" *Review of General Psychology* 2 (1998): 300–19. https://www.ncbi.nlm.nih.gov/pmc /articles/PMC3156001/.

Grewal, Daisy, and Peter Salovey. "Feeling Smart: The Science of Emotional

Intelligence." *American Scientist* 93 (2005): 330–39. http://www
.americanscientist.org/issues/pub/feeling-smart-the-science-of
-emotional-intelligence.

Jones, Marian M. "The Unconventional Wisdom of Emotional Intelligence."
Psychology Today, September 1, 1997. https://www.psychologytoday.com
/articles/199709/the-unconventional-wisdom-emotional-intelligence.

12 PERFORMANCE

Cassidy,T., and R. Lynn. "A Multifactorial Approach to Achievement Motivation: The Development of a Comprehensive Measure." *Journal of Occupational Psychology* 62 (1989):301–12.

Cattell, J. McKeen. "A Statistical Study of Eminent Men." *Popular Science
Monthly* (1903):359–77. https://en.wikisource.org/wiki/Popular_Science
_Monthly/Volume_62/February_1903/A_Statistical_Study_of
_Eminent_Men.

Cattell, R. B., and H. J. Butcher. *The Prediction of Achievement and Creativity.* Oxford, England: Bobbs-Merrill, 1968.

Chamorro-Premuzic, T., and A. Furnham. *Personality and Intellectual Competence.* Mahwah, NJ: Lawrence Erlbaum, 2005.

Chown, S. M. "Personality factors in the formation of occupational choice."
British Journal of Educational Psychology 29 (1959):23–33.

Costa, P. T., and R. R. McCrae. *Revised NEO Personality Inventory
(NEO-PI-R) and NEO Five-Factor Inventory (NEO-FFI): Professional
Manual.* Odessa, FL: Psychological Assessment Resources, 1992.

Cox, Catharine M. *Genetic Studies of Genius: Vol.2. The Early Mental Traits
of Three Hundred Geniuses.* Stanford, CA: Stanford University Press, 1926.

Desrochers, S., and V. Dahir, V. "Ambition as a Motivational Basis of Organizational and Professional Commitment: Preliminary Analysis of a Proposed Career Advancement Ambition Scale." *Perceptual and Motor Skills*
91(2) (2000):563–70. https://www.ncbi.nlm.nih.gov/pubmed/11065319.

"*Drummond*-class Corvette." *Wikipedia.* https://en.wikipedia.org/wiki
/Drummond-class_corvette.

Harnden, Toby. "Dead Men Risen: The Snipers' Story." *Telegraph,* March 13,
2011. http://www.telegraph.co.uk/culture/books/8376808/Dead-Men
-Risen-The-snipers-story.html.

Onuoha, John. "Soldiers Zero In on Sniper Training." US Army, May 11, 2016.

https://www.army.mil/article/167711/Soldiers_zero_in_on_sniper _training.

Slugboy. "British Sniper Training: The Basic Cadre." *Sniper Country*, August 20, 2001. http://www.snipercountry.com/articles/britishsniper training.asp.

Stern, Victoria. "Why We Worry." *Scientific American*, November 1, 2009. https://www.scientificamerican.com/article/why-we-worry/.

"Train Your Mind Like a Sniper." YouTube video, 1:03:09. Uploaded by HDMindMovies, February 7, 2014. https://www.youtube.com/watch ?v=YIs7mjvhWPg.

INDEX